ODDBALL
TEXAS

ODDBALL TEXAS

A Guide to Some Really
STRANGE PLACES

JEROME POHLEN

CHICAGO
REVIEW
PRESS

The author has made every effort to secure permissions for all the material in this book. If any acknowledgment has inadvertently been omitted, please contact the author.

All photographs courtesy of Jerome Pohlen unless otherwise noted.
Cover and interior design: Mel Kupfer

FOr GOrDON,
GABRIELA, KAreN,
AND SANDra

CONTENTS

INtRODUCtiON

*L*et's just get this out of the way up front: Texas is big. Big, big, big, big, big. Everybody happy?

Perhaps not, for as big as Texas is, it isn't *The Biggest*. Yes, Alaska is larger. Still, there are a few things the Lone Star State has that a certain frostbitten moose preserve does not: the World's Largest Six-Shooter, the World's Largest Rattlesnake, the World's Largest Roadrunner, the World's Largest Jackrabbit, and the World's Largest Wooden Nickel.

There's more—take a deep breath. The World's Largest Fire Hydrant, the World's Largest Mosquito, the World's Largest Cornet, the World's Largest Caterpillar, the World's Largest Saxophone, the World's Largest Killer Bee, the World's Largest Red Grapefruit, the World's Largest Fly Rod and Reel, and the World's Largest Oatmeal Box.

These Texas-sized roadside attractions are only part of what this travel guide is all about. *Oddball Texas* will not waste your time discussing antiques in the Hill Country or breathtaking hikes through Big Bend or even—gasp!—the Alamo. It will, however, tell you where to find Barney Smith's Toilet Seat Art Museum, a modern replica of the Munsters' mansion, the world's only Cockroach Hall of Fame, a small town filled with hippo statues, two different replicas of Stonehenge, and a San Antonio suburb with streets named for Charlie Chan, Michael Nesmith, and Gomer Pyle.

And for those readers who feel the need to learn something before they're through, I've included plenty of important Texas history. Did a UFO really crash into a windmill northwest of Fort Worth in 1897? Why did Santa Claus rob the First National Bank of Cisco? What does an Abilene Kinko's have to do with the early retirement of Dan Rather? Could John Wilkes Booth have escaped capture, only to live out his days tending bar in a Granbury saloon? And why was Clay Henry, the mayor of Lajitas, castrated?

Oddball Texas is chock-full of these and other helpful suggestions to make the most of your Lone Star vacation. Why fight the crowds at the Alamo when another Texas shrine—the repository of coach Tom Landry's hat—has free, ample parking? The answer will be obvious.

While I've tried to give clear directions from major roads and landmarks, you could still make a wrong turn. And when you make a wrong turn in Texas, you can end up wayyy out of your way. Or even worse—you could end up in Oklahoma. Here are a few Oddball travel tips to help you reach your destination:

➡ **Stop and ask!** Molly Ivins said it best: "What still makes Texas Texas is that it's ignorant, cantankerous, and ridiculously friendly." Use that third quality to overcome the other two. Admit you're lost, suck up your pride, pull over, and *ask*. Even if you don't find anybody who can point you in the right direction, you'll meet some mighty nice folks.

➡ **Call ahead.** Few Oddball sites keep truly regular hours. Before you hop in the car and take off for El Paso, give the place you're headed for a ring. Gas ain't cheap, not even in Texas.

➡ **Don't give up.** Remember the Alamo's defenders—they didn't surrender when the going got tough . . . though they probably should have. You're not going to be slaughtered by the Mexican army if you don't find Barney Smith's Toilet Seat Art Museum on the first try. Check your map. Reread the directions. *Call*. But don't go home a quitter. Make Davy Crockett proud.

➡ **Don't trespass!** Don't be a Terrible Tourist. If one of the sites in this book is not open to the public, stay on the road. Besides, have you forgotten the Lone Star State's concealed weapons law?

Do you have an Oddball site of your own? Have I missed anything? Do you know of a location that should be included in a later edition? Please write and let me know: c/o Chicago Review Press, 814 N. Franklin Street, Chicago, IL 60610.

THE PANHANDLE

What better place to start a Texas travel guide than the wide-open plains of the Panhandle? Towns and tourist attractions are few and far between, so they stick out like sore thumbs. For example, it might not seem noteworthy that settler Thomas Cree planted a bois d'arc tree beside his Panhandle homestead in 1888 . . . but some claim it was the first tree ever planted in the region. To mark this groundbreaking sapling, a gardening plaque was erected along Route 60 southwest of the town of Panhandle. Unfortunately, Cree's tree was accidentally killed in 1969 by road crews carelessly spraying herbicide; a new tree stands in its place.

Is Thomas Cree's tree odd? Perhaps, but not odd enough. We can do better than that. But be sure to top off your tank—it's going to be a lonnnnnng drive.

Abilene
National Center for Children's Illustrated Literature

Back in 1993 the mayor of Abilene, Gary McCaleb, was reading *Santa Calls* to a group of schoolchildren when he got an idea to contact the book's author and illustrator, William Joyce. What started as a request for Joyce to visit Texas turned into something bigger. Why not establish a museum dedicated to the artists who create picture books, right here in Abilene? In 1997, the National Center for Children's Illustrated Literature (NCCIL) opened its doors.

The NCCIL gallery typically focuses on one illustrator at a time, featuring original sketches and finished artworks, side by side with the books in which they appear. Some of its exhibits are on loan from other museums, and directly from artists, but it also has a substantial collection of its own. Rather than let the art collect dust, the NCCIL lends out its collection to children's museums around the nation.

102 Cedar St., Abilene, TX 79601

(325) 673-4586

E-mail: nccil@bitstreet.com

Hours: Tuesday–Saturday 10 A.M.–4 P.M.

Cost: Free

www.nccil.org

Directions: At N. First St., one block north of the railroad tracks.

ABILENE

It is against the law to flirt or "mash" in Abilene.

Abilene boasts that it has "Texas's Only Atlas Missile Sites."

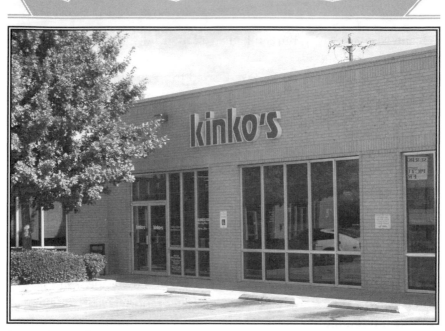

Dan Rather really should check his fax.

Rathergate

Dan Rather can tell you from experience: you better get your facts straight. And your fax. In the waning months of the 2004 presidential campaign, Rather came forward on *60 Minutes Wednesday* with new allegations regarding President George Bush's service, or lack thereof, in the Texas Air National Guard. He cited several newly uncovered documents faxed to him by retired Lieutenant Colonel Bill Burkett of Baird, just east of Abilene.

Who was Burkett? The same man who had also crossed Bush's radar during the 2000 presidential election, claiming that in 1997 he overheard two members of Governor Bush's staff—Joe Allbaugh and Dan Bartlett—arranging to "scrub" Bush's military records at Camp Mabry in Austin. Ten days later Burkett spotted an unidentified political staffer, who claimed to be doing research for Bush's autobiography *A Charge to Keep* (ghostwritten by Karen Hughes), tossing the governor's military pay and performance records into a trash can. The incident took place at what later became the Texas Military Forces Museum (3100 W. 35th Street) on the base. Shortly after making the charge, Burkett's medical disability rating from the Texas National Guard was dropped from 50 percent to 30 percent. Needless to say, Burkett had an ax to grind, and Rather should have been suspicious.

The documents in question were faxed from an Abilene Kinko's and bore a few clues that pointed to forgery. Most damning were a super-scripted "th" and a proportionally spaced font that indicated the memo was re-created on a modern word-processing program, not an early 1970s typewriter. What made the story even more curious was that several conservative blogs posted elaborate, technical refutations of the documents within *hours* of Rather's broadcast, almost as if they had been tipped off in advance. Hmmmmmm . . .

Could this have been a setup? Those who have followed the career of Karl Rove claim that the incident seemed suspiciously "Rovian," though no smoking gun was ever uncovered. What can't be ignored, however, was how well the Rathergate scandal played into the president's reelection playbook; Rather was disgraced and other reporters started taking a wide detour around the National Guard story. After an internal investigation, CBS fired four employees who worked on the story, and Rather moved up the date for his previously planned retirement.

Abilene Kinko's, 4133 S. Danville Dr., Abilene, TX 79605

(325) 698-3300; fax (325) 698-4500

Hours: Always visible; Store, Monday–Friday 7 A.M.–11 P.M., Saturday–Sunday 8 a.m.–8 P.M.

Cost: Free

www.kinkos.com

Directions: Exit north on Buffalo Gap Rd. from I-83/84, then west on Danville Dr., the I-83/84 north-side frontage road, for one block.

Amarillo
Big Texan Steak Ranch

There aren't many places left in Texas where you can still witness a genuine, perfectly legal showdown, except in Amarillo. Here, at the Big Texan Steak Ranch, you can watch a hungry man (and sometimes a woman) go *mano a boca* with a 72-ounce steak. The battle takes place on a platform in the middle of the restaurant, like a prize-fighting ring without the ropes. If the challenger can down four-and-a-half pounds of charred sirloin, and a salad, and a roll, and a cup of shrimp cocktail, and a baked potato, and dessert, all within an hour, the meal is free. About

35,000 have tried, but only one in seven have walked away without picking up the tab. Among the winners are a 69-year-old grandmother and an 11-year-old boy, and one guy who downed it all in under 10 minutes.

Even if you don't have a Texas-sized appetite, there's plenty to enjoy at the Big Texan Steak Ranch. Try an appetizer of diamondback rattlesnake or mountain oysters ("If you think it's seafood, go with the shrimp" warns the menu). The restaurant is decked out like a fancy barn, with wagon wheel chandeliers and dead critter heads mounted on the walls. Stop in on a Tuesday night and they've got a Big Time Opry. They also host an 80-player Texas Hold 'Em Tournament every Wednesday and (gasp!) Sunday. If you want to spend the night, there's the adjacent Western Motel; the pool isn't Texas-sized, but it is Texas-*shaped*. And if you rode in on your trusty steed, they've got a Horse Hotel as well.

7700 I-40 E, Amarillo, TX 79111
(800) 657-7177 or (806) 372-6000; Motel, (806) 372-5000 or (806) 371-0099
E-mail: lee3372@aol.com
Hours: Daily 7 A.M.–10:30 P.M.
Cost: Meals, $9–$30 ($50 for 72-ounce steak meal); Rooms, $39.99–$79
www.bigtexan.com
Directions: East of Lakeside Dr. (Rte. 335) on the north-side I-40 frontage road.

ADRIAN
The MidPoint Café on Historic Route 66 in Adrian is 1,139 miles from both Los Angeles and Chicago. (866) 538-6380, www.midpoint66.com

AMARILLO
You cannot, by law, bathe on the streets of Amarillo . . . during business hours.

Dancer **Cyd Charisse** was born Tula Ellice Finklea in Amarillo on March 8, 1923.

About 15,000 cattle disappeared in an Amarillo blizzard on February 20, 1971.

MORE FOR MEAT LOVERS

If you find yourself in Amarillo with an appetite for beef of the ground variety, stop on by Arnold Burgers (1611 S. Washington Street, (806) 372-1741). If their ¾-pound Arnold Double Burger isn't enough, they've also got a 20-person megaburger for the whole family, plus some—it weighs about 18 pounds and is 24 inches in diameter. They've got a smaller 18-inch version that feeds 12, as well as burgers grilled in the shape of Texas.

Oprah Winfrey probably never had the Arnold Double Burger. During a 1996 broadcast about BSE (Mad Cow Disease) she swore off hamburger forever and was promptly sued, along with her guest Howard Lyman, by a group of Texas cattlemen for defamation of red meat under the Food Disparagement Act. When she wasn't on trial at the federal courthouse (205 E. Fifth Avenue) downtown, Oprah taped new shows at the Amarillo Little Theatre (2019 Civic Circle, (806) 355-9991, www.AmarilloLittleTheatre.org) and relaxed at a local bed-and-breakfast. Though she gained 11 pounds during her stay, she departed a happy host; she was acquitted of all charges.

Still, average Texans and vegetable-eating types aren't always on opposite sides of every meat-related issue; they came together to support a roadkill bill during the 2002 legislative session in Austin. Folks from People for the Ethical Treatment of Animals (PETA) tried to have a law enacted that would make it legal to harvest roadkill. As they saw it, critters run over by cars and pickups were typically *not* tainted by growth hormones and were free-range (perhaps a little too free-range). Though for many years Texans have partaken of such "protein windfalls," the bill never passed. If you want roadkill, *legal* roadkill, you have to order the simulated kind available at kitschy themed restaurants, such as Toad's Roadkill Café in Leakey (Highway 83S, (830) 232-5009).

AMARILLO

Each year Amarillo hosts the World's Largest Calf Fry Cook-Off. Calf fries are bull testicles.

Amarillo was originally named Ragtown.

Cadillac Ranch, the Cadillac of Cadillac creations.
Photo by author, courtesy of Stanley Marsh 3.

Cadillac Ranch

They're hard to miss: 10 Cadillacs planted nose down in a field west of Amarillo along old Route 66. They were put there in May 1974 and were intended to be a demonstration of ". . . sexual freedom, the freedom to make choices, and the ability to just go." Today, the Cadillac Ranch is mostly visited by sullen teens, gun-totin' cowboys, graffiti artists, and music video directors, who are just the folks Stanley Marsh 3 (*not* Stanley Marsh III) had in mind when he financed the project.

Marsh, an eccentric local millionaire who made it onto Nixon's Enemies List, hired a group of California artists known as the Ant Farm to create the work. The Cadillacs were inserted at the same angle as the Great Pyramid of Cheops, and the models were chosen to trace the history of the tail fin from 1949 to 1963: '49, '52, '54, '56, '57, '58, '59, '60, '62, and '64. Bruce Springsteen immortalized the site on his album *The River*. But, contrary to an oft-repeated rumor, the Cadillac Ranch has never been the site of an Evel Knievel stunt.

As Amarillo grew during the 1980s and '90s, the Cadillac Ranch was in danger of being swallowed by urban sprawl. So, in the summer of 1997, Marsh had the Cadillacs uprooted and moved to a new field two miles farther west.

I-40, Amarillo, TX 79101

(806) 372-5555

Hours: Always visible

Cost: Free

www.libertysoftware.be/cml/cadillacranch/crmain.htm

Directions: 12 miles west of downtown on I-40, between Exit 60 and 62 off the north
  frontage road.

A GERMAN IMPORT

Fans of the Cadillac Ranch might want to hop on 1-40 and head to
Conway, about 20 miles east of Amarillo. There, on the south side of
the interstate, there's a German version of Amarillo's most famous
artwork. It's called the Bug Ranch and is made from a half-dozen
bright yellow Volkswagen Beetles.

Helium Central

Approximately 90 percent of the earth's recoverable helium is located in
the ground beneath Amarillo, and in its honor the locals have built a
monument to this most noble gas. Helium makes balloons rise, keeps the
Goodyear Blimp from blowing up like the *Hindenburg* (see page 84), and
will make anybody's voice sound like Betty Boop. Not bad for something
inert.

In 1968, to celebrate the 100th anniversary of helium's discovery by
Sir Joseph Lockyear (a non-Texan), Amarillo erected the International
Helium Centennial Time Columns, designed to represent a giant helium
atom. They contain four stainless steel time capsules to be opened in 1993
(done!), 2018, 2068, and 2968. Each contains 1,000 or so objects, some
donated by corporate America—Kent cigarettes, All detergent, etc.—but
some good stuff, too. One capsule holds dehydrated apple pie, plant seeds,
and Hollywood movies, all protected from rot in a chamber of helium.
Then there's the $10 savings account passbook from an Oklahoma City
bank, which is earning 4 percent interest. When it is turned over to the
U.S. Treasury in 2968, per instructions, it will be worth about
$1,000,000,000,000,000.00, a quadrillion dollars, which just might be able
to solve the budget crisis, if only we can hold out for a thousand years.

International Helium Time Columns & Helium Pavilion, Don Harrington Discovery Center, 1200 Streit Dr., Amarillo, TX 79106

(806) 355-9547

Hours: Monument, always visible; Museum, Tuesday–Saturday 9:30 A.M.–4:30 P.M., Sunday Noon–4:30 P.M.

Cost: Free

www.dhdc.org/helium.html

Directions: One block northwest of Rte. 400/60 Business (Amarillo Dr./Old Rout 66) on the west side of town.

Ozymandias and Lightnin' McDuff

The year was 1819. Percy Bysshe Shelley and his fiancée, Mary Wollstonecraft, were riding across the Great Plains headed for New Spain when they came upon two enormous legs made of stone, outlined against the sky, and what they took to be the face of the shattered statue half-buried in the sand. From this, Shelley penned the poem "Ozmandias," and the future Mary Shelley most likely got her idea for the novel *Frankenstein.*

The face was eventually moved to the Amarillo Museum of Natural History after it was vandalized by students from Lubbock when they lost an athletic competition to an Amarillo team. But the legs of Ozmandias still stand where they have for centuries.

I-27 and Sundown Lane, Amarillo, TX 79119

No phone

Hours: Always visible

Cost: Free

Directions: Just east of I-27 at the Sundown Lane Exit on the south side of town.

BIG SPRING
Actress **Betty Buckley** was born in Big Spring on July 3, 1947.

BORGER
It's illegal to throw rubber balls or confetti in Borger.

". . . two vast and trunkless legs of stone / stand in the desert. Near them, on the sand, / half sunk, a shattered visage lies, whose frown, / and wrinkled lip, and sneer of cold command, / tell that its sculptor well those passions read / which yet survive, stamped on these lifeless things, / the hand that mocked them . . ."
—from "Ozmandias" by Percy Bysshe Shelley, 1819

If you want to learn more about the Ozymandias ruins, there's nobody who knows them better than Lightnin' McDuff, an artist and welder who lives along old Route 66 in Amarillo. McDuff has a gallery where he displays his works, goofy animals made out of old machinery and modern pieces that can sometimes be very large—stop on by and check out his work. (Eccentric patron of the arts Stanley Marsh 3 has, at least once.)

Carey–McDuff Contemporary Art, 508 S. Bowie, Amarillo, TX 79106

(806) 376-5045

Hours: Call ahead

Cost: Free

Directions: One block north of old Route 66 (Sixth Ave.), seven blocks west of Adams St.

BOVINA
Bovina was originally called Bull Town, but it was renamed because its Spanish derivative sounded classier.

Trouble, trouble, trouble.

Anson
No Dancing!

When the WPA mural was unveiled at the Anson post office in 1941, the artist Jenne Magafan was almost run out of town. Why? Not because the mural depicted the town's annual Cowboy Christmas Ball—everybody knew that would be the subject—but because the dancers seemed to be *enjoying* themselves. The town had outlawed dancing in 1933, punishable by a $5–$15 penalty. There was a one-day exception, however: on the weekend before Christmas locals could gather at the Pioneer Hall for the much-anticipated Cowboy Christmas Ball and not fear fine or incarceration.

In a case of life imitating art (if you can call the movie *Footloose* art), a group of young 'uns calling themselves the Footloose Club challenged the statute and eventually succeeded in getting it overturned. In the *1990s.*

Anson Post Office, 1002 11th St., Anson, TX 79501

(325) 823-2241

Hours: Monday–Friday 8 A.M.–4:30 P.M.

Cost: Free

Directions: One block east of Commercial Ave. (Rte. 83) on 11th St., on the northeast corner of the town square.

They're Canadliens.

Canadian
Cockrell's Creations

As you drive north on Route 83/60 toward Canadian, down the last long hill into town, you'll spot a 25-foot-tall green dinosaur atop the bluff on your right.

"That's odd," you'll think.

Actually, that's Aud, as in *Aud*rey, the wife of Bobby Gene "Pig" Cockrell, the man who put that concrete sculpture up there in 1992.

It's the least Cockrell could do for Audrey, considering what she's had to put up with over the years. You'll know what I'm talking about when you see their place near town. The yard is filled with large concrete

sculptures: a buffalo, a burro, a wooly mammoth, a centaur, a two-headed dragon . . . should I go on? All right: Indians on horseback, a cowboy in an outhouse, Barney the dinosaur.

More? A flying saucer with a family of aliens taking a peek around. Jesus ministering to a lion and a lamb. And a Dallas Cowboy cheerleader Cockrell has titled *Once Nude*. She *was* once nude, but Audrey put an end to that.

15115 Marshall Dr., Canadian, TX 79014

Private phone

Hours: Always visible

Cost: Free

Directions: Head east out of town on FM 2388 (Marshall Dr.); watch for the sculptures
   on the north side of the road.

BROWNFIELD
If a Brownfield man jilts his fiancée, the law requires him to leave town within six hours.

CLARENDON
Clarendon was founded as a "sobriety settlement" in 1878, and earned the nickname Saints Roost from local cowpokes.

CLAUDE
Much of the 1963 movie *Hud* was filmed in Claude.

CLYDE
A $60 million treasure of gold plundered by Coronado is believed to be buried on an 80-acre pasture at the Sems Ranch near Clyde.

Canyon
Big Tex Randall

The sign on the base of Big Tex Randall makes a mighty bold claim: "Biggest Texan." Trouble is, that wasn't true when Harry Wheeler built the 47-foot-tall concrete and stucco statue in 1959, and it isn't true today, either. Big Tex at the Texas State Fair (see page 74) has this Canyon cowboy beat by three feet! Big Tex Randall *might* be the Biggest Texan if Dallas's Big Tex wasn't from the Lone Star State, but c'mon, the Fair's statue ain't named Big Pierre.

Biggest Texan? Not even close!

Now any cowboy (or cowgirl) will tell you it's not right to boast about the size of your herd, or anything else for that matter. So is it any wonder this Panhandle braggart was rammed by a semi truck, crushing its left foot? No sooner did he get patched up when somebody shot out the cigarette he held in his right hand. That kind of stunt would get cheers for Annie Oakley, but didn't amuse the owners of this gangly seven-ton monstrosity. When the statue was restored in 1989, a spur was placed in its hand instead.

15th St. and Rte. 60, Canyon, TX 79105

No phone

Hours: Always visible

Cost: Free

Directions: Four blocks east of FM 217 on the south-side Rte. 60 frontage road.

Conlen
Bow-Legged Cowboy

As long as we're talking big Texans, there's another colossal cowboy worth mentioning in the Panhandle town of Conlen. Calling Conlen a town is a bit generous since there isn't much more to this wide spot in the road than a grain elevator, a collapsing shed, and a 20-foot-tall statue of a bow-legged, concrete cowboy. His name is Tex—what else?—or at least that's what it says on his belt buckle. He's got a gun, drawn and ready to shoot, so he's the biggest Texan as far as I'm concerned.

Rte. 54 and Jake Rd., Conlen, TX 79084

No phone

Hours: Always visible

Cost: Free

Directions: On the south side of Rte. 54, one block east of FM 807.

Easy, pardner!

DALHART

Dalhart got its name because it straddles the Dallam–Hartley county line.

The electric fence was invented on the XIT Ranch near Dalhart in 1888.

Built broken to last.

Groom
Leaning Water Tower

You've got to hand it to the folks who owned the Britten U.S.A. truck stop for thinking outside the box. When they built a water tower on the outskirts of Groom, they erected it crooked so that well-meaning travelers would pull off the highway to warn somebody about its impending collapse, or at the very least find out what was going on. Either way, the folks would be out of their cars, and probably fill up their gas tanks or stop in for a bite to eat.

Well, the leaning water tower formula didn't last forever. Britten U.S.A. closed its doors and was bulldozed. But oddly enough, the structure they built to look as if it was on its last legs is still standing. And it's still crooked.

I-40, Groom, TX 79039

No phone

Hours: Always visible

Cost: Free

Directions: On the north side of I-40 at the FM 295 exit.

North America's Second Largest Cross

How would you feel if you spent thousands of dollars erecting a 190-foot cross with a 110-foot wingspan capable of withstanding 140-mph winds, only to find out that it was North America's *Second* Largest Cross? Well, for the record, Steve Thomas feels pretty good.

Thomas built the Cross of Our Lord Jesus Christ in 1995 so that travelers along I-40 would have something to look at and think about, a rarity in this barren stretch of the Panhandle. He keeps the cross illuminated at night so that *nobody* misses it. The cross is surrounded by a dozen life-sized bronze depictions of the Stations of the Cross, circularly arranged in a not-so-merry-go-round. An adjacent museum is dedicated to the Shroud of Turin and is home to one of seven exact replicas made of the mysterious burial cloth.

The Cross of Our Lord Jesus Christ, I-40, Groom, TX 79039

(806) 665-7788

E-mail: info@crossministries.net

Hours: Always visible

Cost: Free

www.crossministries.net

Directions: Exit 112 from I-40, south on FM 295, and follow the signs.

DICKENS

Dickens is the Unofficial Wild Boar Capital of Texas.

What you wear when you're *incredibly* nearsighted.
Photo by author, courtesy of the Buddy Holly Center.

Lubbock
Buddy Holly-ville

Suffering a premature, tragic fate is sometimes a good way for a musician to revive a waning career—just ask Elvis. But when Buddy Holly's plane went down north of Clear Lake, Iowa, on February 3, 1959, his career was still on the way up.

Holly was born Charles Hardin Holley (not Holly) on September 7, 1936, in a house that once stood at 1911 Sixth Street. The house still exists, but has long since been moved to an undisclosed location. While he was growing up his family also lived at 3315 36th Street, 3204 First Street, and 1906 24th Street; all three homes are still standing, but are private residences. Holly attended Roscoe Wilson Elementary (2807 25th Street) from 1943 to '47, Roosevelt Elementary (Route 1, Box 402) from 1947 to '49, and Hutchinson Junior High (3102 Canton Avenue) from 1949 to '52. While attending Lubbock High (2004 19th Street) he signed his first contract with Decca Records. The folks at Decca mistakenly dropped the "e" from his last name on the contract, and the new spelling stuck.

Following his 1956 graduation, Holly's career moved along at about the pace you would expect from a 19-year-old: he played American

Legion halls, roller rinks, grocery store parking lots, and Lubbock's "Sunday Party" on KDAV Radio (6602 MLK Boulevard). But after a visit to the Norman Petty Recording Studios in Clovis, New Mexico, he hit it big. "That'll Be the Day" reached #1 on the *Billboard* chart later that year. Holly was still living in Lubbock with his family at 1305 37th Street (still standing, private residence), so he used the profits to buy his first and final house at 1606 39th Street (still standing, private residence).

After the Iowa plane crash, Holly's body was brought back to Texas and buried at the City of Lubbock Cemetery (31st Street and Teak Avenue), where the name on his headstone has the original "e." Fans leave guitar picks at his grave.

Lubbock has never forgotten its hometown star. In 1980 the city erected a Buddy Holly statue in front of the Lubbock Memorial Civic Center (Eighth Street and Avenue Q) as the centerpiece of the West Texas Musical Walk of Fame. True fans will want to stop at the Buddy Holly Center in the city's old train depot, which sports a pair of the World's Largest Buddy Holly Glasses. The guitar-shaped gallery contains personal items from Holly's short life and remarkable career, including his Cub Scout uniform, marbles, crayons, contact lens case and solution, and Fender Stratocaster electric guitar. They even have the "Faiosa frame" glasses he wore the Day the Music Died, which were recovered from the Iowa cornfield after the crash.

Buddy Holly Center, 1801 Ave. G., Lubbock, TX 79401

(806) 767-2686

E-mail: Pearl@buddyhollycenter.org

Hours: Tuesday–Friday 10 A.M.–6 P.M., Saturday 11 A.M.–6 P.M.

Cost: Adults $5, Seniors (55+) $3, Kids (under 12) Free

www.buddyhollycenter.org

Fan site: www.buddyholly.com

Directions: Two blocks west of I-27 on 19th St.

FLOYDADA

Floydada calls itself Pumpkin Capital, USA, and hosts Punkin Days (not Pumpkin Days) on the last weekend before Halloween each year. (806) 983-3434, www.floydadachamber.com

---

TEXAS MUSICAL DEATH TRIP

One of the stranger items in the collection of the Buddy Holly Center is the rear half of a 1963 Chrysler Newport once owned by **Lank Spangler**. The up-and-coming country musician was driving this very car on February 28, 1968, when it plunged off the caprock northwest of Gail. Some suspect he was distraught over the death of his younger brother in Vietnam. The impact killed Spangler instantly, cutting short a promising career. Neither Spangler nor his car were found right away.

Sadly, Lank Spangler hasn't been the only musician to come to a grisly end in the Lone Star State.

Johnny Ace: Singer Johnny Ace killed himself backstage at the Houston City Auditorium (615 Louisiana Street) on December 24, 1954, the victim of a poorly executed Russian roulette stunt he used to impress women. His final words were spoken to Willie Mae "Big Mama" Thornton: "I'll show you that it won't work." "It" was a pistol, and it *did* work. The auditorium was torn down in 1963; the Jones Hall for Performing Arts stands on the death site today.

Johnny Horton: Best known for his rendition of "The Battle of New Orleans," Horton died instantly when his Cadillac rammed head-on into another car near Milano on November 5, 1960. The crash occurred on Route 79, about 300 yards west of the Route 36 intersection.

Ricky Nelson: The former teen heartthrob was flying over Texas on December 31, 1985, when his DC-3 caught fire. His plane hit two power lines and plowed into a cow pasture east of DeKalb near the intersection of FM 990 and FM 1840, killing Nelson, his fiancée Helen Blair, and five other members of the Stone Canyon Band. (The pilot and copilot survived.) Rumors circulated that Nelson was freebasing cocaine, but the crash was likely caused by a faulty cabin-heating unit. Ironically, the defective plane was once owned by Jerry Lee "Great Balls of Fire" Lewis.

HEREFORD

Hereford is called the Town Without a Toothache because of the high level of fluoride found in its water supply.

Actor **Ron Ely** was born in Hereford on June 21, 1938.

Open wide!
Photo by author, courtesy of Custom Iron Works.

Killer BBQ

If there's anything Texans love more than guns it's barbecue. So why hasn't anyone thought of a way to celebrate them both?

As it turns out, somebody has: Custom Iron Works offers a six-shooter-shaped grill where the food is cooked in the bullet chamber and the smoke curls out the barrel. Just dare anyone to criticize your grillin' skills!

The grills come in several sizes and styles; the largest model looks like it belongs in Dirty Harry's backyard. The only way for Custom Iron Works to possibly improve on its designs would be to rig the cooker to somehow shoot steaks and burgers out the barrel when the meat's done.

Custom Iron Works, 12701 Highway 87, Lubbock, TX 79423

(806) 745-2757

Hours: Always visible

Cost: Free

Directions: Off the east-side Rte. 87 frontage road north of 146th St.

Prairie Dog Town

There was a time when prairie dogs ruled the Panhandle. Around the time the settlers arrived, a single colony in the vicinity of present-day Lubbock covered 37,000 square *miles*, with about 400 million resident rodents.

Well, no more. These critters' burrows can twist horses' or cows' legs, so ranchers systematically wiped the varmints out. Luckily, in 1932, Mrs. K. N. Clapp stepped in to prevent the last of the prairie dogs from being exterminated. Prairie Dog Town was established from the last two burrows from that original megacolony. It has rebounded as far as it is able: to the cement wall erected to prevent it from spilling out onto the surrounding countryside.

The Lubbock prairie dogs do come in handy on occasion . . . as groundhog stand-ins. One of these prairie pests is yanked out on Groundhog Day each year; Prairie Dog Pete serves as the local meteorologist on February 2.

MacKenzie State Park, Fourth St. and Ave. A, Lubbock, TX 79404

(800) 692-4035 or (806) 747-5232

Hours: Daylight hours

Cost: Free

Directions: North on Ave. A from Rte. 82 (Parkway Dr.), then right into MacKenzie State Park, following the signs around to the left.

LEFORS
By law, you may not take more than three sips of beer *while standing* in Lefors.

LITTLEFIELD
Musician **Waylon Jennings** was born in Littlefield on June 15, 1937.

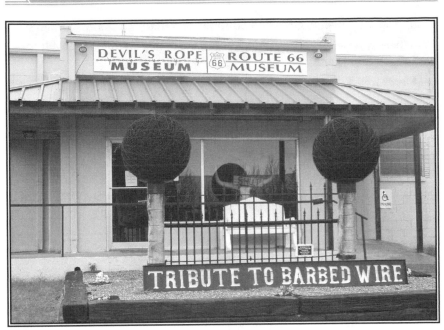

Satan, I contain thee!

McLean
Devil's Rope Museum and Route 66 Museum

Shortly after barbed wire was introduced to the West in the 1870s, it earned the nickname "devil's rope." The U.S. Patent Office has issued 530 unique patents for barbed wire, and there have been thousands of unpatented variations over the years. This small museum has about 6,000 samples of devil's rope in its collection, though not all are on display. They've also commissioned sculptures made from the prickly stuff, including coyotes, rabbits, bird nests, and a cowboy hat they call the Sharp Stetson.

But that's not all. Sitting as it does along the old Mother Road, the museum shares its roof with the Route 66 Museum and the Texas Route 66 Hall of Fame. They've re-created a four-stool "66 Café" lunch counter serviced by a mannequin waitress who is only slightly less responsive than the flesh-and-blood kind. And finally, be sure to check out the large state map with soil samples from each and every Texas county glued to it—fascinating . . . but a little dirty.

The Devil's Rope Museum is located in an old bra factory. Back when it was in business, Marie's Foundations made so many women's undergarments that McLean was known as the Uplift City. Today, to be honest, it's a bit saggy.

100 Kingsley St., PO Box 290, McLean, TX 79057

(806) 779-2225

E-mail: barbwiremuseum@centramedia.net

Hours: March–October, Tuesday–Saturday 10 A.M.–4 P.M.

Cost: Free

www.barbwiremuseum.com

Directions: Off old Route 66 (Graham St.), three blocks east of Main St. (FM 3143).

LUBBOCK

In Lubbock you may not, by law, sleep in a trash can, nor may you drive within an arm's length of alcohol.

Singer **Mac Davis** was born in Lubbock on January 21, 1942.

Lubbock is the Chrysanthemum Capital of the World.

MCLEAN

The founding father of McLean, Alfred Rowe, died aboard the *Titanic*.

MIAMI

Miami hosts the National Cow-Calling Championship on the first weekend in June each year. (806) 868-2202, ww.miamitexas.org/cow_calling.htm

PERRYTON

Perryton calls itself the Wheatheart of the Nation.

What an ass.

Muleshoe
National Mule Memorial

Judging from this town's name, you'd suspect the residents here hold the mule in high regard. And it's true, many refer to this area as the "Greater Muleplex." But most people have long since traded in their mules for automobiles, so you're not likely to see many of the stubborn beasts around town ... except one. The National Mule Memorial portrays a life-sized mule that will neither spit at nor kick you. This 1965 sculpture by Kevin Wolff was modeled after Old Pete, a local favorite.

Any prospector will tell you a mule is what you get when you mate a donkey with a horse, and because two different species have been cross-bred, their offspring are unable to procreate. A mule is tough, as the roadside marker points out: "Indians ate horses hitched to cart or coach, but left tough mule meat go by." *Really?* And they didn't even unhook the horses first?

Muleshoe was not named for the mule, nor its shoes, but the nearby Muleshoe Ranch, one of the offshoots of the enormous XIT Ranch. It's a distinction that few care about; Muleshoe sets aside the last Saturday in August each year to celebrate Mule Day, not Muleshoe Ranch Day.

American Blvd. and First St., Muleshoe, TX 79347

(806) 272-4248

Hours: Always visible

Cost: Free

Directions: On Rte. 84 (American Blvd.) where it meets Rte. 70 (First St.) in the middle of town.

O'Donnell
Blocker-Head

Dan Blocker, Hoss Cartwright on *Bonanza*, wasn't just a large adult. He was *born* big, 14 pounds big, in DeKalb on December 10, 1928. His father and poor, poor, *poor* mother moved to O'Donnell when Bobby Don (Dan was his stage name) was six, where they opened the Blocker Grocery. By the time Bobby Don was 12, he was six feet tall and weighed more than 200 pounds.

Though he studied theater while a student at Sul Ross State University in Alpine, Blocker didn't get his first acting job until *Bonanza* came along. He was able to parlay Hoss's popularity into a successful chain of steak houses; Blocker was part owner of Bonanza.

But Blocker should have hit the salad bar a little more often; on May 13, 1972, he died of a massive heart attack. He was only 43 years old.

O'Donnell wanted to honor its hometown son, so in 1973 they hired sculptor Glenna Goodacre to create a granite bust of the actor in his sig-

nature cowboy hat. It can still be found in a park adjacent to the old Blocker Grocery. The town also opened a small museum where you can see his boxing gloves, Boy Scout pants, and other Blockerabilia. About the only thing they don't have is Blocker himself; he's buried in DeKalb's Woodsmen Cemetery (646 Front Street).

O'Donnell Museum, Heritage Plaza, Eighth and Doak Sts., O'Donnell, TX 79351

(806) 428-3708

Hours: Always visible; Museum, Tuesday–Saturday 10 A.M.–Noon and 1–4 P.M., Sunday
1–5 P.M.

Cost: Free

Directions: One block north of FM 76 (Ninth St.) on FM 2370 (Doak St.).

POST

According to legend, the wind direction at sunrise in Post on March 22 determines the rest of the year's weather. South or SE = a very bad year. West or SW = a bad year. North or NW = a so-so year. East or NE = a very good year.

The town of Post was founded by, and named after, **C. W. Post**, the breakfast cereal magnate. A statue of Post on Main Street may not, per instructions of the Post family, be cleaned.

SEMINOLE

Singer **Larry Gatlin** was born in Seminole on May 2, 1948.

Musician **Tanya Tucker** was born in Seminole on October 2, 1958.

SNYDER

A semi trailer overturned on a Snyder highway on October 4, 2001, spilling 7,600,000 pennies from the Denver Mint.

SPUR

Marshall Herff Applewhite, leader of the Heaven's Gate cult, was born in Spur on May 17, 1931.

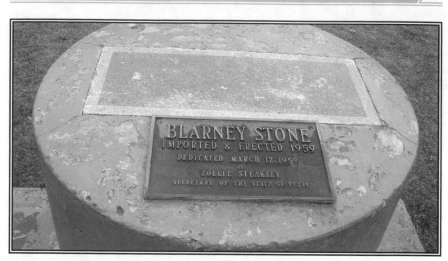

Pucker up, stumblemouth!

Shamrock
The Blarney Stone

If you visit Ireland and want to kiss the Blarney Stone you have to hang upside down, but in Texas you can do the same thing standing upright in a city park or a local motel. Town boosters purchased a piece of the lucky rock from Cork, Ireland's Blarney Castle in 1959 and embedded it into a concrete pedestal for anyone bold enough to put their lips on it. If you're worried about smooching a rock that has seen 40+ years of lips, there's a newer Blarney Stone in the lobby of Shamrock's Irish Inn (I-40 Frontage Road and Route 83, (806) 256-2106), on loan from Dr. D. E. Blackketter. Most of this stone is protected by a plexiglass shield, but it does have a hole for you to stick your head through.

Why would you do such a thing? Legend has it that when you kiss the Blarney Stone you'll be given the gift of eloquence. Back when Elizabeth I demanded Dermot McCarthy surrender his castle to the throne as a sign of loyalty, McCarthy would always come up with an elaborate explanation as to why it couldn't be turned over just yet. His verbal skills impressed the queen, and the myth was born.

Shamrock loves its Irish heritage, perhaps a little too much. Each year the town holds a beard-growing contest. Not just any beard, but an Irish Donegal beard, which is shaved along the chin line, leprechaun style. Contestants have to have a stubble-free face on January 1, then

grow as much hair as they can before St. Patrick's Day. Anyone—well, any adult male—opting not to participate must buy a five-dollar shaving permit *or risk being thrown in jail.* Yikes.

Elmore Park, First and Texas Sts., Shamrock, TX 79079

(806) 256-2501

Hours: Always visible

Cost: Free

www.shamrocktx.net

Directions: Three blocks east of Main St. (Rte. 83) on FM 2033.

Snyder
Albino Buffalo

When a rare albino buffalo was spotted on the plains northwest of Snyder, locals did what they did with all the other buffalo: they shot it. J. Wright Mooar blasted the creature away on October 7, 1876. Mooar was no stranger to the job; he'd killed another white buffalo several years earlier in Kansas. In fact, there have only been seven such animals ever documented, and Mooar killed two of them. (He gunned down an estimated 22,000 brown ones as well.)

Mooar kept the albino pelt and exhibited the hide at the 1904 St. Louis World's Fair. Back in Snyder the town eventually erected a fiber-glass monument in front of the courthouse in the dead critter's honor. After it was destroyed by vandals, a replacement was purchased and placed at the fairgrounds. Several years later descendants of Mooar took a good look at the pelt and realized the animal had actually been a female, though the town's two statues had been male. Snyderians corrected the situation when they commissioned a bronze white buffalo from artist Robert Taylor in 1994. The newest sculpture stands on the northwest corner of the courthouse square.

Scurry County Courthouse, 1806 25th St., Snyder, TX 79549

(325) 573-3558

E-mail: synchcom@snydertex.com

Hours: Always visible

Cost: Free

http://snyderchamber.org

Directions: At College Ave. (Rte. 350) and 25th St. (Rte. 180).

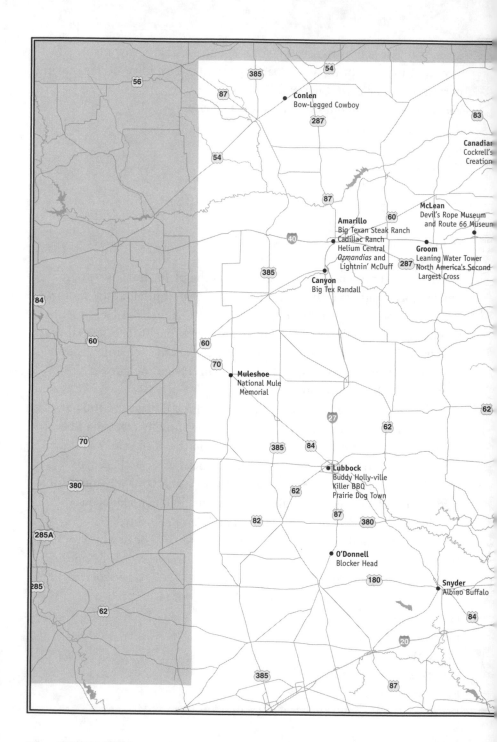

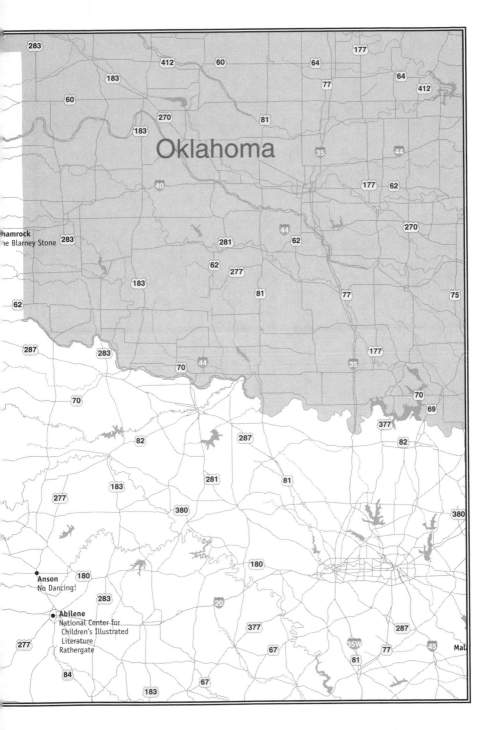

2

NORTH TEXAS

*A*ccording to North Texas lore, a person can be cured of mental illness if he or she takes a sip of water from the Crazy Well in Mineral Wells. Whether or not that's true, damn few people in the region seem to have made the trip. How else can you explain all the strangeness around here? There are people in North Texas who have gone around telling everybody that they were John Wilkes Booth, and Jesse James, and even Peter Pan. There was even a guy who claimed to be Santa Claus . . . so he could rob a bank . . . at Christmastime!

And where do you think people have found "evidence" of cavemen frolicking with dinosaurs? Where did a horned toad live for more than three decades sealed in a building's cornerstone? Where did a man build an airplane with plans he found in the Bible? Where did a Texan—I said *a Texan*—build the state's littlest skyscraper, *on purpose*? That's right, all this craziness happened in North Texas. No wonder that an alien tried to land his airship in these parts. (Too bad he crashed into a windmill.)

What, never heard of any of this? Then read on . . .

Aurora
Dead Alien

On April 17, 1897, a large cigar-shaped "airship" struck a windmill owned by Judge J. S. Proctor near Aurora and then burst into flames. The charred remains of a pilot—some say he looked "not of this world"—were pulled from the wreckage and buried three days later in the local Masonic cemetery. Big deal, you say? Actually, yes!

First of all, this all happened 10 years *before* the first maneuverable lighter-than-air zeppelins took to the skies. Secondly, the crash capped off five months of mysterious airship sightings across the United States, and, though the Aurora crash was barely mentioned outside northern Texas, airship reports ceased after the accident.

The Aurora crash was quickly forgotten. But in 1973 the case was brought back to light by several Dallas-area newspapers. Soon ufologists were flocking to Aurora with metal detectors. More than 20 graves were disturbed or robbed, including that of the pilot, who had been laid to rest beneath the old oak on the south side of the graveyard.

There is an effort being led by Austin mystic Dave Walsh to buy a memorial for the unfortunate, now-missing pilot. It will be inscribed with the same hieroglyphics carved on the original headstone, which had been copied from markings retrieved from the rubble. Until it arrives, you'll have to satisfy yourself with the current historical marker near the cemetery gate, which briefly mentions the pilot. It does not, however, mention another odd headstone in the same cemetery, that of Loreta, the World's Talking Bird. I smell a cover-up.

Cemetery Rd., Aurora, TX 76078

No phone

Hours: Always visible

Cost: Free

http://ufocasebok.com/Aurora.htm

Directions: Head west out of Rhome on Rte. 114, then south on Cemetery Rd. just before Aurora.

ATHENS

Each July Athens celebrates the Black-Eyed Pea Jamboree.

STRANGE THINGS IN THE TEXAS SKIES

The Aurora Airship wasn't the only bizarre craft to cruise through the Texas skies. In fact, the term "flying saucer" *originated* in the Lone Star State. On January 25, 1878, hunter John Martin spotted a dark, circular craft in Grayson County near Denison, which hovered over his location. He described it as the size of a "large saucer." It was the first UFO in Texas but, if you believe the reports, certainly not the last:

★ A UFO crashed near Laredo on July 7, 1948; photos of its charred pilot—dubbed "Tomato Man" because of its oversized head—surfaced in 1978.

★ Another flying saucer reportedly crash-landed at the Laredo Airport in February 1950. The Martian pilot punched out a National Guardsman before collapsing dead.

★ Mysterious blue lights, flying in a "V" formation, were spotted and photographed over Lubbock for several evenings, starting on August 25, 1951. The Air Force claimed they were a flock of birds.

★ A torpedo-shaped UFO flew over the pickup of Pedro Saucedo along Route 114, four miles from Levelland, on November 2, 1957, causing the truck to stall. One day later, a red, egg-shaped UFO landed on a road near town and frightened motorist Jim Wheeler. It was sighted by 20 other witnesses, including police officers and firefighters.

★ Ray Rosi of Austin claimed to have made contact with a blue, cigar-shaped UFO near the Mansfield Dam on June 24, 1967. Rosi used his flashlight to signal pi—3.14—at the craft, and it seemed to respond. He also tried SOS and "shave and a haircut, 2 bits."

★ A UFO was reported to have hovered over an open-pit uranium mine near Karnes City in the summer of 1971.

★ A mutilated cow was found in the center of a crop circle near Whiteface on March 10, 1975. Rancher Darwood Marshall found the cow without any internal organs and its navel "cored out."

★ A Tyler couple was approached by a triangular UFO while driving in their pickup on November 26, 1976. Their wristwatches later showed they had "lost" time.

★ A young man was taking a leak beside his car near Lindale on January 24, 1979, when he was hit by a blast of light from above. He awoke five hours later, beside the road, with holes in his socks and pants and a diamond-shaped burn on his chest.

★ Betty Cash, Vickie Landrum, and Landrum's grandson Colby were stopped by a diamond-shaped UFO on FM 1485 near Huffman on

December 29, 1980. The craft belched a cone of fire, and soon the surface of their automobile became too hot to touch. Both women felt sick afterward, developed sunburns, and displayed symptoms of radiation poisoning. Witnesses claim the saucer was later surrounded, then chased, by 23 black army helicopters. Betty Cash died of cancer 18 years to the day after the sighting.

Cisco
Santa Steals

It sounds like a plot the Grinch might have come up with before his change of heart. Two days before Christmas in 1927, Santa Claus walked into the First National Bank of Cisco with three accomplices and made off with $12,200 in cash and $150,000 in securities. This being Texas, the robbers immediately began to draw gunfire from police and armed citizens, and all four men were wounded. But using two young girls as shields/hostages, the bandits made their way to a stolen car, which they used to escape town.

They didn't get far before their getaway car got a flat tire. One mortally wounded robber, Louis Davis, was left behind while the others carjacked a new vehicle; in their haste the trio left the money behind, too. A short time later they released the girls. Within three days all three surviving criminals—Henry Helms, Robert Hill, and Santa—were apprehended. Back in Cisco, police chief B. E. "Bit" Bedford and officer George Carmichael had died of their wounds, and the trio was in big, big trouble.

Santa turned out to be Marshall Ratliff, a local no-good-un who wore the holiday outfit to avoid being recognized by his neighbors. Ratliff, Helms, and Hill were convicted of a wide number of crimes in separate trials at the Eastland County courthouse (see page 40). Hill got off easy with life in prison; Helms and Ratliff were both sentenced to die and shipped off to the Huntsville death house (see page 218).

Still awaiting execution two years later, Ratliff was returned to Eastland to stand trial for another charge: stealing a car at gunpoint. On November 18, 1929, Ratliff attempted to escape from the Eastland jail (210 W. White Street) and killed officer Thomas Jones in the process.

On hearing the news, locals broke into the jail, took Ratliff, and strung him up in a local vacant lot. You can still see the hanging pole and a historic marker behind the Eastland Hotel (112 N. Lamar Street). The rope is still in the jail, which is now a museum.

First National Bank of Cisco, Conrad Hilton Blvd. and Seventh St., Cisco, TX 76437

No phone

Hours: Always visible (though no longer a bank)

Cost: Free

Directions: One block north of Rte. 208 (Eighth St.) on Rte. 6 (Conrad Hilton Blvd.), on the southwest corner.

ANOTHER CISCO HOLDUP
The Cisco chief of police was once held hostage for 40 minutes by a man armed with two sticks of beef jerky wrapped in a napkin.

CISCO
Conrad Hilton opened his first hotel in Cisco, the Mobley, in 1919. He had come to town to buy a bank, but couldn't get a room at the Mobley . . . so he bought it. Today Cisco has a Hilton Museum (309 Conrad Hilton Avenue, (254) 442-2553, www.ciscotx.com) in his honor.

CLARKSVILLE
Clarksville is the Wild Turkey Capital of Texas.

CORSICANA
Corsicana claims to be the Fruitcake Capital of the World. The Collin Street Bakery (401 W. Seventh Avenue, (800) 292-7400, www.collinstreet.com), founded in 1896, produces more than 1.6 million fruitcakes each year.

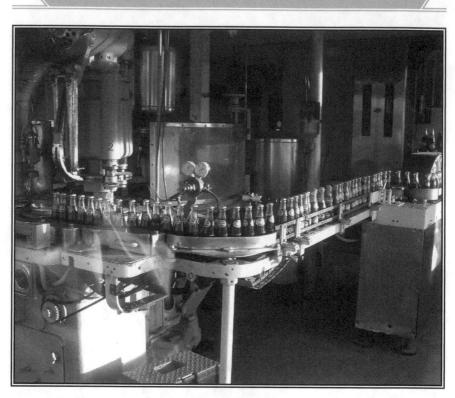

The way it used to be is the way it still is in Dublin.
Photo by author, courtesy of the Dublin Dr Pepper Bottling Company.

Dublin
Dr Pepper Bottling

Dr Pepper might have been invented in Waco (see page 172), but Sam Houston Prim of Dublin helped put it on the map. Back in 1891 Prim convinced the drink's owner, Wade Morrison, to sell the first franchise to his Dublin bottling plant. Over the years it grew to be the largest Dr Pepper bottling operation in the United States . . . and it still is today, probably because they're the *only* Dr Pepper bottler in the nation. No, there are plenty of other companies who peddle a brown concoction they *claim* is Dr Pepper, in *cans*, but only this Dublin operation uses the original formula. The difference is in the sweetener; everybody else uses high-fructose corn syrup, but here they still use Imperial Pure Cane Sugar.

Dublin's bottling operations are open to the public every day, but you'll want to come on Wednesday when they fire up the assembly line to

fill thousands of 10-ounce bottles. You can enjoy a sip or buy souvenirs next door at Old Doc's Soda Shop. And before you leave town, drive around and check out the vintage Dr Pepper billboards and painted-wall advertisements, particularly the Rangerette on a mechanical swing at the corner of Blackjack and Patrick streets.

221 S. Patrick St., Dublin, TX 76446

(888) 398-10-2-4

Hours: Monday–Friday 9 A.M.–5 P.M., Saturday 10 A.M.–5 P.M., Sunday 1–5 P.M.

Cost: Adults $2, Seniors (55+) $1.50, Kids (2–12) $1

www.drpep.com

Directions: One block south of Blackjack St. on Rte. 377 (Patrick St.).

CROSS PLAINS
Author Robert E. Howard, creator of Conan the Barbarian, committed suicide on July 11, 1936, in a car parked behind his family home (625 W. Route 36) in Cross Plains.

DENISON
President Dwight D. Eisenhower was born in Denison on October 14, 1890. You can still see the Eisenhower family quilt in the two-story frame house (208 E. Day Street, (903) 465-8908, www.eisenhower birthplace.org) where the Supreme Allied Baby greeted the world.

EASTON
Easton hosts a Turnip Green Festival each June.

ELECTRA
Each year on Mother's Day, Electra hosts the Electra Goat Barbeque Cook-Off. www.electratexas.org

FROST
The sports teams at Frost High School are named the Polar Bears.

It's an imposter!

Eastland
Old Rip

Growing up, Ernest Wood had always heard that the horned toad (which is actually a lizard) could hibernate for years—decades perhaps—without food or water. What better way to test this theory than by placing a live horned toad in the time capsule being sealed at the new courthouse in Eastland? So, during the building's cornerstone-leveling ceremony on July 29, 1897, Wood dropped his son's pet into a small cavity in the stone, along with a small Bible.

Fast forward 31 years to February 28, 1928. The old courthouse was being torn down so that it could be replaced with a larger structure, and 3,000 people had gathered to witness the reopening of the time capsule. Had the horned toad survived? Reverend Frank Singleton was tapped to be the first to peer into the hole after crews pulled down the wall atop the stone, and Judge Ed Pritchard was given the responsibility of reaching in and extracting the critter. Yes, Singleton announced, there was something inside. Pritchard pulled it out, blew off a layer of dust, and the horned toad inhaled a mighty breath—it was alive!

Locals dubbed the lizard Old Rip in honor of Rip Van Winkle. Wire services picked up the story, and this reptilian Lazarus became an instant celebrity. He embarked on a cross-country tour, attended a Broadway play as the guest of honor, and visited the White House where he met Calvin Coolidge. Years later Old Rip became the inspiration for Michigan J. Frog, in the 1955 Looney Tunes cartoon "One Froggy Evening."

Sadly, Old Rip was better off sealed in his tomb than he was in the outside world. After contracting pneumonia, he died on January 19, 1929. Old Rip was embalmed and placed in the front window of the Barrow Furniture Company in Eastland, laid out in a tiny coffin donated by the National Casket Company. He was later placed on permanent display at the new courthouse.

It was here, during a 1960s campaign stop, Governor John Connally reportedly broke a leg off Old Rip while picking him up. Connally was later cleared of the charges when a child confessed to having snapped the limb in half before the politician ever touched it. Then, on January 16, 1973, Old Rip was toadnapped. Although a ransom letter was sent to the *Abilene Reporter-News*, the famous reptile was never returned. The Old Rip on display in the courthouse lobby today is, to be accurate, an Old Rip-Off.

On the third Saturday in September each year the town celebrates Old Ripfest in honor of its celebrated former citizen. Maybe some day he'll return.

Eastland County Courthouse, Seaman and Main Sts., Eastland, TX 76448

Contact: Eastland Chamber of Commerce, 102 S. Seaman St., Eastland, TX 76448

(877) 2-OLD-RIP or (254) 629-2332

E-mail: ecofc@eastland.net

Hours: Always visible

Cost: Free

www.eastland.net/eastland/parade.htm

Directions: Between Seaman and Lamar Sts. on Rte. 80 (Main St.).

Stamp Mural

Marene Johnson Johnson (yes, that's her name) was the Eastland postmaster from 1957 to 1968. For seven years, after all the mailboxes were stuffed and the packages delivered, Johnson would work on a pet project in the back room: an enormous mural made entirely of postage stamps. By the time she finished she'd used 11,217 stamps, so don't waste your time counting. No, just stand back and admire her hard work.

The centerpiece of the mural is a replica of the United Nations seal surrounded by stamps from around the world. Johnson also re-created portraits of Abraham Lincoln and Benjamin Franklin (our nation's first postmaster general), as well as a map of Texas and the Confederate flag, all surrounded by a frame of yellow roses.

Eastland Post Office, 400 W. Main St., Eastland, TX 76448

(254) 629-2383

Hours: Always open

Cost: Free

www.eastland.net/eastlad/mural.htm

Directions: Four blocks west of the courthouse on Rte. 80 (Main St.), at Daugherty St.

Glen Rose
Creation Evidence Museum

Since the 1930s folks have been coming to Glen Rose, the Dinosaur Capital of Texas, to check out the amazing tracks left by the prehistoric creatures along the Paluxy River (see below). The scientific party line has long been that the earth is billions of years old and that life on this planet is the result of constant and continuing evolution.

In 1984 Carl Baugh, Ph.D., decided he'd had just about enough of *that* malarkey. As he saw it, the religious party line—that the world was created in six days—had been around for a whole lot longer, and since the Bible was divinely inspired, who were you going to trust, Darwin or *God*? So, armed with his mail-order doctorate in philosophy (not paleontology), Baugh set out to prove the theory of evolution wrong, and he was going to use the scientific method to do it!

As luck or wishful thinking would have it, Baugh and his team discovered 90 *human* footprints in the same rock formations as the dinosaur prints were found, proving that humans and dinosaurs walked the earth at the same time. Paleontologists dismissed the human tracks as either fakes or misinterpreted erosion patterns. First of all, some of the footprints were three feet long and seven feet apart, clearly not of human origin. The creationists had an answer: they were made by the giants mentioned in the book of Genesis. Paleontologist Glen Kuban gave the best explanation for the tracks in the 1980s: they were the prints of a dinosaur that walked on the pads of its feet, not its toes. Sure enough, faint, filled-in toe prints were later uncovered around the prints.

Baugh's research marches on. You can see the fruits of his labor at the Creation Evidence Museum, just down the road from the state park. This double-wide museum is only temporary until the permanent structure is finished. What it lacks in style it more than makes up for in "evidence." Look over there—a replica of a petrified human finger embedded in Cretaceous stone. And check out the oil painting of cave men frolicking in a river with a friendly dinosaur—see, it could happen! And what about that human tooth somebody found next to the dinosaur tracks or the iron hammer encased in stone or the petrified human foot still stuck in a cowboy boot?

None of it is as interesting, however, as Baugh's ongoing experiments with the Hyperbaric Biosphere. By re-creating the earth's atmosphere to pre-Flood levels, Baugh will show that common reptiles can be transformed into dinosaurs. He's just in the prototype stages—there's a small iron lung–like chamber in the museum, but Baugh's working on an even larger tank in the half-finished new museum. In the meantime, Baugh has been searching high and low for living dinosaurs who might have survived the Great Flood and was recently hacking his way through the jungles of Papua New Guinea in pursuit of pterodactyls.

Finally, for those of you who find the biblical Flood story hard to swallow, Baugh also plans to build a full-sized Noah's Ark, just to show doubters it can be done. Even if it proves nothing, it still might come in handy if global warming continues unabated.

3102 FM 205, PO Box 309, Glen Rose, TX 76043

(254) 897-3200

Hours: Tuesday–Saturday 10 A.M.–4 P.M.

Cost: Adults $2, Kids $2, Families $5

www.creationevidence.org

Directions: Four miles west of town, first on Rte. 67, then north on FM 205, at the Paluxy River Bridge.

GAINESVILLE
Forty-four Gainesville residents were murdered by their neighbors in October 1862 after expressing sympathy for the Union.

I don't think those fences are going to hold them.

Dinosaur Valley State Park

Around 113 million years ago this region of Texas was at the edge of a giant sea, and a bunch of dinosaurs made an awful mess as they trod around in the muddy swamps along the shore. Nobody figured this out until 1909 when the first dinosaur tracks were uncovered along the Paluxy River. But not until 1938 did paleontologist Roland Bird figure out that one set of tracks showed a meat-eating dino chasing a plant eater. Bird promptly jackhammered up the evidence and carted it off to the American Museum of Natural History in New York, where it remains today.

It turns out the species being hunted was a pleurocoelus, a relative of the apotosaurus. (The pleurocoelus is the official Texas State Dinosaur—a *vegetarian* dino, mind you.) The hungry predator was an acrocanthosaurus, a smaller version of the Tyrannosaurus rex. A year after the area was designated a state park in 1969, Atlantic Richfield donated two full-sized fiberglass dinosaurs left over from the 1964 New York World's Fair: a brontosaurus and a tyrannosaurus. They were built by Louis Paul Jonas for the Sinclair Oil Corporation, which later merged with Atlantic Richfield. While not entirely accurate representations of the dinosaurs that once called Texas home, they were close enough . . . and they were free. In 1985 the brontosaurus was modified to look like an apatosaurus, which made a few nerds happier. Then, because so many people complained that its new noggin looked too small, the old head was screwed back on—science be damned.

FM 205, PO Box 396, Glen Rose, TX 76043

(254) 897-4588

Hours: Park, daily 8 A.M.–10 P.M.; Visitors Center, daily 8 A.M.–5 P.M.

Cost: Adults $5, Kids (12 and under) Free

www.tpwd.state.tx.us/park/dinosaur/dinosaur.htm

Directions: Five miles west of town, first on Rte. 67, then northwest on FM 205, just past the Paluxy River Bridge.

Granbury
John St. Helen or John Wilkes Booth?

John Wilkes Booth shot President Abraham Lincoln in Ford's Theater on April 14, 1865. But was Booth killed 12 days later in a Virginia tobacco barn? Some people in Granbury don't think so.

Blame John St. Helen . . . or should I say, blame John Wilkes Booth? St. Helen showed up in Texas in 1870, arriving from parts unknown, and eventually settled in Granbury where he worked as a bartender at the Black Hawk Saloon and, later, the Gay Lady Saloon. St. Helen was known around town for reciting Shakespeare and getting rip-roaring drunk each April 14. Hmmmmm . . . *curious* . . .

One day St. Helen fell ill and summoned his lawyer, Finis J. Bates, to his deathbed. He confessed that he was really John Wilkes Booth and wanted Bates to contact his brother Edwin. St. Helen/Booth also told his employer, Alfonso Gordon, where he could find the gun used to assassinate the president. Gordon found it wrapped in a newspaper announcing Lincoln's murder. Unfortunately for St. Helen, or Booth, he survived his illness. His cover blown, the bartender fled Texas.

Bates was understandably intrigued about the story told by his former client, but what could he do? Then, on January 13, 1903, a housepainter named David George committed suicide in Enid, Oklahoma. Jessica Harper of El Reno, Oklahoma, came forward and claimed George had confessed to her that *he* was Booth. The news got back to Bates who then rushed to view the body, which he identified as Granbury's missing John St. Helen. Bates tried to claim a $50,000 reward offered by the federal government for evidence on assassination conspirators, but the feds never paid out.

Since nobody claimed the body, and since it was too interesting to bury, St. Helen/George/Booth's mummified corpse was placed on public display. He was posed, seated in a chair while reading a newspaper, in the front window of the Penniman Funeral Home, the Enid establishment that had embalmed him. In 1905 Bates was granted custody of the body and had it shipped to his home in Memphis where he stored it in his garage. Bates rented the mummy out to various sideshows, but when he died in 1923 his widow sold the mummy for $1,000. The assassin's body toured the South (where else?) for years before disappearing from sight sometime in the 1970s. ABC's *20/20* did a story on the St. Helen case, which Barbara Walters called "intewesting."

You can visit the old Gay Lady Saloon, now the Nutshell Eatery, where St. Helen tended bar, and admire a mural to Lincoln's killer. The B&B upstairs is located in the room where St. Helen first let the cat out of the bag.

Nutshell Eatery and Alfonso's Loft, 137 E. Pearl St., Granbury, TX 76048

(817) 573-3308

Hours: Daily 7 A.M.–5 P.M.

Cost: Free

www.alfonsosloft.com

Directions: At the intersection of Rte. 377 (Pearl St.) and Crockett St., on the southeast corner of the town square.

J. FRANK DALTON OR JESSE JAMES?

John St. Helen wasn't the only old geezer in Granbury who wanted the world to know he was a murderous fugitive. The headstone of J. Frank Dalton in the Granbury Cemetery (Crockett and Moore streets) doesn't list his real name at all, but proclaims:

CSA
Jesse Woodson James
Sept. 5, 1847
Aug. 15, 1951
Supposedly killed in 1882

It's not for licking.

Grand Saline
The Salt Palace

The town of Grand Saline sits atop a 16,000-foot-thick salt dome that is 1.5 miles across and contains enough salt to season the world for the next 20,000 years—hence the town's name. In honor of Grand Saline's main industry, local visionary C. O. Dixon cut salt blocks from a nearby quarry, coated them with silicone, and erected a Salt Palace in 1936.

To be honest, the Salt Palace is more of a Salt *House*, only slightly larger than a two-car garage—kind of disappointing in a state where things are supposed to be B-I-G. As you can imagine, rain has been tough on the Salt Palace, as is having the occasional tourist lick its walls. This particular palace was built in 1993, the third version of Dixon's original. Please resist any temptation to taste it; they only have building material for the next 200 centuries.

Garland and Main Sts., Grand Saline, TX 75140

(903) 962-5631

Hours: Tuesday–Saturday 8:30 A.M.–5 P.M.

Cost: Free

Directions: At the intersection of Rte. 80 (Garland St.) and Rte. 110 (Main St.).

To boldly build where no one had built before.

Italy
World's Largest Caterpillar in Outer Space

You might not think there were many different ways to use a "monolithic dome" to build a structure, but you'd be wrong. Just check out the two establishments built by the Monolithic Dome Institute in Italy. The first is a series of domes linked end to end to form the World's Largest Caterpillar. Drivers on I-35 south of Dallas have all seen it—the seven-dome, 350-foot-long creature is hard to miss with its antennae, cowboy boots, and garage door mouth.

The second structure in Italy has been dubbed the Starship *Pegasus*. This Trek-like spaceship has landed just east of the overpass and beams down sandwiches, salads, and pizzas seven days a week.

Monolithic Dome Institute, 177 Dome Park Place, Italy, TX 76651

(972) 483-7423

Hours: Always visible

Cost: Free

www.monolithic.com and www.starshippegasus.com

Directions: Exit east on Rte. 34 from I-35 (for Pegasus), then turn north on Kinfolk Rd. (for caterpillar).

If you think that's big, you should see Grandma.
Photo by author, courtesy of Texas Hill Country Furniture.

Lipan
World's Largest Rocking Chair

Folks, don't try this at home. If you want a World's Largest Rocking Chair, leave it to a professional. Somebody like Larry Dennis. As owner of Texas Hill Country Furniture and Mercantile, Dennis knows how to make a rocker; once he'd selected the appropriate cedar logs, it only took him five and a half days to put it together. A standard rocking chair could take that long.

The Star of Texas Rocker, as it's officially known, is 29 feet, 10½ inches tall, and 12 feet, 7⅜ inches wide, or about six times the size of the rocking chairs he sells in his store . . . and 216 times the weight, tipping the scales at more than four tons.

Texas Hill Country Furniture and Mercantile, 19280 Rte. 281 S, Lipan, TX 76462

(254) 646-3376

E-mail: txcount@lipan.net

Hours: Always visible; Store, Tuesday–Saturday 9 A.M.–6:30 P.M., Sunday 1–5 P.M.

Cost: Free

www.txhcountry.com

Directions: On Rte. 281 north of Rte. 4, west of town.

Mineral Wells
Washing Machine Museum

Who says a trip to the laundromat can't be educational? In Mineral Wells you can wash a load of laundry or two while you're visiting a museum— they're in the same building!

This informative washateria is the brainchild of owner Fred Wilson. Over the years he's collected more than 50 antique washing machines that he has mounted on high shelves above the rows of washers and dryers in his store. Most of the models are hand operated, one dating back to 1885. Wilson also has several dozen antique washboards hanging from the rafters. Imagine all the scrubbing and cranking and wringing required to use these domestic dinosaurs, and be thankful to live in an era of modern appliances.

The Laundromat, 700 W. Hubbard St., Mineral Wells, TX 76067

(940) 325-3404

Hours: Daily 7 A.M.–9 P.M.

Cost: Free

Directions: Two blocks west of Rte. 281 (Fifth St.) on Rte. 180 (Hubbard St.).

HAWKINS
Hawkins is the Pancake Capital of Texas.

HENDERSON
Actress **Sandy Duncan** was born in Henderson on February 20, 1946.

KARNAK
Lady Bird Johnson was born Claudia Alta Taylor on December 22, 1912, three miles southwest of Karnack on Route 43. When she was five, her mother died after breaking her neck; she tripped over a collie and fell down the stairs.

KINGSTON
The most decorated soldier of World War II, **Audie Murphy**, was born in Kingston on June 20, 1924.

What, would you have preferred a beret?

Paris
Eiffel Tower, Texas Style

Red-state Texans, by and large, aren't the type of folks you would think of as Francophiles, not even in Paris, the "Second Largest Paris in the World." Attitudes toward France have changed a lot since this town was incorporated in 1844. (The original settlement was called Pinhook.)

The name was not without some historical precedent; the French flag once was one of the six flown over Texas, when that country snagged the territory from Spain between 1685 and 1690.

For years this 65-foot replica of the Paris landmark, built by the Boilermakers Union Local #902, stood unadorned near the town's convention center. Then in 1998 the city decided to give it a Texas makeover, and installed a gigantic red Stetson atop the spire. Laugh all you want—you wouldn't be the first.

Love Civic Center, Jefferson Rd. and S. Collegiate Dr., Paris, TX 75460

(800) PARIS-TX or (903) 784-2501

Hours: Always visible

Cost: Free

www.paristexas.com

Directions: Adjacent to the Convention Center at the east end of FM 1507 (Jefferson Rd.).

LINDEN
Musician **Don Henley** was born in Linden on July 22, 1947.

LONGVIEW
Actor **Forest Whitaker** was born in Longview on July 15, 1961.

MARSHALL
Marshall hosts a Fire Ant Festival each October, which includes a Fire Ant Calling Contest. (903) 935-7868, www.marshalltxchamber.com

MERIDIAN
Each June Meridian hosts an insect celebration called Chiggerfest.

MINEOLA
Mineola was originally named Sodom. It was changed in 1873 to reflect the names of two railroad executives' daughters: Minnie and Ola.

Texas is no place for sandals.

Jesus in Cowboy Boots

Texas is no place for sandals, even if all you're doing is standing watch over a grave. At least that's what Willet Babcock thought, which is why he gave special instructions to stonemason Gustav Klein in 1880: Babcock wanted a statue of a mourning figure to place over his future burial plot, but he wanted it to be properly shod in cowboy boots. Though Klein's statue is draped in a full-length robe, its left foot peeks out from beneath the garment to reveal the heel-end of a cowboy boot.

Oddly enough, locals refer to this monument as "Jesus in Cowboy Boots," even though the marble mourner seems to be female and is not, as many have claimed, carrying a cross up Calvary. (The figure is leaning against the cross.) Further confusing the situation, Babcock's grave faces west, rather than east—a cemetery no-no—and the torches on the statue's base have been mounted upside down.

Evergreen Cemetery, 560 Evergreen St./Jefferson Rd., Paris, TX 75460

(903) 784-6750

Hours: Daily Sunrise–Sunset

Cost: Free

Directions: At the corner of Church St. (Rte. 19/24) and Evergreen St. (FM 1507).

Pittsburg
Ezekiel Airship

If you think the Wright brothers invented the first airplane, you might want to keep that opinion to yourself in Pittsburg. A local Baptist minister/inventor named Burrell Cannon built a powered flying machine a year *before* the Wright Brothers flew at Kitty Hawk, North Carolina. How did he do it? Cannon claimed he was divinely inspired and based his craft on descriptions of flying machines in the Book of Ezekiel. The Bible does not come with blueprints, so Cannon drew upon 20 years of prayer and divine guidance.

The Ezekiel Airship was a wheel-within-a-wheel contraption, with four "paddles" turned by a small engine. True believers claimed that the helicopter-like device actually took off and flew 100 feet during its maiden voyage in 1902 but eventually struck a fence. Doubting Thomases report that it lurched a few inches into the air above a cow pasture, shuddered violently, then crashed back to the ground after a second or two.

Whatever the case, Cannon felt triumphant and arranged to ship his invention to the 1904 St. Louis World's Fair. It got as far as Texarkana where a tornado blew the train, and the airship, off the tracks. Cannon took this as a warning from above. "God never willed that this airship should fly; I want no more to do with it," he announced before abandoning the crushed vehicle beside the tracks.

But Cannon lied. Nine years later he rebuilt the airship in Illinois, but God (or something) sent the craft veering into a utility pole.

The minister never challenged divine providence again, but the Pittsburg Optimists Club did. They built a faithful re-creation of Cannon's airship, though nobody ever took it out for a spin. Engineers who have

studied the device find Cannon's claim that it lifted off the ground to be dubious at best. The faithful find the engineers' scientific dismissal to be blasphemy at worst. Come to Pittsburg and make up your own mind.

Cotton Belt Depot Museum, Northeast Texas Rural Heritage Center, PO Box 157, 200 W. Marshall St., Pittsburg, TX 75686

(903) 856-0463

E-mail: PittsburgMuseum@cs.com

Hours: Thursday–Saturday 10 A.M.–4 P.M.

Cost: Adults $4, Seniors $3, Kids (12–17) $2

www.pittsburgtxmuseum.com/airship.html

Directions: One block south of Rte. 11 (Jefferson St.), two blocks west of Loop 238 (Mt. Pleasant St.).

MINEOLA
Each spring Mineola hosts a May Days Bean Fest.

MT. VERNON
Footballer **Don Meredith** was born in Mt. Vernon on April 10, 1938.

The Bankhead Highway Visitor Center in Mt. Vernon is housed in the 1868 home of Henry Clay Thruston who, at 7 feet, 7.5 inches tall, was the tallest Confederate soldier in the Civil War.

NEW LONDON
On March 18, 1937, the New London Consolidated School, a public junior/senior high, exploded and killed 293 students, teachers, and staff. The building had been using raw (or "wet") natural gas from a local oil field for heating. Since it had not been odorized, nobody detected a leak until a spark from an electric belt sander in a shop class ignited the gas, lifting the entire structure off its foundation. A young UPI reporter, **Walter Cronkite**, reported on the disaster.

Have a cow . . .

Stephenville and Sulphur Springs
Cow Towns

Fort Worth calls itself a cow town, but Stephenville and Sulphur Springs have the mighty mooers to back up their claims.

Stephensville's Moo-la the Cow was installed on the courthouse square on September 23, 1972, in honor of a local industry that generates

"$223,000,000.00 in milk sales annually." That's how Moo-la got her name. Sadly, that figure has decreased over the last three decades as dairy production consolidates in the upper Midwest, and one day Moo-la could be sold off for fiberglass steaks.

Erath County Courthouse, Graham and Washington Sts., Stephenville, TX 76401

No phone

Hours: Always visible

Cost: Free

Directions: On the corner of Rte. 377 (Washington St.) and FM 108 (Graham St.).

. . . or two.

Buttercup and Creampuff stand a better chance of weathering the changing agricultural climate—each is much larger than Moo-la, and they have the advantage of numbers. Buttercup, a Holstein, and Creampuff, a Jersey, stand guard over a museum dedicated to the region's dairy industry. There's plenty to learn here; at one point you're guided by a robotic skeleton name Cal C. Umm, who will tell you how milk is essential to combat osteoporosis. Hmmmmm . . . what do you have to drink to keep your skin and muscles, too?

Southwest Dairy Center and Museum, 1200 Houston St., PO Box 936, Sulphur Springs, TX 75482

(903) 439-MILK

E-mail: swdairycenter@geocities.com

Hours: Always visible; Museum, Monday–Friday 9 A.M.–4 P.M.

Cost: Free

www.geocities.com/Heartland/Ranch/3541/

Directions: On FM 11 (Houston St.) west of FM 154.

Sulphur Springs
Music Box Gallery

Years ago Leo St. Clair of Sulphur Springs received a music box from the Belgian royal family. It sparked his interest in the devices and he began collecting until he had amassed more than 150. St. Clair eventually donated them to the local library, which today displays his best pieces in the building's foyer.

You'll have to take their word that these really are music boxes since it's not as if you can wind them up and listen. Many of the boxes are classic, ornate, and a little dull, but others are downright bizarre. One depicts a single monkey wearing a hat, while on another a monkey plays an accordion. One more shows a group of rats and squirrels sitting in a classroom—who knew they could read? The best, however, is a music box with a Turkish sultan; its label says that smoke will come out the sultan's mouth if you put a cigarette in the hookah beside him. Sadly, this is a non-smoking facility.

Sulphur Springs Public Library, 611 N. Davis St., Sulphur Springs, TX 75482

(903) 885-4926

Hours: Monday–Wednesday and Friday 9 A.M.–6 P.M., Thursday 11 A.M.–8 P.M.

Cost: Free

www.sslibrary.org

Directions: One block north of Houston St., two blocks west of Church St. (Rte. 154).

NOONDAY

Each June, Noonday throws an Onion Festival.

Texarkana
Making a Run for the Border

Texas and Oklahoma have had a long and celebrated rivalry, but Texas and Arkansas? They seem to be able to get along . . . at least in Texarkana. In fact, when this town on the Texas–Arkansas border was established in 1873, the founders even tried to incorporate Louisiana into the name (TEXas–ARKansas–louisiANA), even though that state is 20 miles from town.

The greatest symbol of this rapprochement is the city's Bi-State Justice Center, which straddles the Texas/Arkansas line. The building was constructed with Texas pink granite and Arkansas limestone and houses the government offices of two counties, two cities, and two states. It is located on State Line Avenue, which is unique all by itself; since the Texas side of Texarkana is dry, the liquor stores are all located on the Arkansas side of the street.

Another government building sits atop the border: the town's federal center/post office (500 N. State Line Avenue). Though there is only one post office, it has two zip codes. Those mailing to Arkansas use zip code 71854, but Texas is 75501.

Bi-State Justice Center, 100 N. State Line Ave., Texarkana, TX 75501

(903) 798-3000

Hours: Always visible

Cost: Free

www.texarkana.org

Directions: Five blocks south of Rte. 67 (Seventh St.) at Broad St. (Second St.).

OLNEY

Each September Olney hosts an annual sporting festival for amputees called the One-Armed Dove Hunt.

PALESTINE

Palestine hosts a Hot Pepper Festival each October, which includes a Macho Man Pepper Eating Contest. www.visitpalestine.com

The wonders of welding.

Vernon
Home of the Junkyard Critters

Johnny Sue Big Rivers knew how to handle a welding torch. Years ago he spotted an expensive sculpture in a catalog and bragged to a friend that he could do better. "Prove it," the friend replied, and Big Rivers accepted the challenge.

Working with cast-off objects, machine parts, and old propane tanks, Big Rivers assembled an impressive menagerie in his front yard. He built lobsters and insects and centipedes, a full-size gun-totin' sheriff and matching banjo player, and several totem poles. His largest pieces were two dinosaurs: a stegosaurus at the curb and a T. rex to guard the front door.

Big Rivers has passed away, but his sculptures were built to last, which is why you can still find them on a quiet side street in Vernon.

1620 Turner St., Vernon, TX 76384

Private phone

Hours: Always visible

Cost: Free

Directions: Two blocks north of Wilbarger St. (Rte. 287 Business), three blocks east of Bentley/Tolar St.

Mabel Frame, before and after.

Waxahachie
Fearsome Faces

Mabel Frame should have known better than to play with the emotions of a stonecarver. If you can believe the story—and who knows if you can—her boyfriend was working on the Ellis County Courthouse in Waxahachie in 1895. To demonstrate his affection, he chiseled her angelic face into the ornamental stonework around the building's porch entryways. But as the courthouse progressed, Frame's affection for her boyfriend did not. Each new face the brokenhearted man carved was uglier than the one before it. The last was downright scary.

Ellis County Courthouse, Main and College Sts., Waxahachie, TX 75165

(972) 938-9617

Hours: Always visible

Cost: Free

www.waxacofc.com

Directions: One block southeast of Rte. 77 (Elm St.) on Rte. 287 (Main St.).

Munster Mansion

There are classic TV fans, and there are fanatics. When it comes to *The Munsters*, Charles and Sandra McKee are fanatics. How so? Would mere fans spend a quarter million (and counting!) building a modern replica of the Munsters' mansion? Though not as creepy and run-down as the original, this place does have a dungeon, an electric chair in the living room, a revolving bookcase, a secret passageway, and a fire-breathing dragon (Spot) under the front stairway. And the McKees are always adding features.

Why do they do it? Why not! In a nation of boring subdivisions filled with cookie-cutter homes, isn't it refreshing that somebody would think outside the box (and by "box" I mean "coffin")?

The Munster Mansion is visible from a road on the north side of Waxahachie, though you have to look quickly past the main gate while driving along the busy road. Each Halloween the McKees host a party to raise funds for local charities. Both Al Lewis (Grandpa) and Butch Patrick (Eddie) have attended. Check out their Web site for next year's ghoulish guest of honor.

"1313 Mockingbird Lane" (3636 FM 813), Waxahachie, TX 75165

Private phone

Hours: Always visible

Cost: Free

www.munstermansion.com

Directions: The Mockingbird Lane address is from the show; the mansion is really located on east side of Brown St. (FM 813), east of the Rte. 287 Bypass, not far past the road's sharp turn to the left.

TIOGA

Gene Autry, "King of the Cowboys," was born Orvon Grover Autry in Tioga on September 29, 1907. Autry offered to donate a considerable sum to the town in 1936 if it changed its name to Autry Springs. Tioga declined.

EDIFICE COMPLEX

The McKees' Munster Mansion continues a long tradition of Texans with edifice complexes. "If you can't beat 'em, build 'em," seems to be the motto for these folks:

Mount Vernon (Lawther Drive, Dallas): Dallas millionaire/nutball H. L. Hunt thought of himself as a modern-day George Washington, and what better way to convince others than to live in a home that resembled Mount Vernon? His former mansion sits on the northwest shore of White Rock Lake.

White House (515 Bayridge Road, La Porte): Texas Governor Ross Sterling also thought of himself as cut from presidential cloth, so he had a ³/₅ths replica of the White House built in the 1920s. Actually, he only half-built the executive residence, the back half. Sterling's streetside entrance looks like a regular mansion, but the side that faces Galveston Bay off Morgan's Point has the familiar Washington facade. The property is off-limits to the public, so to see the White House side of the building you have to rent a boat and view it from the water.

Falkenstein Castle (7400 Park Road 4, Marble Falls, www.falkenstein castle.com): Why not reach a little further back in history for architectural inspiration? This 1996 structure northwest of Marble Falls is based on Mad King Ludwig II's Neuschwanstein Castle in Bavaria. Though not open to the general public, you can rent it out for weddings . . . and you don't even have to be crazy to do so. Rent it, I mean. But get married? Well . . .

Famous Rooms (Douglas MacArthur Academy of Freedom, Howard Payne University, Austin Avenue and Coggin Street, Brownwood, (325) 646-2502, www.hputx.edu): Located on the grounds of Howard Payne University, this military academy has study rooms that resemble the interior of Independence Hall, the Magna Carta castle room, and an Egyptian pharaoh's tomb.

Liberty Bell (Humphreys Cultural Center, 1710 Sam Houston Street, Liberty, (936) 336-8901, www.libertydaytonchamber.com/lrc.htm#ghcc): If the fake Independence Hall in Brownswood needs a fake Liberty Bell, it can find a bogus bell in Liberty. This big ringer was cast in 1960 from the same mold as the original Liberty Bell, only this one didn't crack. It was intended as a monument of hope for those seeking a cure for muscular dystrophy. In 1976 it was placed atop its own tower for the nation's Bicentennial. Liberty's Liberty Bell is only rung on special occasions: New Year's Day and the Fourth of July.

Niña, the *Pinta*, and the *Santa Maria* (Corpus Christi Museum of Science and History, 1900 N. Chaparral Street, Corpus Christi, (361) 884-8085, www.cctexas.com/?fuseaction=main.view&page=200): No, they're not buildings, but they are faithful replicas of the three ships that brought Christopher Columbus to the New World in 1492. These re-creations were built in Spain in 1992 for the historic voyage's 500th anniversary and are now docked at a re-created Spanish coastal village.

The Alamo (400 Creekside Lane, Holiday Lakes): And finally, there's no better way to show you're a Texan than to build your home to look like the Alamo. The late Ken Freeman did just that and constructed a second building on the property that looks like the mission's barracks.

UNCERTAIN
Nobody knows for sure how the town of Uncertain got its name. Really.

VERNON
Whitewater Special Prosecutor **Kenneth Starr** was born in Vernon on July 21, 1946.

WAXAHACHIE
Rocker **Jerry Lee Lewis** attended Southwestern Bible Institute in Waxahachie, but was expelled for playing "My God Is Real" as a boogie-woogie.

I won't grow up!

Weatherford
Peter Pan Statue

Peter Pan didn't really hail from this small Texas town, though tiny
actress Mary Martin did. Martin was born at 414 W. Lee Avenue on
December 1, 1913, to Preston and Juanita Martin. As a child she was
obsessed with Buster Brown; Martin named her dog Tige and had her

hair cut in a pageboy bob. She even refused to wear a bow in her hair until she learned a cruel truth. She explained her disillusionment in her memoir: "Buster Brown was a midget, not a little boy."

How ironic, then, that Martin played a boy who would never grow up until she was well into her fifties. In 1976, sculptor Ronald Thomason was commissioned to create a life-sized bronze of Martin in her signature role for the Weatherford Public Library. Martin/Pan fans can see a display of memorabilia in the library's Heritage Gallery.

Sadly, not even Tinkerbell's fairy dust could keep Martin going forever, and she died in 1990. Her body was returned to Weatherford where she was buried in the family plot in Greenwood Cemetery (Mill and Water Streets).

Weatherford Public Library, 1014 Charles St., Weatherford, TX 76086

(817) 598-4150

Hours: Statue, always visible; Library, Monday–Thursday 10 A.M.–8 P.M., Friday–
 Saturday 10 A.M.–6 P.M.

Cost: Free

Directions: Two blocks east of S. Bowie Dr., one block north of Mockingbird Ln.

WEATHERFORD
The Parker County Courthouse in Weatherford cost $55,555.55 to build in 1884.

WICHITA FALLS
Dancer **Tommy Tune** was born in Wichita Falls on February 28, 1939.

Wichita Falls hosts the 100-mile Hotter 'n Hell Hundred bike race each August.

A tornado killed 42 Wichita Falls residents on April 10, 1979, and left another 20,000 homeless.

Wichita Falls
The Littlest Skyscraper

Back in 1918, swindler J. D. McMahon used Texas's reputation for thinking big to scam investors of hundreds of thousands of dollars. Here's how it worked: McMahon made the rounds of the moneyed class showing off plans for a Wichita Falls skyscraper. The skyscraper in the blueprints was clearly labeled as 480" tall. Of course, a skyscraper would more likely be in the 480' range, not 480", a mere 40 *feet*. That's just four stories tall.

To his credit, McMahon went through with the construction. Each floor on "The Littlest Skyscraper" is 8 by 12 feet, but only the ground level is accessible—the building has no staircases. When the skyscraper was finished, McMahon skipped town with the balance of the investors' contributions. The building's current owner plans to restore the skyscraper, including adding stairs. Nice touch!

"The Littlest Skyscraper" is not the only fraud perpetrated in this North Texas town. In fact, not even the falls of Wichita Falls are real. The original five-foot waterfall on the Wichita River, from which this town draws its name, washed away in 1886. In 1987 a new waterfall was built, but at a different point in the river. The new waterfall is 54 feet tall—10 times the original—gushes 3,500 gallons a minute, and is controlled by a switch.

701 LaSalle St., Wichita Falls, TX 76301

No phone

Hours: Always visible

Cost: Free

www.cwftx.net

Directions: Three blocks northeast of Scott Ave. (Rte. 287), two blocks southeast of Fifth St. (Rte. 479), at the railroad tracks.

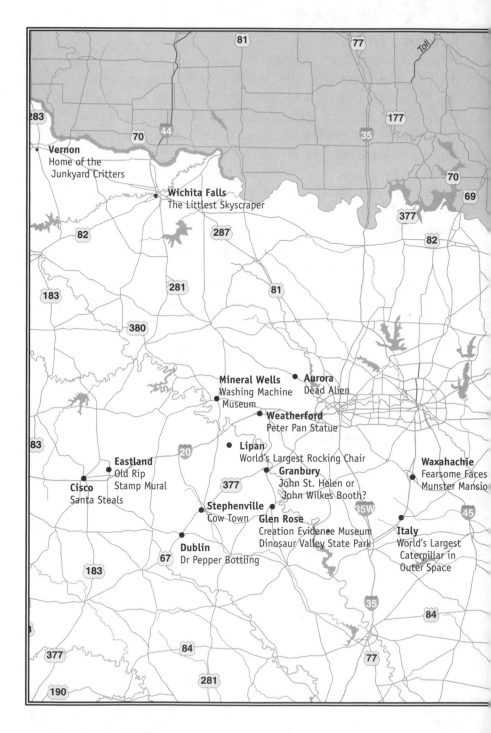

Vernon
Home of the
Junkyard Critters

Wichita Falls
The Littlest Skyscraper

Mineral Wells
Washing Machine
Museum

Aurora
Dead Alien

Weatherford
Peter Pan Statue

Lipan
World's Largest Rocking Chair

Eastland
Old Rip
Stamp Mural

Granbury
John St. Helen or
John Wilkes Booth?

Waxahachie
Fearsome Faces
Munster Mansion

Cisco
Santa Steals

Stephenville
Cow Town

Glen Rose
Creation Evidence Museum
Dinosaur Valley State Park

Dublin
Dr Pepper Bottling

Italy
World's Largest
Caterpillar in
Outer Space

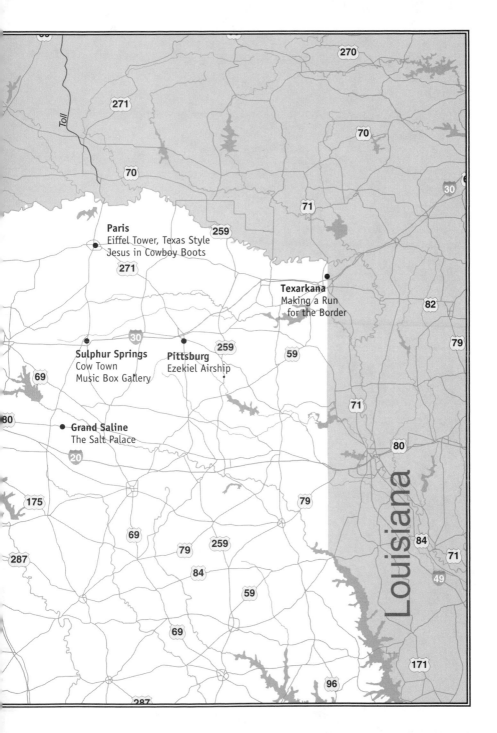

3

DaLLaS/Fort WortH Area

Back in 1997 Dr. Hon-Ming Chen moved his Chen Tao (True Way) Church, sometimes called the God and Buddha Salvation Foundation, or the God Saves the Earth Flying Saucer Foundation, to the Dallas suburb of Garland. Why Garland? Dr. Chen claimed "Garland" sounded like "God-Land" to him.

The group's Taiwanese followers were, by all accounts, good neighbors. But then Dr. Chen started making unusual proclamations: God would appear on Dallas TV's Channel 18 on March 25, 1998, to announce that he would inhabit Chen's body, effective March 31, at 10 a.m. Central Standard Time. Soon thereafter a nuclear war would break out between China and Taiwan, but few would die because they'd be transported by UFO to Gary, Indiana, just before the blasts. (Some improvement!)

Well, as you probably know, none of this came to pass. Unlike so many self-proclaimed prophets before him, Dr. Chen actually *admitted* his mistake. "I would rather you don't believe what I say any more," he announced before disbanding his followers. And this is why, sadly, you will not be able to visit the Chen Tao Church on your oddball trip to Dallas.

But I do have a few other strange suggestions . . .

We risked nuclear Armageddon for this?

Dallas
America Won . . . Burgers!

When the Soviet Union collapsed in 1989, it immediately found itself with a surplus of slightly dented statues of Vladimir Lenin. For a while it was a true buyer's market, and you could pick up one of these works of

art for about $500. That's what Texan Harvey Gough paid for his Lenin statue, which he purchased from the Odessa Crane Factory in the Ukraine. Gough then paid 10 times that amount to ship the 800-pound concrete and rebar statue back to the States.

Now I know you're wondering, "What in the *world* was Gough thinking when he blew more than five Gs rescuing a Commie monument so he could erect it in Dallas? Dallas!?!" The answer is simple: he did it to taunt this nation's former Cold War foe. Lenin now graces the parking lot of a 100 percent free market burger joint, mounted on a pedestal with a plaque that reads, "America Won."

Goff's Charcoal Hamburgers, 5702 W. Lovers Ln., Dallas, TX 75209

(214) 351-3336

Hours: Always visible; Restaurant, daily 10 A.M.–11 P.M.

Cost: Free; Meals $4–$7

Directions: One block west of the Dallas North Tollway on Lovers Ln., at Devonshire Dr.

DALLAS

Dallas hosts a Corn Dog Festival each October. One of the event's most popular competitions is the Celebrity Look-Alike Contest where the *corndogs* are chosen for their famous characteristics. www.corndogfestival.com

---

Musician **David Crosby** was busted for freebasing cocaine at Dallas's Cardi's nightclub on April 12, 1982.

The Texas State Fair is home to the 212-foot-tall Texas Star, the Largest Ferris Wheel in the Western Hemisphere.

"Everything in Dallas looks as if it's been built in the last thirty minutes. . . . If the Alamo had been in Dallas, it would be the Hyatt-Alamo today." —Dan Jenkins

Biblical Arts Center

Though churches have historically been big supporters of the arts, in the last few centuries a rift has grown between the creative community and the religious establishment. The Biblical Arts Center aims to close that gap. Of course, it's not interested in paintings of Campbell's soup cans or Thomas Kinkade cottages but focuses instead on depictions of Jesus Christ and other holy subjects.

You enter the museum through a re-creation of St. Paul's Gate in Damascus and pass galleries filled with parable paintings and ancient artifacts. Another space, titled Experience Israel, allows you to "walk where Jesus walked" through a re-created Holy Land, though when you get to the Garden Tomb you're not allowed to "rise where Jesus rose."

You'll want to keep your eye on your watch during your visit, because the museum's main attraction—*The Miracle at Pentecost* by Torger Thompson—is only unveiled once an hour, on the half-hour. If you had three of these 124-by-20-foot murals, you could cover a football field, but then you'd be penalized for too many men on the field—the painting has more than 200 Biblical figures in it. Thompson's work appears from behind a curtain during a "dramatic sound and light show." Who needs Laser Floyd?

7500 Park Lane, Dallas, TX 75225

(214) 691-4661

Hours: Tuesday–Saturday 10 A.M.–5 P.M., Sunday 1–5 P.M.

Cost: Free; Mural, Adults $7, Kids (5 and under) Free

www.biblicalarts.org

Directions: Four blocks north of Northwest Hwy., two blocks west of I-75.

Big Tex

Laugh all you want, but little by little Big Tex is coming to life. Back in the 1940s, the folks in the town of Kerens built a 50-foot-tall Santa to promote local businesses. He was billed as the World's Largest Santa. But as tall as he was, Santa wasn't very tough: he was blown over in a windstorm a year later. Rather than repair him, the town sold Santa to the Texas State Fair for $750. In Dallas, Jack Bridges transformed the jolly old elf into the World's Largest Texan by shaving off his hemp-rope beard and adding a 75-gallon cowboy hat, which made him two feet taller.

Big Tex was unveiled at the 1949 fair. He wore size 70 boots, a tailored Williamson-Dickie shirt, and size 23/23 (feet) Lee jeans. That's some inseam!

Then, over the years, Big Tex started to change. In 1952 he got a mechanical jaw, and began shouting "Howdy folks!" every hour, on the hour. Then, in 2000, somebody got the bright idea to make his arm wave. What's next—is the fair going to remove his feet from cement, allowing him to roam the midway, stomping on guests? If we've learned anything from *Westworld* it's that the more freedom you give a robot, the more it'll take. Fairgoers beware!

Fair Park, The Midway, 1300 Robert B. Cullum Blvd., Dallas, TX 75210

(214) 565-9931

E-mail: pr@bigtex.com

Hours: Always visible

Cost: Free (except during State Fair)

www.bigtex.com/2002/history/bigtexhitory.html

Directions: North two blocks from the Grand Ave. gate.

BIG LONGHORN

What's a cowboy without cows? Just a boy, I guess. So where's Big Tex's herd? Well, at least one of them—a 25-foot fiberglass longhorn—has found a home on the southwest side of downtown Dallas, at the north end of the Houston Street viaduct.

DALLAS

Paintings by **Pablo Picasso** and **Diego Rivera** were removed from the Dallas Museum of Art (1717 N. Harwood Street, (214) 922-1200) in the 1950s because it was not the museum's policy "to knowingly acquire or to exhibit the work of a person known . . . to be now a Communist or of Communist-front affiliation."

The evil OCP Headquarters in *Robocop* is actually the Dallas City Hall (1500 Marilla Street).

The old Barrow home.

Bonnie and Clyde

The story of Bonnie and Clyde has been glamorized, exaggerated, and distorted so often in popular culture it's sometimes difficult to separate the fact from the fiction. It's always been this way, even while they were still on the lam. But the idea that they were Depression-era Robin Hoods, knocking off banks on behalf of the little guy, is laughable. Sure, they pulled their share of bank heists, but they robbed more gas stations and mom-and-pop stores than anything else. Oh, and they killed at least a dozen innocent victims—mostly "little guys"—in the process. It's worth a look back on the *real* story.

Clyde Barrow was born six miles west of Telico on March 24, 1909. In 1922 the Barrows moved to the Cement City neighborhood of Dallas (after a short stay beneath the Houston Street viaduct) where they lived in the back half of the Star Service Station at 1221 Singleton Boulevard. Clyde attended Sidney Lanier High School, though he dropped out to get a job in a mirror factory when he was 17 years old.

After buying his first car in early 1927, Clyde launched his life of crime by robbing an Oak Cliff drugstore at gunpoint. Brother Marvin "Buck" Barrow helped Clyde roll other establishments in Dallas, Sherman, and Waco. Their successful string of robberies ended in October 1929 when, following a Denton heist, Clyde ran his car off the road while being pursued by police. Clyde escaped capture, but Buck was shot, apprehended, tried, convicted, and packed off to Huntsville for a five-year sentence.

★

Bonnie Parker was born in Rowena on October 1, 1910. Her father died before she turned five, and her mother moved the family to Dallas. Bonnie grew up at 1406 Cockrell Street (since demolished) and later attended Cement City High School where she was an honor student. At 16 years old, she married a petty criminal named Roy Thornton, moved to a house on Olive Street, and was abandoned a year later. Thornton was later sent to prison for murder.

In January 1930 she met Clyde at the home of a friend. It was love at first sight, and Bonnie brought Clyde home to meet her mother. After spending the night sleeping on Mrs. Parker's couch, Clyde was wakened the next morning by police who promptly took him into custody for further questioning in the Denton heist. Bonnie's mother was suddenly less enamored with her daughter's new boyfriend, but did Bonnie listen to her mama?

Though never charged in the Denton job, Waco officials asked that Clyde be released into their custody on March 2, 1930. They charged him with a variety of offenses. Awaiting trial, Clyde convinced the love-struck Bonnie to slip him a gun, launching her into what would become a short career in crime. He escaped from Waco's McClennan County jail on March 9. Bonnie waited in Dallas while Clyde embarked on a quick crime spree through the Midwest. He was eventually arrested in Middleton, Ohio, on March 19.

After being extradited to Texas, Clyde was convicted of five car thefts and two robberies in Waco, as well as the armed escape, and was given 14 years at hard labor. He was sent to Huntsville on April 21, but soon transferred to the Eastham Prison Farm near Crockett. Bonnie took a job as a waitress in Dallas and pined for her true love . . . though she did date other men.

Two years later, Clyde came up with a brilliant plan to get out of Eastham's work detail: he had another prisoner use an ax to chop off two of his toes in an "accident." Clyde's mother had been petitioning the governor to parole her son, and the injury helped secure his release. On February 8, 1932, he hobbled out of prison and back to his old ways.

Over the next two years Bonnie and Clyde, and their compatriots, robbed banks, stores, and individuals throughout the South and Midwest and killed at least 12 police and bystanders in the process. In Texas, their murders included

★ Hillsboro gas station owner John Bucher, murdered by gang member Raymond Hamilton on April 30, 1932, (intersection of Routes 77 and 81 north of town)

★ Howard Hall, manager of the Little Food Store in Sherman, who was gunned down on October 11, 1932, for $60 (Vaden Street and Wells Avenue)

★ Doyle Johnson, who was shot by W. D. "Deacon" Jones while stealing a car from Johnson's driveway in Temple on December 23, 1932 (606 S. 13th Street)

★ Deputy Sheriff Malcolm Davis, who was killed by Clyde on the front porch of Hamilton's sister Lillie McBride's house after police tried to ambush the couple at her home, just around the corner from the Barrow service station in West Dallas, on January 6, 1933. The pair escaped. (3111 N. Winnetka Street)

On June 10, 1933, Bonnie and Clyde (and W. D. Jones) ran off Route 203 six miles east of Wellington on the way to Quail, at a bridge over the Salt Fork River. The car rolled over several times before coming to rest atop Bonnie. The car caught fire and Bonnie's legs were badly burned as her nylons melted onto her flesh. It took a while, but she eventually recovered in a motor court in Fort Smith, Arkansas.

Back on the road, the duo's woes went from bad to worse. Buck Barrow was shot twice in the head on July 18, 1933, during a gun battle in Platte City, Missouri. Five days later the gang was attacked again, this time near Dexter, Iowa; Buck and Blanche Barrow were captured, and Buck died six days later. In January 1934 Texas Ranger Frank "Pancho" Hamer was enlisted to bring Bonnie and Clyde justice, one way or

another. But before he stopped them, the gang killed again. Accomplice Henry Methvin gunned down two Grapevine policemen on Easter Sunday, April 1, 1934; the motorcycle cops stopped to investigate the gangsters' car, which was parked just off Dove Road, east of Route 114. A granite monument now marks the spot where officers E. B. Wheeler and H. D. Murphy died.

Hamer eventually ambushed the couple on May 23, 1934, near Gibsland, Louisiana. Their bullet-filled corpses were returned to their families in Dallas. Bonnie's body was viewed at the McKamy-Campbell Funeral Home on Forest Avenue, then planted in Fish Trap Cemetery as biplanes flew overhead, dropping flowers. In the 1940s she was moved to Crown Hill Memorial Park. Her mother refused to honor Bonnie's request that she be buried beside Clyde. Her epitaph reads: "As the flowers are made sweeter, by the sunshine and the dew, so the world is made brighter, by the likes of folks like you."

Crown Hill Memorial Park, 9700 Webb Chapel Rd., West Dallas, TX 75520

(214) 946-5133

Hours: Always visible

Cost: Free

Directions: Just east of Webb Chapel Rd. at Lombardy Ln.

Clyde's body was viewed by 30,000 visitors at the Sparkman-Holtz-Brand Funeral Home in Dallas, the same establishment where Buck was viewed a year earlier, and he was buried beside his brother in the Western Heights Cemetery. During the graveyard ceremony, the throng grew so large that they nearly pushed the Barrow family into Clyde's open grave. Over the years Barrow's tombstone has been stolen no less than five times, usually during the weekend of the Texas–Oklahoma football game, but it has always turned back up somewhere.

Clyde and Buck Barrow's Grave, Western Heights Cemetery, 1617 Fort Worth Ave.,
  West Dallas, TX 75208

No phone

Hours: Always visible

Cost: Free

Directions: Just north of I-30 on Rte. 260 (Fort Worth Ave.).

WHAT ABOUT THE REST OF THE GANG?

Though they died as a pair, Bonnie and Clyde rarely worked alone. Those who helped them on their crime sprees met their ends in other not-so-glamorous ways.

Marvin "Buck" Barrow: Buck Barrow was already in bad shape when he was taken into custody after a shoot-out near Dexter, Iowa, on July 23, 1933. Though shot twice, he had already been mortally wounded a week earlier in Platte City, Missouri. Witnesses in Dexter reported that his brains were oozing out of a hole in his skull. Buck died of pneumonia in the King's Daughters Hospital in Perry, Iowa, six days later. His body was returned to Dallas and buried at the Western Heights Cemetery (1617 Fort Worth Avenue).

Blanche Barrow: Sentenced to prison in Missouri, she was paroled in 1939. Blanche remarried in 1940, died on December 24, 1988, and was buried in Dallas's Grove Hill Memorial Park (4118 Samuell Boulevard).

Raymond Hamilton: The pair's former sidekick was first sentenced to 362 years for crimes that included murder, armed robbery, and escape. But it was the death sentence that did him in; he was executed in Huntsville on May 10, 1935, and was buried in Elmwood Memorial Park in Dallas (1315 Berkley Avenue).

W. D. Jones: Clyde's childhood friend was shot and killed during a dispute in Houston on August 20, 1974. He was buried in Houston's Brookside Memorial Park (13401 Eastex Freeway).

DALLAS

The Icee was invented in Dallas by Dean Sperry and Omar Knedlik in 1959. Then, in 1965, 7-Eleven came up with its own version of the Icee: the Slurpee.

Children's Medical Center Train

It's supposedly the largest permanent train display in the nation, but what makes it special is not its size, but its elevation. While most train layouts spread out, the eight trains in the Children's Medical Center rise up and around several large mountains. In fact, to best appreciate them you have to take the stairs to a second-floor platform where you can survey them all at the same time.

There are about 1,000 feet of track rolling through the mini-mountains, over the tiny trestles, and into the dinky depots. Part of the layout is supposed to represent Arizona's Grand Canyon (which real railroads have always avoided), but there are some recognizable Texas landmarks as well, namely the Dallas skyline. The view is from the west side of downtown, near the Triple Underpass (see page 322), though you won't find the Three Teeny Tramps in the railyard. Because of it, I suspect the layout's creators are part of a vast, albeit miniaturized, assassination conspiracy.

1935 Motor St., Dallas, TX 75235

(214) 920-2000

Hours: Daily 8 A.M.–8 P.M.

Cost: Free

www.childrens.com

Directions: One block north of I-77 (Stemmons Fwy.) on Motor St.

TINY TOWN

As long as you're at the Children's Medical Center, check out its other exhibit: dozens of dollhouses from the American Museum of Miniature Arts (www.minimuseum.org). The museum, which currently doesn't have a venue of its own, rotates its large collection of dollhouses, scale models of famous Texas homes, room boxes, and other tiny structures, between several Dallas institutions. In addition to the Children's Medical Center, you can also see the collection at the Dallas Public Library (1515 Young Street, (214) 670-1740), the Dallas Fireman's Museum (3801 Parry Avenue, (214) 821-1500), and the Hall of State at Fair Park (Washington and Parry Avenues, (214) 421-4500).

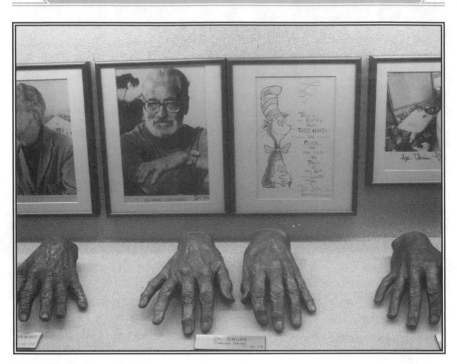

I sure do like these hands of Seuss.
Left hand, right hand, yes I doose.
Photo by author, courtesy of Baylor University Medical Center.

Hands of the Masters

Dr. Adrian E. Flatt is fascinated with hands, as well he should be—he's a hand surgeon! In 1962 he started making bronzed casts of his fellow surgeons' hands, and before long everyone was getting into the act, from presidents to movie stars to astronauts. His somewhat creepy, but still fascinating collection is on display in a lobby of the Baylor University Medical Center.

So whose hands does he have? Ethel Merman, Katharine Hepburn, Paul Newman, Greer Garson, Winston Churchill, Mary Martin, Billy Graham, Walt Disney, Louis Armstrong, Dr. Seuss, Joe DiMaggio, Walter Cronkite, Margaret Thatcher, Tom Landry, Andre the Giant, Kathy Rigby, Charles Schulz, Nolan Ryan, Larry Hagman, Martina Navratilova, Norman Rockwell, David Copperfield, Willie Shoemaker, Wilt Chamberlain, and every U.S. president from Harry Truman to George H. W. Bush. A few of the casts reveal amputations; astronaut Deke Slayton is missing his

left ring finger past the first knuckle, and mountain climber C. Beck Weathers, who was left for dead on Mt. Everest in 1996, has little more than stumps.

Baylor University Medical Center, Truett Building, 3500 Gaston Ave., Dallas, TX 75246

(800) 4-BAYLOR or (214) 820-7499

Hours: Daily 9 A.M.–5 P.M.

Cost: Free

www.baylorhealth.com

Directions: Two blocks southwest of Washington Ave. on Gaston Ave.; in the Truett Lobby bearing right from the Gaston Ave. entrance.

DALLAS

Mitch Maddox of Dallas had his name legally changed to DotComGuy (www.dotcomguy.com) in 1999, then spent the entire year of 2000 in his Dallas condo with his DotComDog. Everything they needed he accessed via his computer, and Web fans watched his every move on 24 cameras.

Owen Wilson based his *Rushmore* screenplay on his 10th-grade expulsion from St. Mark's Academy (10600 Preston Road, www.smtexas.org) in Dallas.

Dallas pawnbroker Rocky Goldstein sold **John Hinkley** a .22-calibre revolver that he later used to shoot **President Ronald Reagan**.

Musician **Stevie Ray Vaughan** grew up at 2557 Glenfield Street in Dallas. He is buried at Laurel Land Memorial Park (6000 S.R.L. Thornton Freeway, (214) 371-1336).

Hindenburg Junk

About all that's left.
Photo by author, courtesy of Frontiers of Flight.

You've seen the newsreel footage over and over again, the 803-foot-long *Hindenburg* zeppelin exploding in flames as it moved in for a landing in Lakehurst, New Jersey, on May 6, 1937. How could anyone, or anything, have survived that conflagration? Well, 62 of the *Hindenburg*'s 97 passengers and crew did make it out alive, but very little of the craft itself was left untorched. However, Dallas's Frontiers of Flight Museum has the largest unburned artifact recovered from the disaster: the radio operator's chair. It also owns a fragment of its propeller and a cigarette case and lighter (!) from a passenger.

Now you can imagine that, as an aircraft museum, Frontiers of Flight doesn't devote too much space to a disaster like the *Hindenburg*; the majority of its displays focus on those aircraft that didn't go down in flames. The museum starts with a swatch of fabric from the Wright brothers' Flyer and continues through the Space Race with the *Apollo 7* Command Module. Even non-ghouls will find its collection interesting.

Frontiers of Flight Museum, 6911 Lemmon Ave., Dallas, TX 75235

(214) 350-3600

E-mail: info@flightmuseum.com

Hours: Monday–Saturday 10 A.M.–5 P.M., Sunday 1–5 P.M.

Cost: Adults $8, Seniors (65+) $6, Kids (3–17) $5

www.flightmuseum.com

Directions: One block north of Mockingbird Ln. on Lemmon Ave.

Medieval Times

If eating dinner with your bare hands, wearing a paper crown for an entire evening, or cheering on Fabio wannabes as they battle on horseback doesn't sound appealing, then you should avoid Medieval Times. Then again, maybe you should lighten up. This 11th century dinner theater is surprisingly entertaining, if you let it be.

Your banquet is served by teenage serfs and wenches in a 1,000-seat arena divided into six colored sections. Each section cheers for its designated knight. The show begins with a display of the horses used in the tournament and a visit from the Royal Falconer, followed by a parade of the night's knights. At the behest of the king, the men spear rings with their lances at a full gallop and heave javelins at a target. Soon they are locked in hand-to-hand battle, striking each other with swords, maces, and battle-axes—yet *you* do not receive so much as a fork for your meal! The victorious knight is allowed to choose the Queen of Love and Beauty from the audience, usually a girl about five years old. This child is brought to the throne where she watches her Prince Charming battle with the Black Knight and eventually threaten to chop off his head. Talk about entertainment!

If Medieval Times has a fault, it is the constant pestering you receive at the hands of strolling merchants. Over the course of the evening, you're given the opportunity to purchase a photo of yourself with the king and queen (nobody gets through the front gate without them snapping it), flags for your knight, glowing necklaces, a photo of yourself with the members of your party, nonlethal swords and shields, and illuminated plastic roses, not to mention all the junk in the gift shop.

2021 N. Stemmons Fwy., Dallas, TX 75207

(888) WE-JOUST or (214) 761-1800

Hours: Wednesday–Thursday 7:30 P.M., Friday 6 P.M., Saturday 6 and 8 P.M., Sunday 5 P.M.

Cost: Adults $46.95, Kids (12 and under) $32.95

www.medievaltimes.com

Directions: East of Market Center Blvd. on the south-side I-77 frontage road.

Fort Worth
American Airlines C. R. Smith Museum

If you're like most people, your experience with aviation is limited to the commercial variety. It is surprising, then, that most air museums focus on the military and experimental aspects of flight. The American Airlines C. R. Smith Museum is the exception to the rule.

As president of American Airlines, C. R. Smith helped transform the fledgling company into the nation's second largest airline. This private museum traces not only Smith's 34-year career, but American's corporate history, starting on April 15, 1926, when a young Charles Lindbergh flew the first mail bags from Chicago to St. Louis for the Robinson Aircraft Corporation. Robinson and 80-some other puny carriers merged in 1930 to form American; Smith became its president in 1934 at the age of 35. (OK, suddenly I feel like a slacker. . . .)

The museum covers all aspects of commercial aviation, from the flight deck to the maintenance crews to the passengers. If you've always opted for Coach, plop on down in one of the comfy First Class seats in the IWERKS Theater for a cinematic aerial tour of the globe. And if your kids express an interest in the airline business, sign them up for the Eagle Aviation Academy, a weeklong camp for budding aviators, run by the museum.

4601 Highway 360, Fort Worth, TX 76155

(877) C-R-SMITH or (817) 967-1560

Hours: Wednesday–Saturday 10 A.M.–6 P.M., Sunday Noon–5 P.M.

Cost: Adults $4, Seniors (55+) $2, Kids (2–12) $2

www.crsmithmuseum.org

Directions: On the west side of Rte. 360, just south of Rte. 183 (Airport Fwy.), at FAA Blvd.

FORT WORTH

Thirty-four fish fell from a dark cloud onto the front yard of Fort Worth resident Louis Castoreno on May 8, 1985.

Kids these days.

Bicycle Tree

George Hilton knows that bicycles don't grow on trees—that's why he had to put them in one. Just off a quiet side street north of downtown you'll find this artist's hackberry tree filled with bicycles, a few tricycles, and a motorcycle. Why did he do it? Well, does it really matter?

609 Grand Ave., Fort Worth, TX 76106

Private phone

Hours: Always visible

Cost: Free

Directions: Four blocks west of Main St. (Rte. 287), one block south of North Side Dr., at Circle Park Blvd.

Seriously cool.

Jackalope and Sno-Cone

Fort Worth is often dismissed as a cow town, but truth be known, it is home to several impressive museums and works of public art. Case in point: a few years ago a large jackalope statue on Fort Worth's west side was in danger of being bulldozed for a car dealership. That business recognized its duty to the city's cultural landscape and preserved the artwork. The horned hare was mounted atop the dealer's main showroom, where you can still see it today.

RLB Sales & Leasing, 5929 Camp Bowie Blvd., Fort Worth, TX 76101

(817) 731-8777

Hours: Always visible

Cost: Free

Directions: On Rte. 377 (Camp Bowie Blvd.) at Bryant Irvin Rd.

As long as you're visiting the jumbo jackalope, head east three blocks to check out another Fort Worth landmark: the supersized Sno-Cone. This roadside stand is only open during the summer, but is visible year-round.

Locke Ave. and Home St., Fort Worth, TX 76101

No phone

Hours: Always visible

Cost: Free

Directions: One block north of Camp Bowie Blvd., three blocks east of Bryant Irvin Rd.

BORN IN FORT WORTH

Kate Capshaw (Kathy Sue Nail)—November 3, 1953

Larry Hagman—September 21, 1931

George "Spanky" McFarland—October 2, 1928

Fess Parker—August 16, 1927

Bill Paxton—May 17, 1955

Rex Reed—October 2, 1940

Mary Elizabeth "Liz" Smith—February 2, 1923

FORT WORTH

"Fort Worth is where the West begins; Dallas is where the East peters out." —Amos G. Carter

To get that pink Cadillac, you've got to make some sacrifices.
Photo by author, courtesy of Mary Kay International.

Suburbs
Addison
Mary Kay Museum

Mary Kay Ash once said, "If you think you can, you can. If you think you can't, you're right." Well, to look at her company's headquarters north of Dallas, she obviously thought she could, and did. Ash launched her cosmetics empire from her kitchen table in 1963, which in four decades has expanded to include 300,000+ direct-market beauty consultants across the globe.

You can trace the company's history, from its humble beginnings to its current operations, at a museum in the lobby of its headquarters. One gallery traces the evolution of the Independent Sales Directors' business suits, and another contains Ash's collection of fine porcelain. See her pink hard hat, rhinestone-covered gowns, and photos of her white poodles, which she lovingly called "fur people."

For those of you who have been awarded pink Cadillacs, or who dream of one day owning one, you'll want the full Mary Kay experience; tours of their manufacturing facility can be arranged by calling (972) 687-5720. And if you want to pay your respects to Ms. Ash, you'll find her buried at Sparkman-Hillcrest Memorial Park (7405 W. Northwest Highway) in Dallas. Ash's ashes to ashes, Ash's dust to dust . . .

Mary Kay International, 16251 Dallas Pwy., Dallas, TX 75247

(972) 687-6300 or (972) 687-5720 (Tours)

Hours: Monday–Friday 9 A.M.–5 P.M.

Cost: Free

www.marykay.com/Headquarters/Company/Headquarters.asp

Directions: Exit Keller Springs Rd. westbound from the Dallas North Tollway, then
  north on Mary Kay Way.

Arlington
George Bush and the Texas Rangers

When he was owner of the Texas Rangers, Eddie Childs explained his predicament to a friend: "I'll try to sell, but sooner or later there aren't going to be any suckers left out there." Well, he was wrong on two counts: there *was* a sucker—George W. Bush—and it turns out that he wasn't a sucker after all. The taxpayers of Arlington were.

As with so many business deals before, Bush assembled the investors, and when the deal was sealed in 1989 he was rewarded by being named the club's managing general partner. He loved every minute of the job, remarking, "I want the folks to see me sitting in the same kind of seat they sit in, eating the same popcorn, peeing in the same urinal." And, hopefully, washing the same hands.

A year and a half after the sale, the investors were looking to upgrade the stadium. By threatening to take the team elsewhere, the Rangers were able to strong-arm the residents of Arlington into approving a half-cent sales tax increase to raise $191 million for a new facility. Arlingtonians approved the measure by a two-thirds margin. The Rangers, for their part, kicked in $30 million . . . which they collected from fans through a $1 surcharge on each ticket sold.

The land for the park was appropriated by the Arlington Sports Facilities Development Authority (ASFDA), a quasi-governmental agency empowered by the Texas legislature with the right of eminent domain. The ASFDA, little more than a front for the baseball franchise, condemned 18 acres of prime real estate and bought it back for the low, low price of $812,220. A jury later forced the ASFDA to pay $4.2 million to the original landowners, which was closer to the fair market value.

Now before you start feeling sorry for the team's owners, listen to the rest of the deal. Once the Texas Rangers paid $60 million in rent, they were given the title to the $191 million facility. Bush, who owned 11 percent of the franchise, had turned his original $606,000 investment into a $15.4 million buyout in just nine years—not too shabby!

Ameriquest Field (formerly the Ballpark in Arlington), 1000 Ballpark Way, Arlington, TX 76011

(817) 273-5099

Hours: Call ahead for tour times

Cost: Free

www.texasrangers.com

Directions: Four blocks west of Rte. 360 on Randol Mill Rd.

ARLINGTON
Arlington hosts the Texas Scottish Festival each June.

DENTON
A woman claimed to have spotted **Elvis**, still alive, riding the parachute drop at a roadside carnival in Denton. The King was wearing a fake mustache.

Actress **Ann Sheridan** was born Clara Lou Sheridan in Denton on February 21, 1915.

Hitler was in *Casablanca*?
Photo by author, courtesy of the Palace of Wax.

Grand Prairie
Palace of Wax and Ripley's Believe It or Not!

It was a sad day in 1988 when the Palace of Wax and Ripley's Believe It or Not! museum burned to the ground. But, like a kitschy phoenix, a new odditorium rose from the ashes. As the name suggests, this Texas Taj Mahal is really two museums, either of which would be worth the cost of the combined ticket price.

Ripley's Believe It or Not! has all those things you'd never expect to see in your lifetime, but thankfully now can. It's got the only shrunken head known to have been made from a European's noggin, a painting of *The Last Supper* done in postage stamps, a stuffed two-faced kitten playing with a ball of yarn, a vest made from human hair, a sneaker-wearing goose named Andy, a bedpan banjo, a one-headed–two-bodied calf, a painting of *The Angelus/Millet* made with burnt toast by a Japanese artist, and a display case answering the age-old question: Mermaids, Fact or Fantasy? And if you'd like to feel what it's like to live through a twister, but without all of the flying cows, step into the museum's Tornado Alley.

After being blown out into the gift shop, you tour continues through the Palace of Wax. In addition to the 225+ statues you'll find an impressive collection of Hollywood memorabilia: W. C. Fields's "Poppy" outfit, William Shatner's Captain Kirk uniform, Dan Rowan's *Laugh-In* suit, Christopher Reeves's *Superman* cape, and Charlton Heston's *Ben-Hur* costume. The museum's wax celebrities are divided among six galleries: A Galaxy of Stars, The Asylum of Fear, A Child's Garden of Fantasy, The Life of Christ, The Spirit of Man, and Colonel Bill's Wonderful Wild West Wax Works. Interestingly, The Spirit of Man gallery pits humankind's best citizens against its worst: Mahatma Gandhi, Martin Luther King Jr., and Walt Disney on the blue side of the room face off against Adolf Hitler, Joseph Stalin, and Ayatollah Khomeini on the red side of the room. Who wins? Well, I'm pulling for the blue.

601 E. Safari Pwy., Grand Prairie, TX 75050

(972) 263-2391

Hours: Monday–Friday 10 A.M.–5 P.M., Saturday–Sunday 10 A.M.–6 P.M.

Cost: Combo/single, Adults $18.95/$15.95, Seniors $16.95/$13.95, Kids (4–12) $9.95/$8.95

www.palaceofwax.com

Directions: Exit Belt Line Rd. north from I-30, then left on Safari Pwy.

GRAND PRAIRIE
American Idol runner-up **Justin Guarini** was charged with reckless Jet Skiing after nearly running down a five-year-old swimmer in Grand Prairie on June 28, 2003.

Irving
The Movie Studios of Las Colinas Tour

When you think about movie studios, you probably don't think about Irving, Texas . . . but you should. The Movie Studios at Las Colinas have snagged more than a few productions from Hollywood, including *JFK*, *Silkwood*, *Born on the Fourth of July*, and *Robocop*, among others.

Of course, once these projects wrapped, the studio had plenty of props and sets left over and, to its credit, has preserved many pieces that you can now see on its studio tour. The studio has the Oval Office from *JFK*, the model submarine from *The Hunt for Red October*, and the park bench from *Forrest Gump*. You'll also get to see props and costumes from films made far from the Lone Star State, like the Von Trapp children's play clothes from *The Sound of Music* and Dorothy's blue gingham dress from *The Wizard of Oz*.

Building One, 6301 N. O'Connor Rd., Irving, TX 75039

(800) 914-0006

E-mail: tours@studiosatloscolinas.com

Hours: September–March, Monday–Friday Noon and 2 P.M., Saturday Noon, 2 P.M., and 4 P.M.; April–August, Monday–Thursday 10 A.M., Noon, and 2 P.M., Friday–Saturday 10 A.M., Noon, 2 P.M., and 4 P.M., Sunday Noon, 2 P.M., and 4 P.M.

Cost: Adults $12.95, Seniors (65+) $10.95, Kids (5–12) $8.95

www.studiosatlascolinas.com

Directions: One block south of Royal Ln. on O'Conner Blvd.

Lake Worth
Lake Worth Monster

Boaters, you're off the hook—the Lake Worth Monster isn't of the Loch Ness variety; it's more of a Bigfoot type of creature. The white-haired, goat-bearded, seven-foot biped—some call him Goatman—was first spotted near the lake on July 9, 1969, when it jumped on the hood of a car in which two couples were necking. The next night, four police units and 40-odd critter hunters returned to the Mosque Point area to investigate. According to reports, the creature howled and chucked a car tire (with the rim still on it) at a group . . . tossing it more than 500 feet!

As Texans often do when threatened, they armed themselves. Hundreds of gun-toting teens converged on the area, and one was eventually

shot—a teenager, not a monster. The young man survived, but learned an important lesson: never wear white overalls on a Goatman hunt. Interest waned in the wake of the shooting, but on November 7 the Lake Worth Monster attacked Charles Buchanan as he snoozed in a sleeping bag in the open bed of his pickup. Buchanan tossed a bag of fried chicken at the beast, which then swam off toward Greer Island clutching the greasy sack in its mouth.

The monster has never been captured or killed, so beware of where you park. Or bring a bucket of Original Recipe.

Jacksboro Hwy., Lake Worth, TX 76135

(817) 237-6890

Hours: Always visible

Cost: Free

www.n2.net/prey/bigfoot/articles/lakeworth.htm

Directions: On both sides of Rte. 199 (Jacksboro Hwy.) northwest of I-820 (Jim Wright Fwy. NW); Mosque Point is to the south, and Greer Island is to the north.

Parker
Southfork Ranch

Call it the Magic Bullet Theory, Part II: when J. R. Ewing was shot on the final episode of the 1979–80 season of *Dallas*, CBS made it once again acceptable to talk about "gunshots in Dallas" without making people cringe. With hostages in Iran and the Soviet Union in Afghanistan, you'd think there would have been more important national questions than "Who shot J.R.?" But you'd be wrong. (In an weird twist of incredibly bad taste, or callous insensitivity, J.R. was rushed to Parkland Memorial Hospital after being gunned down—see page 323.)

When the truth was revealed on November 21, 1980, three of four American televisions were tuned in to find out. It was Kristin who pulled the trigger, played by Mary Crosby, who was pregnant with J.R.'s baby. Interestingly, Ewing was shot five times during the show's 10-year run, but only once did anyone care.

Though the show was filmed in Hollywood, the Southfork Ranch seen in the opening credits is an actual ranch near Dallas. At the time it was owned by a man named J. R. Duncan, but that J.R. didn't appreciate the attention; he sold the estate to a company that turned it into a

museum and conference center. Dallas fans can see the gun that almost killed that smug bastard, Lucy's wedding dress, and Jock's Lincoln Continental. Still not enough? Rent the place out for your next wedding, and if your dad's not available, you can hire a J.R. look-alike to walk you down the aisle. The place is also available for corporate events (perhaps hostile takeovers) and retreats.

3700 Hogge Rd., Parker, TX 75002

Contact: PO Box 516009, Dallas, TX 75251

(972) 442-7800

Hours: Daily 9 A.M.–5 P.M.

Cost: Adults $7.95, Seniors $6.95, Kids (5–12) $5.95

www.southfork.com

Dallas Fan Site: www.ultimatedallas.com

Directions: Parker Rd. east from I-75 (North Central Expressway) to FM 2551 (Hogge Rd.), then south to the ranch.

GRAPEVINE
The Dallas/Fort Worth Airport in Grapevine is larger than the island of Manhattan.

Former Dallas Cowboys head coach **Barry Switzer** was arrested in 1997 at the Dallas/Fort Worth Airport in Grapevine for carrying a loaded pistol.

HIGHLAND PARK
Though Highland Park Village (Mockingbird Lane and Preston Road) opened in 1931, it took 20 years to finish; many claim it is the world's first shopping mall.

MESQUITE
Children may not, by law, have unusual haircuts in Mesquite.

PLANO
Cyclist **Lance Armstrong** was born in Plano on September 18, 1971.

Sure he's a roach, but he's *fabulous*!
Photo by author, courtesy of the Pest Shop.

Plano
Cockroach Hall of Fame

Most cockroaches, like most humans, lead quiet, uneventful lives. They eat a little garbage, have a few thousand offspring, and die in roach-filled motels. But there are a few bugs that make it to the big time. For years this museum's creator, Michael "Cockroach Dundee" Bohdan (a working exterminator), has been collecting mini-dioramas of these celebrity pests, such as Elvis Roachley, artist Norman Roachwell, Imelda Marcoroach (in gold shoes), Liberochi (at the piano), billionaire Ross Peroach, John Wayne Bobroach (post-amputation), Marilyn Monroach, and *Psycho*'s Combates Roach Motel. Bohdan also has scenes that salute daily American life, such as dioramas of a day at the beach and a barbecue cookout.

The Pest Shop, 2231-B W. 15th St., Plano, TX 75075

(972) 519-0355

E-mail: mbohdan54@hotmail.com

Hours: Monday–Friday Noon–5 P.M., Saturday Noon–3 P.M.

Cost: Free

www.pestshop.com

Directions: One lock west of Custer Rd. on Rte. 544 (15th St.).

BUG MAN

Believe it or not, Plano's Michael Bohdan is only the state's *second* best-known bug exterminator. Who holds the top title? None other than House Majority Leader **Tom DeLay**, who got into national politics because the EPA had banned his favorite insecticide, Mirex.

DeLay started a pest control business named Environmental Services in 1974, based in the Houston suburb of Sugar Land. He later bought out another operation called Albo Pest Control and kept the name because he thought it sounded a lot like the popular dog food Alpo. Even with that dynamic name, his business struggled along, never hitting the bug big time. DeLay blamed environmental regulations for his failure to succeed, though presumably all his competition had to comply with the same regulations.

DeLay decided to supplement his income by running for the state legislature in 1978, and he won. He was known as a "back bencher" in Austin, more interested in the after-hours, good-ol'-boy party culture than he was in the day-to-day dance of legislation. (He was even nicknamed Hot Tub Tom by his statehouse colleagues because of his well-known patronage of an Austin massage parlor.)

When the EPA banned Mirex, DeLay's chemical weapon of choice against fire ants, DeLay vowed to go to Washington and change the regulation from within. He was elected to the U.S. Congress in 1984 and has served ever since. Unless indicted for corruption, which, as of this writing, is a very real possibility, he'll be in Washington for some time to come.

4

West Texas

*E*arly reports from settlers in West Texas say that the grass here was as tall as the cows' bellies. What better place to raise cattle? Then, in pretty short order, the entire region was overgrazed, leaving what you see today: mile after mile of desert, or something darn close to it.

That's not to say there's nothing here to see; it's just that what you find tends to mimic the harsh landscape. The World's Largest Six-Shooter. The Odessa Meteor Crater. The death site and grave of John Wesley Hardin. And, if you're a Democrat, the hometown of President George W. Bush.

Then again, if you're a Republican, the grass around Midland looks as green and as tall as it ever did.

Del Rio
Goat Testicles

Dr. John Brinkley was a bit of an odd bird. He received his medical training the way so many doctors, thankfully, do not: through the mail. Armed with a diploma from the Eclectic Medical University of Kansas City, he set out on a mission to rid the world of male impotence . . . and make a few bucks while he was at it. His secret? Goat testicles!

Brinkley believed male goats to be the most virile of animals, so wouldn't it be logical that something in their testicles was the secret to virility? Of course. So Brinkley devised a procedure to help impotent men willing to pay $200 (and up to $1,500 once word got around) to be transformed back into 20-year-old horndogs. Here's how it worked: Brinkley would slice up the testicles—though he referred to them only as "glands"—of Toggenberg goats and then implant small slivers of the tissue into his willing patients.

Brinkley started his practice in Kansas in the 1920s, but when the state medical association came after him in the early 1930s, he fled to this border town. He opened a clinic on the mezzanine level of Del Rio's Roswell Hotel, while just over the river in Villa Acuna, Mexico, unfettered by U.S. broadcasting restrictions, he launched radio station XER. The station grew until it reached 500,000 watts of pure, unadulterated quackery. In addition to his gland operation, Brinkley hawked 45 different patent medicines to cure everything what ails ya. Some of XER's advertisers got into the spirit, hawking autographed pictures of Jesus, electric bow ties, and wind-up John the Baptist dolls whose heads popped off on command.

Brinkley used some of his profits to build two waltzing water fountains in front of his Del Rio mansion. Folks would line up each night to watch the light and water show and check out Brinkley's menagerie of penguins, flamingos, and other exotic creatures. There was also a clearly visible 12-foot-tall statue of a she-wolf, with Romulus and Remus suckling on her teats. Yep, Brinkley was *classy*.

The U.S. government eventually convinced Mexican officials to shut down Brinkley's operations, so the doctor decided he would run for Congress from Texas to change the system from within. He had previously run for the governorship of Kansas and nearly won—how hard could it be?

Apparently too hard. He lost the race and died in 1942. His elaborate mansion is still visible, but the penguins, flamingos, statues, and fountains are long gone.

512 Qualia Dr., Del Rio, TX 78840

Private phone

Hours: Always visible

Cost: Free

Directions: Head south from Garfield St. for 10 blocks on Pecan St., then right on Qualia Dr. for four blocks.

WHO NEEDS A RADIO?

During a brief period in the 1930s, XERA (the former XER), broadcast at one million watts of power and reached the entire continental United States. Local ranchers said the transmission caused their wire fences to pick up the station, and some Del Rio residents heard music coming from their dental work.

ANTHONY

Anthony, the Leap Year Capital of the World, hosts a Leap Year Festival every four years.

BIG BEND

The cult movie classic *Race with the Devil* was filmed in Big Bend.

DEL RIO

Robert Weston Smith, best known as **Wolfman Jack**, first broadcast in 1960 on the 250,000-watt XERF radio station in Ciudad Acuna, Mexico, just across the border from Del Rio.

EL PASO

Every public establishment in El Paso is required have a spittoon.

Johnny Cash spent a night in the El Paso jail on October 4, 1965, for trying to smuggle speed and tranquilizers from Mexico through the El Paso International Airport. He pled guilty and paid a $1,000 fine.

Stick 'em up! Wayyyyyyyy up!
Photo by author, courtesy of Bob Wade.

World's Largest Six-Shooter

Texans love their guns. Understanding that, the six-shooter outside Humphrey's Gun Shop might just be the most loved gun in the state—its barrel is 20 feet long! Build by Bob Wade in 1981, this Colt single-action revolver looks mighty dangerous, but don't worry, Wade didn't build two-foot-long bullets to fit into its chambers.

This gun might look familiar to anyone who followed the debate over the Brady Bill in the 1980s. Journalists, ever interested in raising the bar of public discourse, used this gun as a backdrop for many man-on-the-street interviews.

Humphrey's Gun Shop, 124 E. Garfield St., Del Rio, TX 78840

(830) 775-1983

E-mail: coltwalker@humphreysgunshop.com

Hours: Always visible

Cost: Free

www.humphreysgunshop.com

Directions: One block east of Pecan St. on Garfield St.

El Paso
Alligators in El Paso?

In case you're wondering, no, alligators are *not* native to West Texas, though a colony of these creatures lived in a downtown plaza for eight decades, starting in 1883. But in 1967 these poor penned creatures were finally given a reprieve from the El Paso winters, which can sometimes see temperatures below freezing, and were moved to the El Paso zoo. (They had also suffered at the hands of small-brained humans; two alligators were stoned to death in the 1960s, and another had a spike driven into its eye.) In 1972 they were returned to the plaza, but two years later they went back to the zoo, which is where they remain today.

Artist Luis Jiménez visited the alligators as a child, and in 1995 created a fiberglass statue, *Plaza de los Lagartos*, in their honor. Considering that these reptiles probably looked at the young Jiménez as a just-out-of-reach snack, the monument seems all the more magnanimous.

San Jacinto Plaza, Mesa and Main Sts., El Paso, TX 77902

(800) 351-6024

Hours: Always visible

Cost: Free

www.visitelpaso.com

Directions: In the plaza surrounded by Main, Mesa, Mills, and Oregon Sts. along Rte. 20 (Mesa St.).

Death Site and Grave of John Wesley Hardin

Even the Fastest Gun in the West can have a bad day. For John Wesley Hardin, that day was August 19, 1895. Hardin was playing a dice game called Ship, Captain, and Crew in El Paso's Acme Saloon (now the Old Lerner Store, 227 E. San Antonio Avenue), and he had his back to the door. A rookie mistake, sure, but Hardin didn't have any reason to believe he was in any danger. In walked Marshal John Selman, who drew his gun and fired a bullet into the back of the gunslinger's skull. Selman claimed Hardin had spotted him in a mirror and was reaching for his holster. That story didn't quell rumors that he had cowardly fired on Hardin from behind. Soon Selman was put to rest, too, filled with lead by another El Pasoan, Deputy Marshal George Scarborough.

Why did Selman do it? Most believe it was because of a falling-out over reward money for the apprehension of cattle thief Martin Morose. Hardin, Selman, and a few friends brought the no-good rustler to justice in a condition more dead than alive. Though it earned the gang the reward, it also earned Selman and two others an indictment for murder; Hardin, however, was not charged. Selman and the others were eventually acquitted of the killing, and after their release Selman headed to the Acme to settle an old score.

Hardin and Selman were laid to rest in El Paso's Concordia Cemetery, not far from one another. Over time Hardin became a folk hero of the Jesse James variety, his bloody history glossed over by dime novel myths. In truth, today Hardin might be classified a serial killer, callously murdering near strangers for no real reason, though his unabashed racism seems to have been a contributing factor.

Hardin was born in Bonham on May 26, 1853, and killed his first victim when he was only 15 years old. Major "Mage" Holshousen, an African American law enforcement officer, bested Hardin in a wrestling match, so Hardin ambushed Holshousen on a trail near Moscow the next day. Before he turned 25, he'd killed dozens—exact numbers are hazy— including a circus roustabout, a Mexican card dealer, an albino cow, and a man named Charles Cougar who snored too loudly in the room next to Hardin's at the American Hotel in Abilene, Kansas. In 1878 Hardin was tried and convicted of killing Comanche Sheriff Charles Webb. Behind bars he wrote his autobiography and studied law, and upon release in 1894, passed the Texas bar exam. Some guys go from bad to worse.

Concordia Cemetery, Yandell Dr. and N. Stevens St., El Paso, TX 79901
No phone
Hours: Daylight hours
Cost: Free
www.famoustexans.com/johnwesleyhardin.htm
Directions: Take Copia St. (Loop 478) north from I-10, then right (east) onto Yandell Dr.; cemetery is just west of Rte. 54.

EL PASO
It is illegal to throw faded bouquets into El Paso trash cans.

U.S. Border Patrol Museum

Each year 1.3 million people are caught crossing the border illegally from Mexico and turned away, though another 2.8 million slip past the U.S. Border Patrol. You might think a .255 batting average is nothing to crow about, but you won't hear anyone here who's the least bit self-conscious about it.

This museum traces the agency's history from the Wild West to the modern organization, including equipment, agents, and procedures. It's got dioramas of border patrol agents in friendly meetings with Canadian Mounties, contraband confiscated at crossing points, and weapons used by human traffickers. You'll see examples of makeshift boats used to ferry people across the Rio Grande and a car hood used as a raft to escape Cuba.

4315 Transmountain Rd., El Paso, TX 79924

(915) 759-6060

E-mail: nbpm@borderpatrolmuseum.com

Hours: Tuesday–Sunday 9 A.M.–5 P.M.

Cost: Free

www.borderpatrolmuseum.com

Directions: On Loop 375 (Transmountain Rd.), a half-mile west of the Patriot Fwy. (Rte. 54).

EL PASO

Each year El Paso gets more sunny days—over 300—than any other U.S. city.

The town of El Paso celebrates Thanksgiving on the last weekend in *April*. Citizens claim they began the practice on April 28, 1598, 23 years before the Pilgrims, at what is now San Elizario on the edge of town.

Can a World's Largest Coyote be far behind?
Photo by Jean Fung.

Fort Stockton
World's Largest Roadrunner

Beep-beep! Blink your eyes and you'll miss most roadrunners . . . except Paisano Pete. Even if he were moving, which he's not, he couldn't very well hide in the sagebrush—he's 11 feet tall and 22 feet long from beak tip to tail feathers!

Paisano Pete is posed mid stride, built in 1979 by Creative Displays (now F.A.S.T.) of Sparta, Wisconsin. Locals wanted to honor this native species, known to some as the "Clown of the Desert" even before he was tricking Wile E. Coyote to run through scenery backdrops and off cliffs or down tunnels into speeding locomotives.

In the 1980s, folks around here worried that a new jumbo roadrunner might upstage Paisano Pete. Angelina College in Lufkin hired artist I. W. Ferguson to create a model of their school mascot, the roadrunner. Ferguson sculpted a large painted steel bird along Route 59, but it in no way upstaged Pete.

Rte. 290 and FM 1053, Fort Stockton, TX 79735

(432) 336-8052

Hours: Always visible

Cost: Free

www.ci.fort-stockton.tx.us

Directions: At the intersection of Dickinson Blvd. (Rte. 290) and Main St. (FM 1053).

Iraan
Alley Oop's Fantasyland

The *Alley Oop* comic strip was created in 1927 by Iraan resident V. T. Hamlin, and it will likely be the only thing of national significance to come out of this dusty, West Texas town. Local boosters probably realized this, so they built a seven-acre park dedicated to Oop and his friends.

Fantasyland has oversized statues of Alley Oop and his girlfriend Ooola, but it's the huge dinosaur, Dinny, that the kids enjoy most. Dinny was built by Bernie Ayers in 1965; he's 65 feet long, 16 feet tall, and weighs 40 tons. With little trouble you can climb astride his back for a great photo. But don't expect much more from this roadside park; take away the Oops and Dinny and it's not much more than a playground.

Fantasyland does come to life, however, for the biannual Alley Oop Day celebration where Miss Iraan and Miss Ooola are crowned. Contestants need not have a unibrow to participate.

Fantasyland (Alley Oop City Park), 1000 Park Side St., Iraan, TX 79744

No phone

Hours: Daylight hours

Cost: Free

Directions: On the west side of town off Rte. 190.

Lajitas
Mayoral Dynasty

America has a long history of political dynasties: the Kennedys, the Bushes, the Daleys, the Tafts, the Henrys . . . What, never heard of the Henrys? Then you've never been to Lajitas. Since 1986 this border town has been led by a mayor named Clay Henry. Mayor Clay Henry Sr. was a bit of a lush, often knocking back 30 or 40 beers a day, and his son was no better. Being constantly inebriated, it was only a matter of time before something when wrong. In 1992 Clay Henry Jr. attacked and killed his father in an argument over who could have sex with a she-goat. And whom did the voters of Lajitas select to replace their fallen mayor? His killer!

Did I forget to mention that the Henrys are goats?

Yes, in an effort to show that *anybody* can get into politics, the local population elected its most famous resident to the town's highest office. That celebrity happened to be a beer-drinking goat at the local trading post, Clay Henry. His son held office for another eight years before dying of natural causes in 2000. He was replaced by Clay Henry III.

Clay Henry III survived an assassination attempt on a Sunday in August 2002. A local nut named Jim Bob Hargrove castrated Henry as the mayor was knocking back brews in his pen. It's unclear whether Hargrove was angry because Henry was drinking beer on the Sabbath, or whether Hargrove was upset that local laws prevented *him* from joining the mayor for a round of brews. Whatever the motive, the result was the same: Hargrove was charged with animal cruelty, and the Henry dynasty came to the end of the line . . . unless he chooses to adopt a kid.

Henry is still the mayor of Lajitas, but he has turned his alcoholism into a force for good: today each beer he chugs raises money for the Terlingua Common School District.

Lajitas, the Ultimate Hideout, HC 70, PO Box 400, Lajitas, TX 79852

(432) 424-5000

E-mail: clay@clayhenry.com

Hours: Daily 7 A.M.–8 P.M.

Cost: Free

www.clayhenry.com

Directions: Heading into town on FM 170, turn left on the road to the state park, drive one mile to the Boardwalk, then enter the Ultimate Hideout through the Badlands Motel behind the Boardwalk.

FORT STOCKTON

Fort Stockton Sheriff A. J. Royal was shot and killed by one of six leading citizens in 1894. They had drawn lots for the honor of shooting the corrupt lawman. Nobody was ever indicted for the crime.

Each Memorial Day Fort Stockton hosts a Menudo Cook-Off competition.

Langtry
Judge Roy Bean Visitor Center

Few post-revolution Texans have made as big an impression on this state's psyche as Judge Roy Bean. This self-proclaimed "Law West of the Pecos" was not too concerned with the law, but was more of a businessman with a gavel. As train crews pressed westward during the late 1800s, Bean set up barrooms along the tracks. To show their appreciation, the work crews proclaimed him Justice of the Peace.

That was all Bean needed. He established a courtroom/bar in Langtry in 1882 dubbed the Jersey Lilly, which he claimed was named for actress Lillie Langtry. (Too bad he didn't spell her name correctly.) His rulings were legendary and bizarre. When a body was found with a gun and $40 on it, he fined the corpse $40 for carrying a concealed weapon. Bean also embodied the racist nature of the times—though that flaw in his personality often is glossed over. He once tossed out a murder case because the victim was Chinese; by his reading of Texas law, there was "not a damn line here nowheres that makes it illegal to kill a Chinaman." Bean always ended his sentences with the same phrase: "May God have mercy upon your soul." Back at ya, Judge!

As the West settled down, Bean became a tourist attraction, holding mock trials for drink-buying customers. He died in the back room of the Jersey Lilly on March 16, 1903. Ten months later, Lillie Langtry visited the saloon and retrieved the gun Bean had left for her. Judge Bean is buried behind the Whitehead Memorial Museum in Del Rio (1308 S. Main Street, (830) 774-7568). His story was made into a movie starring Paul Newman, *The Life and Times of Judge Roy Bean.*

Bean's original saloon has been moved to a Texas Welcome/Information Center named in his honor. A small museum depicts events in the Judge's life through dioramas and with ghostlike projections, such as "The Magic of Pepper's Ghost Revealed."

Rte. 90 at Torres Ave., Langtry, TX 78871

(432) 291-3340

E-mail: TIC-Langtry@dot.state.tx.us

Hours: Daily 8 A.M.–5 P.M.

Cost: Free

www.dot.state.tx.us/trv/trvtics.htm?pg=lytic

Directions: At Loop 25 (Rte. 90) and Torres Ave.

Marfa
Birthplace of Tex-Mex

Culinary historians have traced the history of Tex-Mex cooking back to a small restaurant in Marfa, the Old Borunda Café. There, in 1887, Tula Borunda Gutierrez first brought traditional Mexican dishes—tacos, enchiladas, tamales—into the mainstream. Her Number 1 Dinner was either an enchilada or a taco served with rice and refried beans, essentially the same formula used today.

Then, in 1899, the Farnsworth family of San Antonio opened the Original Mexican Restaurant at 231 Losoya Street. Though its titular claim was not entirely accurate, it did raise the bar for Tex-Mex, adding mole poblano, chiles rellenos, and pescado. The Original Mexican Restaurant closed its doors in 1961, but reopened on the River Walk in the 1980s (528 River Walk Street, (210) 224-9951).

Back in Marfa, the Old Borunda Café on Route 90 closed its doors in August 1985. Thankfully, it has since been resurrected downtown.

Old Borunda Café, 113 S. Russell St., Marfa, TX 79843

(432) 729-8163

Hours: Wednesday–Saturday 5–10 P.M.

Cost: Meals $6–$10

Directions: Two blocks east of FM 17 (Highland St.), one block north of Rte. 90/67 (San Antonio St.).

MORE TEX THAN MEX

The Texas Legislature has proclaimed tortilla chips and salsa as the Official State Snack, though nobody claims the snack originated in the state. Texans have, however, advanced other Tex-Mex traditions over the years. Here are a few:

Fritos (701 Leona Street, San Antonio): Elmer Doolin was eating at a San Antonio greasy spoon in September 1932 when he noticed a 5¢

---

bag of homemade snack chips for sale. Doolin tried them, liked them, and went looking for the person who was supplying them to the café. (Though unconfirmed, some credit a Mexican national named Don Gustavo Olguín.) Doolin bought the recipe and equipment—a modified potato ricer—for $100, then went back to his mother's place on Roosevelt Street and made his first batch. The secret ingredient in Fritos was masa, cornmeal brought to San Antonio by Bartolo Martinez in 1896 and manufactured at a mill at 701 Leona Street. (The mill burned down in 1986.) Doolin went on to found Frito-Lay.

Margarita: There is considerable debate regarding the birthplace of the margarita. Was it created at the Caliente Racetrack in Tijuana, Mexico, in 1920 or at the Garci Crespo Hotel in Puebla, Mexico, in 1936? Or perhaps it was first mixed at the Kentucky Club in Juarez (629 Avenida Juarez), just over the river from El Paso, becoming the drink of choice for servicemen at Fort Bliss during World War II. (This establishment is also known as the place where Marilyn Monroe came to celebrate her Juarez divorce from Arthur Miller.) Another margarita story links the cocktail to singer Peggy Lee, who sipped bartender Santos Cruz's concoction at a Galveston bar in 1948. Whether or not it was born in Texas, or just over the border, it certainly was perfected here.

Frozen Margarita (Mariano's, 5500 Greenville Avenue, Dallas): There is little debate, however, regarding the birthplace of the *frozen* margarita. That honor goes to Mariano Martinez, owner of Marino's restaurant in Dallas. One afternoon in 1971 Martinez stopped by a 7-Eleven and noticed how popular the store's Slurpee machine was with the kids. Why not an adult version of the Slurpee? Martinez rigged up his own crushed-ice drink machine, added tequila and lime juice instead of Coke or cherry syrup, and the frozen margarita was born! Martinez never patented the machine or the idea, and after Jimmy Buffet sung its praises in his 1976 song, there's been no looking back . . . or at least not without blurred double vision. Mariano's closed its doors in 2003.

Nachos (Piedras Negras, Mexico): The folks of Piedras Negras claim nachos were invented here in 1943 by Ignacio "Nacho" Anaya, owner of the Victory Club, just over the Rio Grande from Eagle Pass. Each October the town hosts a Nachos Festival.

Marfa Spook Lights

Before you go dismissing the Marfa Spook Lights as automobile head-lights, you should at least listen to the whole story.

Settler Robert Ellison was the first person to report seeing unexplain-able glowing orbs bobbing around in the Chinati Mountains, in *1883*. And though Ellison often gets the credit for the first report, the Apache had been talking about the lights for even longer. They claim they are the spirit of Chief Alsate, held in limbo by the gods he offended while walk-ing the earth.

Well, a disembodied spirit is about as logical an explanation as you'll hear here. Could they be young *brujas*—witches—who are learning to fly, as some Mexican folk tales have suggested? Or perhaps they're caused by burning bat guano, mini-volcanoes, St. Elmo's fire, stellar mirages, ball lightning, piezoelectric rocks, "earthquake lights," or swamp gas. (See any swamps around here?) Ignoring their long history, others have posited James Bond–like theories. Maybe light energy somehow "got loose" from an experimental death ray the army was developing to fight Hitler. My favorite, however, is a theory that they're irradiated jackrabbits that have escaped from a military lab and are still hopping around in the hills.

Whatever they are, they most certainly exist. The locals have built a viewing area where, most nights, tourists can watch as several lights of varying colors seem to dance in the hills over, and just beyond, Mitchell Flat. The show can go on for hours, and you're likely to have company—they're a popular attraction. If you come to Marfa around Labor Day, the town throws a Marfa Lights Festival.

Marfa Mystery Lights Viewing Center, Route 90, Marfa, TX 79843

Contact: Mystery Lights, PO Box 195, Alpine, TX 79831

(800) 650-9696 or (432) 729-4942

E-mail: info@marfacc.com

Hours: After dark

Cost: Free

www.marfacc.com

Directions: On Rte. 90, eight miles east of town, on the way to Alpine; look toward the mountains beyond the airport.

Midland
Aviation Art Gallery

When you first see the parental warning on the doors to the Aviation Art Gallery, it seems a bit odd; what kind of art *is* this? Then you enter, turn the corner, and va-va-voom! Bosoms here, bosoms there, all perked up and aimed to destroy the Fascist menace. Confused? These nude or scantily clad pinups were painted on the nose cones of World War II aircraft and have been rescued and restored before the planes they once graced were sold off for scrap. Among the 33 stunning panels on display are Easy Maid, Sloppy but Safe, Southern Comfort, Yankee Girl, Forever Amber, Flamin' Mamie, and Target for Tonight, whose nipples conveniently align with two of the aircraft's larger rivets. The most unusual, however, is Lady Luck, no doubt painted by somebody who was as easily distracted by a poker game as a sexy dame; her breasts are eight balls and her hoo-ha is a four-leaf clover. From the gallery you can watch newly acquired works being restored in a conservation laboratory built for just that purpose.

The Aviation Art Gallery is just one part of this amazing museum, home of the Commemorative Air Force. The planes in the CAF's hangars (here and across the nation) constitute the nation's largest collection of flyable World War II aircraft. The museum's goal is to have one of each U.S. aircraft that participated in the conflict, as well as any Allied or Axis planes they can get a hold of.

In addition to the aircraft, the museum has a large exhibit space where you can get an up-close look at an unexploded German incendiary bomb, a Japanese pilot's uniform, and replicas of Fat Man and Little Boy, suspended mid-drop.

American Airpower Heritage Museum, Midland International Airport, 9600 Wright Dr., PO Box 62000, Midland, TX 79711

(432) 563-1000

Hours: Monday–Saturday 9 A.M.–5 P.M., Sunday Noon–5 P.M.

Cost: Adults $9, Seniors (65+) $8, Teens (13–18) $8, Kids $6

www.airpowermuseum.org

Directions: Head north on Wright Dr. from I-20 Business, toward the airport, and watch for signs on the service roads.

GERONIMO GEORGE!

Ever wonder why **George H. W. Bush** seems to throw himself out of an airplane every few years? Stop into the "Bush Mission" exhibit at the American Airpower Heritage Museum and wonder no more. During World War II, Bush piloted a Grumman TBF Avenger named *Barbara* on bombing runs in the South Pacific. On September 2, 1944, his plane was hit by antiaircraft fire while bombing a Japanese radio transmitter on Chichi Jima, one of the Bonin Islands. As Bush told it, he bailed out of the burning plane as it went down in flames and struck his forehead on the tail as he tumbled backward in the slipstream. *Barbara* had two other crew aboard; ordinance officer Jack Delaney jumped out, too, but his parachute never opened, while the plane's gunner, Ted White, never made it out of the aircraft. Bush bobbed around in an inflatable raft before being rescued by the USS *Finback* submarine.

Bush's story was later contradicted by a man named Chester Mierzejewski during a 1988 interview. Mierzejewski was a rear turret gunner in the plane just ahead of Bush's during the mission. He claimed Bush ejected prematurely when he could have attempted a water landing, that *Barbara* was never on fire, and that neither of the other crew ever made it out. Though several airmen raised similar questions back in 1944, Bush was awarded the Distinguished Flying Cross by the U.S. Navy.

Regardless of what happened at Chichi Jima, Bush did fly 58 combat missions even though he was one of the navy's youngest pilots. That's plenty to be proud of. He received an honorable discharge in December 1944 and returned to Connecticut and Yale.

If you'd like to see the parachute Bush used for the jump on his 72nd birthday in 1997, it's at the Bush Library in College Station (see page 208).

MIDLAND

Actor **Woody Harrelson** was born in Midland on July 23, 1962.

Midland got its name for being the midway point between Fort Worth and El Paso.

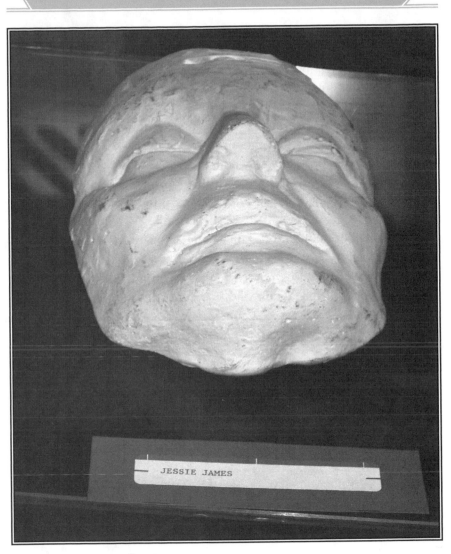

Here's lookin' at you, Jesse!
Photo by author, courtesy of the Midland County Historical Museum.

Faces and Heads

Seems like everyone's losing his head, or face, in Midland. If you've lost yours, go to the Lost and Found: the Midland County Historical Museum.

Take Midland Man. This fella wandered these parts about 22,000 years ago, but his head didn't turn up until 1953, discovered on a ranch southwest of the city. Though Midland Man's skull is now in the possession of Southern Methodist University in Dallas, the museum has an exact replica in a glass case near the front door. Bring along one of your local friends and compare noggin sizes—has Modern Midland Man advanced all that much? You decide.

In another of the museum's display cases you'll find a genuine shrunken head. And do you know the secret to shrinking a head? Simple: remove the bones! Guys, think about taking a long swim in the cold, cold ocean. A shrunken head suddenly doesn't seem as remarkable, does it?

The most interesting case in the museum contains some familiar faces. In the Old West, it wasn't uncommon for folks to make a plaster cast of a gunslinger's face *after* he was freshly filled with lead but *before* he was planted in Boot Hill. This museum has six of these death masks—replicas, actually—each revealing a certain stoic quality. OK, maybe "dead" is the word. They've got Jesse James, Wild Bill Hickok, Clay Allison, George Parker, Bill Dalton, and Bob Ford (the guy who shot Jesse James). Collect 'em all.

Midland County Historical Museum, 301 W. Missouri Ave., Midland, TX 79701
(432) 688-8947

Hours: Monday, Wednesday, and Friday–Saturday 2–5 P.M.

Cost: Free

www.visitmidlandtx.com/sections/attractions/museum.asp

Directions: Two blocks north of Front St. (Rte. 80), one block east of Big Spring St. (Rte. 349), on the south side of the library.

MONAHANS AND SEYMOUR
The thermometer in Monahans reached 120°F in the shade on June 28, 1994, tying the Texas record set by Seymour on August 12, 1936.

NOTREES
Notrees was named by founder Charles Brown because the town had no trees.

Home of two presidents and two governors.

George W. Bush's Childhood in Midland

This story starts in Odessa (see page 124).

After a brief tour of duty among various Dresser Industries subsidiaries in California, and the birth of a baby girl, Robin, in December 1949, the Bush family returned to Texas in the last days of 1949. They landed in Midland at the George's Court Motel on Main Street. A short time later they bought a home at 405 E. Maple Street, part of "Easter Egg Row," nicknamed for the homes' pastel colors. In 1952 the Bushes moved to a new home at 1412 W. Ohio Street, the home Georgie considers his childhood home.

After the move, Babs gave birth to a second son, Jeb, in February 1953. Babs later reflected on the joys of motherhood in Midland: "I would think, well, George is off on a trip doing all these exciting things and I'm sitting home with these absolutely brilliant children who say one thing a week of interest." Ouch.

The Bushes suffered a devastating blow when Robin was diagnosed with leukemia in the spring of 1953. Robin died on October 11 of that year. Young Georgie, who they were then calling Junior, was not told of his sister's condition until after she died. Twenty-eight-year-old Barbara's hair turned prematurely gray after Robin's death, and she developed a two-pack-a-day cigarette habit. Around this time George Sr. started the Zapata

Petroleum Corporation, using the name of the popular Brando movie.

More kids came along: Neil (1955), Marvin (1956), and Dorothy (1959). Around the Bush house, mother Barbara was known as the Enforcer, never shy to dole out a spanking or physically break up a fight between the kids. But her talent for discipline apparently didn't extend to the kitchen. "My mother never cooked," Junior remembered fondly. "The woman had frostbite on her fingers—everything right out of the freezer." And though Babs would later champion literacy, friends remember (with some surprise) that the Bushes did not own a set of encyclopedias. The family attended the First Presbyterian Church (800 W. Texas Avenue) where George and Babs taught Sunday school.

Junior attended Sam Houston Elementary (2000 W. Louisiana Avenue). In third grade he tossed a football through a window after being told the class wouldn't be allowed out for recess due to rain. In fourth grade he once decorated his face to look like a clown . . . with a ballpoint pen. He also like to blow up frogs with firecrackers.

How do we know these details of life on Ohio Street? Later in life the Bush kids seemed to take cruel pleasure in exposing their siblings' childhood secrets. George revealed on *The Tonight Show* that Marvin once peed in the family's steam iron. Jeb confessed that George liked to shoot his younger, unarmed siblings with a BB gun. The Cleavers they weren't.

In 1957 the Bush family moved to their third Midland home, 2703 Sentinel Drive (privately owned), about the time George entered San Jacinto Junior High (1400 N. "N" Street) where he was elected seventh grade class president. The family moved to Houston in 1959 so that Zapata could focus on a new venture: offshore drilling. Shortly thereafter, George was packed off to prep school in Andover, Massachusetts.

The Permian Basin Board of Realtors has purchased the Bush's Ohio Street home and is in the process of restoring it to its 1950s appearance. It eventually will be opened to the public as a mini-museum.

1402 W. Ohio St., Midland, TX 79701

No phone

Hours: Always visible

Cost: Free

www.midlandtxchamber.com/midland/start_files/bush/bush.htm

Directions: One block west of "F" St., three blocks north of Wall St. (Rte. 158).

George W. Bush, All Growed Up . . . Sort Of

After receiving his MBA from Harvard in 1975, George W. Bush returned to his hometown in his five-year-old Olds Cutlass. He lived at two converted garage apartments (both entered from the alley), at 2008-A Bedford Street and 2006-A Harvard Street, and played a lot of golf at the Midland Country Club (6101 N. State Highway 349, (432) 682-4378), where they still have a Worst Dressed Golfer Trophy named in his honor. In June 1977 George met Laura Welch at a barbecue hosted by Joe and Jan O'Neill. Their first date was a round of miniature golf, and they were engaged six weeks later. George and Laura wed on November 5, 1977, at the First United Methodist Church (305 N. Baird Street, (432) 682-3701) and moved into a home they'd purchased at 1405 W. Golf Course Road.

Laura Welch grew up in Midland on Humble Street. Really—that was the name of the street. She led a fairly uneventful youth until November 6, 1963, when she ran a stop sign on Route 349 in her Chevy sedan and struck a Corvair driven by classmate Michael Douglas. The impact broke his neck, killing him instantly. Though she was at fault, she was not charged in the accident. The Douglas family later installed a memorial cannon in the courtyard of Robert E. Lee High School (1800 E. Wall Street) where their son had been a star athlete.

But back to our story . . .

Five months before he married Laura Welch, George Bush founded Arbusto Energy with funding from members of the extended Bush family and folks who were, or wanted to be, their friends. Arbusto's operations were soon put into a holding pattern when Bush decided in July to run for Congress. His opponent was down-home Democrat Kent Hance, who wasted no time portraying Bush as the son of privilege, an East Coast transplant with ties to Yale and Harvard, a man who didn't understand the concerns of Texas's 19th Congressional District.

Bush's campaign was managed by his brother Neil. George could blame him for some of what went wrong, but he made plenty of mistakes on his own. During an interview Bush was asked what qualifications he possessed that Hance did not. "I've got more hair," he replied. When Laura criticized a campaign speech he'd given, Bush, who was pulling into their garage when she gave her blunt assessment, drove his car through the back wall. The nail in the coffin of his campaign, however, was a rally/kegger Bush hosted at Texas Tech. "FREE BEER" the flyer promised. Hance enlisted a Lubbock lawyer, George Thompson III, to send out a mass mailing to the district's churchgoing electorate that began, "Dear Fellow Christians," and went on to detail his concern over what looked like an alcohol-for-votes scheme. Bush lost, though not by much.

The defeat seemed to fuel Bush's problems with alcohol, though the birth of their twins on November 25, 1981, slowed him down a little. Bush claims that a talk with Rev. Billy Graham in 1986 started him thinking about turning his life around, but his religious conversion began a year earlier when he met Arthur Blessitt, a traveling evangelist. Blessitt had been dragging a 12-foot cross around Midland to advertise an upcoming revival. He met with Bush in the coffee shop of the Midland Holiday Inn (4300 W. Wall Street, (432) 697-3181) and asked Bush whether he wanted to live with or without Christ. Bush chose the former. Don Evans, a Midland friend who would later be named Secretary of Commerce, encouraged Bush to attend Bible study. Then, when he woke up with a hangover following his 40th birthday bash, Bush swore off the bottle forever.

All this time Arbusto was struggling along. By 1982 it was almost bankrupt when Philip Uzielli gave it a $1 million cash injection for a 10 percent interest in the $300,000 firm. (Why would Uzielli overpay by $970,000? Perhaps because Uzielli was the former college roommate of James Baker, longtime associate of Bush Sr. . . . just *perhaps*.) Arbusto, which many in the industry were calling Ar-BUST-o, was renamed Bush Exploration. Two years later, still hemorrhaging cash, Bush Exploration was absorbed/rescued by Spectrum 7, and Bush was named Spectrum 7's CEO.

The Bushes moved to their final Midland home, at 910 Harvard Street, in 1985. With Spectrum 7 still failing, the company was purchased by Harken Energy in 1986. Why? Harken investor George Soros put it bluntly: "We were buying political influence. That was it. [Bush] was not much of a businessman." The family moved to Dallas in 1986 when Bush took on his new responsibilities with Harken.

George and Laura Bush's first home has been purchased by the Presi-

dential Museum of Odessa and the Geraldine T. Box Foundation and will be opened as an education center some time in the future.

1405 W. Golf Course Rd., Midland, TX 79701

No phone

Hours: Always visible

Cost: Free

Directions: Four blocks west of "A" St., at Western Dr.

Jessica McClure Falls Down a Well

It was the feel-good rescue of the 1980s: on October 14, 1987, toddler Jessica McClure fell down an unsecured well in the backyard of her aunt's home in Midland. The 18-month-old girl became wedged 22 feet below the surface in the 8-inch-diameter pipe. To extract her, rescuers had to dig a parallel shaft beside the first to pull Jessica out from below. Fifty-eight hours after she fell in, Jessica was pulled out by paramedic Robert O'Donnell on live national TV—CNN's ratings were stupendous!

The media frenzy following the rescue did more damage than the abandoned well. Jessica's parents, Chip McClure and Sissy Porter, were widely criticized when it was reported they had spent $80,000 of the money donated by well-wishers to start a tractor company. The couple divorced in 1990. Firefighter Robert O'Donnell found it difficult to be the focus of national attention one day and forgotten the next. He killed himself eight years later on April 23, 1995, after becoming depressed watching rescuers at the Oklahoma City bombing.

As for Jessica, "Everybody's Baby," she went on to live a typical childhood, soon to be followed by an atypical early adulthood; on her 25th birthday she'll collect about $1 million from a trust fund set up for her with donations.

3309 Tanner Dr., Midland, TX 79703

Private phone

Hours: Always visible; view from street

Cost: Free

www.jessicamcclure.com

Directions: Head northwest on Thomason Dr. from Rte. 80 Business, in two blocks turn right on Holly Dr., then left on Cunningham Dr. for three blocks, then one block to Tanner Dr.

The Petroleum Museum

Face it, if it wasn't for all the oil in the Permian Basin, Midland would be just another dusty town between Dallas and El Paso, if that. Thank goodness for all the sealife that lived and died, was covered in sediment, and compressed over millions of years, or Midlanders would have nothing to pump out of the ground.

The Petroleum Museum will show you how it all began with a 200,000–sea creature diorama of the area's ancient sea. Then fast-forward 230 million years to (almost) the present day and the discovery of black gold in west Texas. Watch as a mannequin operates a crude cable-tool drilling rig, and learn that it was invented by the Chinese. Didn't know that? Well then, you're in for an oil-ducation. The dummy also explains that wildcatters needed girlie pictures to help them through those lonely nights on the range. Ummmm . . . OK . . . perhaps it's time to move along to the next gallery.

What's this? A nitro-laden pickup truck? When they say "Do Not Touch," they mean it! Derricks, pipes, pumps, this place has it all. Feel what it's like to have a blowout in the Wild Well room, assuming the simulator is not blown out during your visit. There's even a special exhibit for the kids starring Dr. Petro, a puppet who knows just how to keep a pump in tip-top shape.

Believe it or not, one of the best reasons to visit the Petroleum Museum isn't the equipment you'll see, but the *art*. The museum commissioned dozens of works from artist Tom Lovell in 1969. From early native cultures to the rise of the drilling industry, each painting is stunning in its own right.

1500 I-20 West, Midland, TX 79701

(432) 683-4403

E-mail: info@petroleummuseum.org

Hours: Monday–Saturday 9 A.M.–5 P.M., Sunday 2–5 P.M.

Cost: Adults $8, Seniors (65+) $6, Teens (12–17) $6, Kids (6–11) $5

www.petroleummusem.org

Directions: Between Rankin Hwy. (Rte. 349) and Cotton Flat Rd., on the north-side I-20 Frontage Rd.

Odessa
George, Babs, and Georgie

In 1948, George and Barbara Bush and their two-year-old son Georgie left New Haven, Connecticut, in their maroon 1947 Studebaker, heading west. They landed in Odessa, where the future president worked as the equipment clerk for the International Derrick and Equipment Company (IDECO), sweeping floors and painting equipment. In 1983 George Bush reminisced, "If I were a psychoanalyzer, I might conclude that I was trying to not compete with my father, but do something on my own."

Nice try, George. This oft-repeated Horatio Alger story typically leaves out one significant detail: IDECO was a subsidiary of Dresser Industries, headed by H. Neil Mallon, a.k.a. "Uncle Neil" to the Bush family. Mallon was installed as president of Dresser in the 1930s by the company's investors. One of those investors was Prescott Bush, George's father. Prescott Bush and Neil Mallon had been in Yale's Skull and Bones Society together. Yep, Odessa's a long way from Connecticut, but not so far that strings couldn't be pulled by elite East Coast types.

The Bushes lived at three different homes in Odessa, first at 1519 E. Seventh Street, then 1523 E. Seventh Street, and finally 916 E. 17th Street. They shared the first home with a pair of hookers, a mother-daughter team who frequently entertained paying guests. Any wonder that Barbara initially "thought Texans were barbarians"? The Bushes left Odessa in April 1949 when Mallon transferred George Bush to a series of Dresser-owned operations in California. Before the end of the year they would return to Texas, but to Midland this time. (See page 119.)

The Bushes' first two Odessa homes have been razed, but their 17th Street address survived long enough to be purchased by local investors and moved to the grounds of the Presidential Museum, where it was restored and opened to the public in 2004. You can see the home's original hardwood floors, kitchen cabinets, and bathtub.

Presidential Museum, 4919 E. University Blvd., Odessa, TX 79762

(432) 363-PRES

Hours: Exterior always visible; Interior, Tuesday–Saturday 10 A.M.–5 P.M., Sunday 2–5 P.M.

Cost: Adults $8, Seniors (65+) $5, Kids (K–12) $5 (Includes Presidential Museum)

www.odessacvb.com/gwbush/main.htm

Directions: Four blocks north of Second St. (Rte. 820) on Headlee Ave. (Loop 338), then one block west on University Ave.; the home is north of the museum, across the footbridge.

ODESSA
Odessa's professional hockey team is known as the Jackalopes.

Odessa Meteor Crater

There's a six-foot-deep hole several miles southeast of Odessa.

So what?

Well, it's also about 550 feet in diameter.

Still not impressed?

What if I told you it was once 100 feet deep . . . and was created by . . . a meteorite?!?!!

Yes, about 50,000 years or so ago, give or take a few thousand years, a large nickel-iron meteorite struck the west Texas plains and blasted 100,000 cubic yards of earth into the sky. That's equivalent to a football field covered in 18 feet of soil.

Keep those stats in mind because you'll need to use your imagination here, though the adjoining museum helps some. But as for the crater, this desert divot looks a lot like the surrounding landscape. Take a walk along the Crater Trail and you'll learn even more . . . perhaps about rattlesnakes. Watch your step.

Odessa Meteor Crater Museum, FM 1936, Odessa, TX 79763

(432) 381-0946

Hours: Tuesday–Saturday 10 A.M.–5 P.M., Sunday 1–5 P.M.

Cost: Free

www.odessacvb.com/museums.htm

Directions: Exit 180 from I-20 west of town, then south two miles on FM 1936.

Presidential Museum

Following the Kennedy assassination, many Texans felt a bit guilty about the whole . . . um . . . *situation*, so they decided to make it up to the nation. Solution? Odessa's Presidential Museum and Leadership Library.

The museum doesn't have as many commander-in-chief artifacts as you might imagine—mostly campaign ribbons, buttons, and commemorative plates—but they do have a few one-of-a-kind items: James Buchanan's straight-edge razor, casts of Abraham Lincoln's hands, a thin plastic "Nixon's the One" record, and a brick, spike, and floor plank left over from the White House restoration under Truman. For GWB fans, there's a gray beanie he once wore, a butterfly-ballot voting machine from Florida, and one of his childhood homes from Odessa (see page 124).

THE SKY IS FALLING!

The meteorite that created the Odessa Meteor Crater isn't the only chunk of space material to fall on the Lone Star State. In fact, Texas records more meteorite strikes than any other state. Here are a few other falls:

★ A football-sized meteorite landed on the front lawn of a Monahans home on March 22, 1998. Seven boys who were playing baseball across the street, and who witnessed the fall, sold the three-pound space rock for $23,000. NASA scientists found small pockets of water in the meteorite, the first-ever discovery of extraterrestrial *agua*.

★ A meteorite struck the home of Reverend Howard Cameron of Beaumont on May 2, 1997. It embedded itself in a closet wall.

★ Hollywood chose the Big Bend town of Shafter to be wiped out by an alien virus carried to earth on a crashed space probe in *The Andromeda Strain*. The near–ghost town looks remarkably unchanged today.

★ Parts of a Soviet satellite fell on a ranch near Adrian in August 1970.

★ And from the Eastern Hemisphere (as opposed to outer space), Japanese-launched balloon bombs fell on Woodson and Desdemona on March 23 and 24, 1945.

Fans of the First Ladies can marvel at dolls showing off their miniature inaugural gowns. Call ahead to find out what traveling exhibit you can expect. Recent programs include Pets of the White House, the White House in Miniature (a 60-foot replica), and They Also Ran (losers, each and every one).

Presidential Museum and Leadership Library, 4919 E. University Blvd., Odessa, TX 79762

(432) 363-PRES

Hours: Tuesday–Saturday 10 A.M.–5 P.M., Sunday 2–5 P.M.

Cost: Adults $8, Seniors (65+) $5, Kids (K–12) $5 (Includes Bush Home)

www.presidentialmuseum.org

Directions: Four blocks north of Second St. (Rte. 820) on Headlee Ave. (Loop 338), then one block west on University Ave.

OZONA

Each July 4 the men of Ozona compete in the Old Time Beauty Pageant, where they model Victorian swimsuits.

Shakespeare's Globe Theatre

Theater today might have been very different had William Shakespeare grown up in West Texas instead of England. But he didn't, which is why this venue on the Odessa College campus is named the Globe Theatre of the Southwest and not Billy Boy's Dinner Thee-Ater and Country Western Hoedown. The structure is a fairly faithful reproduction of the Bard's famous stage, given modern fire safety regulations and building codes, and is the first of its kind (after the original). Adjacent to the theater is another Elizabethan structure, the Anne Hathaway Cottage, which houses a Shakespeare library.

Odessa's Globe hosts Shakespeare productions throughout the year, as well as musical acts and traveling Broadway productions. Each spring it throws a Shakespeare Festival, sometime around April 23, the playwright's birthday. And on alternate Sundays during the summer it hosts bull-riding competitions.

No, wait . . . the bulls are over at Dos Amigos Cantina (4700 Golder Ave., (432) 368-7556, www.dosamigoscantina.com). I'm *always* mixing those two up.

Globe Theatre of the Southwest, 2308 Shakespeare Rd., Odessa, TX 79761

(432) 332-1586

E-mail: Hamlet@GlobeSW.org

Hours: Tours by appointment, Monday–Friday 9 A.M.–5 P.M.

Cost: Adults $5, Kids $5

www.globesw.org

Directions: Three blocks north of the intersection of Kermit and Andrews Hwys., north of Rte. 302 (Kermit Hwy.).

PECOS

You can be arrested in Pecos for walking or sitting on the wrong side of the street.

Pecos throws a Cantaloupe Festival every June.

Jack Ben Rabbit Classic.

World's Largest Jackrabbit

As bunnies go, jackrabbits are pretty big. And as jackrabbits go, Jack Ben Rabbit is the biggest of the bunch. Installed in 1962, this eight-foot-tall concrete statue honored not only this popular stew ingredient but the city's first Jackrabbit Roping Contest, held in 1932 at the corner of Third and Grant Streets. The event drew "out-of-town do-gooders" who protested the unnecessary cruelty; the local sheriff also objected, but was overruled by the Odessa mayor. Cowgirl Grace Hendricks lassoed one of the critters in five seconds, beating out all the male competitors.

Whether or not the contest was canceled in later years to spare the egos of local cowboys, or to avoid further controversy, is anybody's guess. It was revived once, in 1977, with similar outcries. Animal rights activists raided the cages on the morning of the contest, freeing the captives. Several jackrabbits returned later in the day and the competition was back on. Cowboy Jack Torian snagged one in six seconds.

In 1978 a judge declared the contest inhumane, leaving Jack Ben Rabbit to stand as the sole reminder of the town's jackrabbit-roping heritage . . . until a few years ago. Somebody got the hare-brained idea to erect dozens of Jack Ben replicas around town, each embellished by a local artist. And though civic pride and urban beautification are admirable goals, the project diminished the stature of the town's original mascot, not to mention that it confuses visitors.

So, oddball traveler, do not accept imitations. There's only one *true* Jack Ben Rabbit, and he's on Houston Avenue.

802 N. Sam Houston Ave., Odessa, TX 79761

(800) 780-HOST or (432) 333-7871

E-mail: info@odessacvb.com

Hours: Always visible

Cost: Free

www.odessacvb.com/historic_sites.htm

Directions: Three blocks west of Grant Ave. (Rte. 385) on Eighth St.

San Angelo
Miss Hattie's Bordello Museum

This might not be the best-known little whorehouse in Texas, but it's the only one that's a museum. This establishment opened as a "Gentlemen's Social Center" in 1896 and had a good 50-year run. It was so popular, rumors circulated that it had a tunnel in the basement that led to the nearby bank. Then, in 1946, those killjoys known as the Texas Rangers put an end to it all. The house's Miss Hattie stayed in town, and died in 1982 at the very ripe age of 104.

Today, guides dressed (but not *undressed*) in period outfits tell you the history of this local institution and others like it. Maybe you want to open a bordello of your own? You could probably pick up a few pointers here.

18½ E. Concho Ave., San Angelo, TX 76903

(325) 653-0112

Hours: Thursday–Saturday 1–4 P.M.

Cost: Adults $5

www.sanangelo.org/tourism/atract.html

Directions: One block west of Oakes St., just north of the Concho River.

MORE ON WHORES

Legalized prostitution was first introduced to Texas in (believe it or not) Waco, the second town in the United States to establish a regulated red-light district. Starting in 1889, prostitutes were licensed to work along Two Street, better known as The Reservation. Working gals had to obtain a license and get a monthly medical exam. San Antonio adopted a Bawdy House Ordinance later in 1889. The Waco laws were repealed in 1917, but the San Antonio red-light district survived until 1941.

The **Sundance Kid** (Harry Longabaugh) is believed to have met his future wife, **Etta Place**, on San Antonio's cathouse row. Though nobody knows for sure, most believe Place worked in the whorehouse run by Fannie Porter at 503 S. San Saba Street. Or maybe Place was a schoolteacher—stories vary. A lot.

Now if you think these establishments have never contributed to society, consider this: Grace Woodyard, who made her fortune running one of Port Arthur's most popular whorehouses, once loaned the city of Beaumont $30,000 to pay its overdue utility bill.

SAN ANGELO

By law, San Angelo politicians must wear long pants while campaigning.

Survivor Outback runner-up **Colby Donaldson** was arrested in San Angelo for public intoxication on September 10, 1999. He had been found by police, passed out in a puddle of his own vomit, on the north side of an ATM at Southwest Plaza (3524 Knickerbocker Road).

Freshwater pearls, some pink or purple, can be found in the Concho River near San Angelo. A statue of a mermaid, pearl in hand, titled *The Pearl of the Concho* stands on a rock in the middle of the river near the Celebration Bridge.

San Angelo typically celebrates Independence Day on July 3 because it doesn't have first dibs on the cannon from the local armory.

Wink
Roy Orbison Museum

Though Roy Orbison was born in Vernon on April 23, 1936, he grew up in Wink. As a teenager he led a group named the Wink Westerners, and when he graduated from Wink High School in 1954, he announced his ambition in the yearbook: "To lead a western band is my after school wish, and of course to marry a beautiful dish."

It didn't take him long . . . for the band, that is. Orbison went off to North Texas State University to major in geology, but soon dropped out to form the Teen Kings. They caught the ear of Sam Phillips at Sun Records, and Orbison was launched on the road to stardom.

The folks of Wink are doing their best to keep Orbison's memory alive. Each year, during the second weekend in June, they host a Roy Orbison Festival, which includes a Pretty Woman Pageant. And they recently opened a Roy Orbison Museum. It has more albums and bumper stickers than genuine Orbisonabilia, but they do have a pair of his trademark sunglasses, *which they allow you to put on!* See if the stuffy Smithsonian allows you to do *that.*

205 E. Hendricks Blvd., Wink, TX 79789

(432) 527-3622

Hours: By appointment

Cost: Free

www.rootsweb.com/%7Etxwinkle/wink.htm

Roy Orbison Fan Site: www.orbison.com

Directions: Downtown on Rte. 115 (Henricks Blvd.), one block south of First St.

WINK

The ghost of a Russian Cossack named Nicholi has been spotted walking down Hendricks Boulevard in Wink. Even **Roy Orbison** claimed to have spotted him on the road near the edge of town.

MUSICAL MUSEUMS & MONUMENTS

Roy Orbison isn't the only Texas musician with his (or her) own museum or monument, not by a long shot. This guidebook also has entries on Buddy Holly (see page 18), Janis Joplin (see page 227), and Selena (see page 286). And here are a few more:

Lefty Frizzell Museum & Monument (Museum, 912 W. Park Avenue, Corsicana, (903) 654-4846, www.rootsweb.com/~txnavarr/pioneer_village/lefty_frizzell_museum.htm; Monument, Beauford Jester Park, 700 W. Park Avenue): Frizzell was a musician's musician, an even bigger songwriter than he was a performer. (He wrote "If You've Got the Money, Honey, I've Got the Time.") His museum is filed with his signature outrageous cowboy boots, costumes, and original sheet music. A bronze statue of Frizzell is located two blocks east of the museum, where you'll also find handprints of country western stars such as Merle Haggard, who recorded many of Frizzell's tunes. Why is this museum in Corsicana? Frizzell was born here on March 31, 1938.

Woody Guthrie's "This Land Is Your Land" Fence (M. K. Brown Civic Auditorium, 1101 N. Hobart Street, Pampa): Balladeer Woody Guthrie lived at 408 S. Russell Street in Pampa from 1929 to 1937, when he wasn't off riding the rails. In his honor, Russell "Rusty" Neef created a 150-foot-long musical bar fence showing the chorus of "This Land Is Your Land," in 4/4 time, in the key of G. It is illuminated with red, white, and blue lights at night. Guthrie fans will also want to visit Bound for Glory Park at Cuyler Street and Craven Avenue, along the railroad tracks.

Lightnin' Hawkins Statue (Lightnin' Hawkins Park, Camp Street Café, 215 S. Third Street, Crockett, (936) 544-8656, www.campstreetcafe.com): This statue of legendary blues guitarist Sam "Lightnin'" Hawkins is posed on the same corner where Hawkins once played for tips from passersby.

Jim Reeves Memorial (Three miles east of town on Route 79, Carthage): Country music's Jim Reeves perished in a plane crash near Nashville on July 31, 1964. A granite statue of Reeves, guitar in hand, guards his grave in his hometown of Carthage, as well as the plot of his faithful collie, Cheyenne, who joined him three years later.

Tex Ritter Museum (Texas Country Music Hall of Fame, 300 W. Panola Street, Carthage, (903) 693-6634, www.carthagetexas.com/TX_web/

index.html): Though Tex Ritter is only part of the Texas Country Music Hall of Fame, he's certainly the star. Ritter was one of the most popular cowboy actor/singers of the 1950s, and this place is filed with his memorabilia, as well as items from the careers of Tanya Tucker, Kris Kristofferson, Willie Nelson, Gene Autry, and others.

Stevie Ray Vaughan Statue (South side of the First Street Bridge, Austin, (512) 478-0098): Vaughan was born in Dallas, but made a lasting mark on the Austin music scene. Three years after his death in 1990, Austin folks dedicated a full-size statue of Vaughan by artist Ralph Helmick near a Town Lake stage where Vaughan often performed.

Bob Wills Museum & Monument (Museum, Sixth and Lyles Streets, Turkey, (806) 423-1253, www.turkeytexas.com; Monument, W. Main Street, Turkey): Bob Wills, "The King of Western Swing," hailed from Turkey, where you'll find a three-room museum filled with fiddles, costumes, sheet music, and more. There's also a 30-foot pink granite monument in town, with a spinning guitar perched on top. The guitar revolves 24 hours a day, 7 days a week, 365 days a year, while the sounds of Bob Wills waft out from a looped tape. On the last Saturday every April, Turkey hosts a Bob Wills Reunion, which lacks only one thing: Bob Wills.

Heart of Texas Country Music Museum (16th and Bridge Streets, Brady, (325) 597-1895, www.bradytx.com/sites/countrymusic.com): If you're not interested in a single performer, but would like a nice cross-section, come to Brady. This museum doesn't focus just on Texas musicians, but country music performers from all over, including Johnny Cash, Mel Tillis, Loretta Lynn, Tammy Wynette, and Merle Haggard.

Ysleta
Mary of Ágreda

When Father Alonso de Benavides set out to convert the population around Ysleta to Catholicism, he found a few who were already open to the idea. What made this strange was that Benavides arrived in 1625, and was the first known missionary in the region. He thought it strange when the Jumanos Indians, who lived 300 miles west of Ysleta, showed up at his doorstep and asked that he send a priest to baptize their tribe. How had they learned about Christianity?

Fr. Benavides was shorthanded and couldn't spare a priest, so the

request went unanswered until 1629 when a curious story arrived from Don Francisco Manso, the Archbishop of Mexico. It seems a poor Clares nun named María de Jesús de Ágreda—Mary of Ágreda—who lived in a Spanish convent, had visions of teleporting to the New World where she preached to a tribe of Native Americans. The archbishop ordered Fr. Benavides to investigate.

"You mean the Lady in Blue?" the Jumanos asked, describing a nun's habit. (They had not yet told Benavides a person had visited them.) Two friars went to their village and were greeted by a procession that carried a decorated cross. The Lady in Blue had just left, they claimed, after preparing them for the priests' visit.

Fr. Benevides returned to Spain and met with Mary in 1631; she claimed to occasionally fall into a trance after receiving communion. Though she never left the convent, she felt as if she levitated, flew over the ocean, and landed in the Jumanos' village—a process called bi-location, or transvection. She confirmed places and dates that convinced Fr. Benevides she had actually visited the New World.

Mary of Ágreda never returned to the Jumanos and died in 1665. Her body was placed in a crypt in her Spanish convent. Those who have examined her body, some as recently as 1989, claim she has never decomposed. A permanent mission church was built in Ysleta in 1682.

Ysleta Mission, Zaragoza Rd. and Alameda St., Ysleta, TX 79907

(915) 859-9848

Hours: Daily 8 A.M.–5 P.M.

Cost: Free

http://missiontrail.elp.rr.com

Directions: South of I-10 on FM 659 (Zaragoza Rd.) to Rte. 20 (Alameda St.).

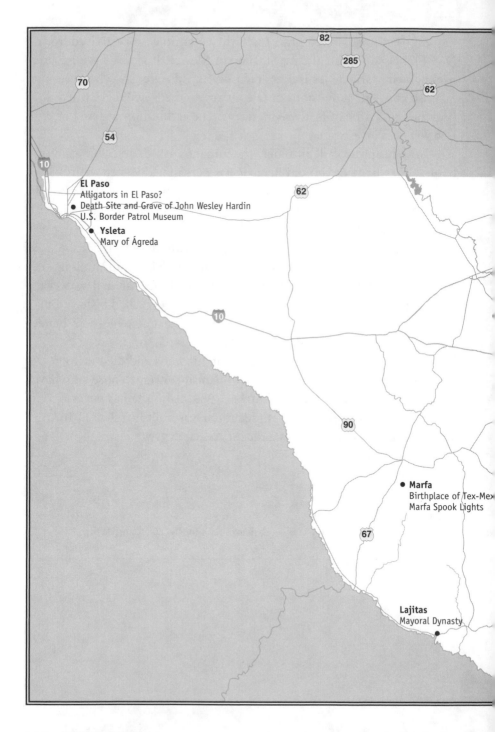

El Paso
Alligators in El Paso?
● Death Site and Grave of John Wesley Hardin
U.S. Border Patrol Museum
 ● **Ysleta**
Mary of Ágreda

● **Marfa**
Birthplace of Tex-Mex
Marfa Spook Lights

Lajitas
Mayoral Dynasty

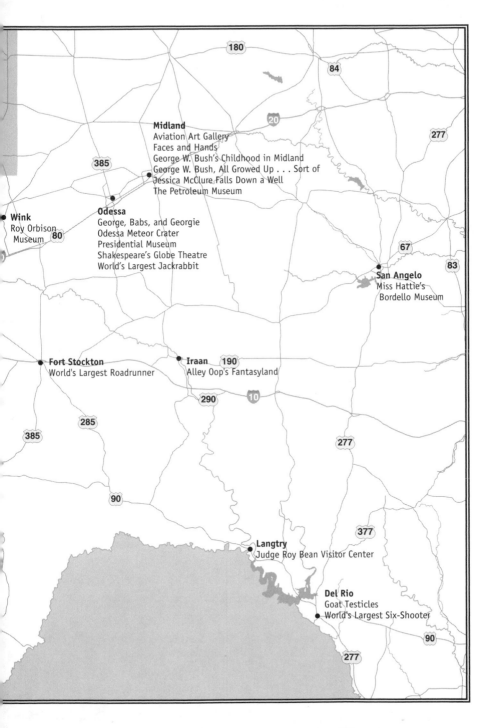

Midland
Aviation Art Gallery
Faces and Hands
George W. Bush's Childhood in Midland
George W. Bush, All Growed Up . . . Sort of
Jessica McClure Falls Down a Well
The Petroleum Museum

Wink
Roy Orbison
Museum

Odessa
George, Babs, and Georgie
Odessa Meteor Crater
Presidential Museum
Shakespeare's Globe Theatre
World's Largest Jackrabbit

San Angelo
Miss Hattie's
Bordello Museum

Fort Stockton
World's Largest Roadrunner

Iraan
Alley Oop's Fantasyland

Langtry
Judge Roy Bean Visitor Center

Del Rio
Goat Testicles
World's Largest Six-Shooter

central texas

*T*he Central Texas Hill Country is the state's most popular tourist destination. Every other building, it seems, is a quaint antique store. In fact, there are so many antique emporiums that it's probably safe to assume if you run across an old piece of junk that isn't nailed down, it's probably for sale. Just ask—your trunk will be filled before you know it.

But then what will you do?

Maybe you should consider a trip that doesn't revolve around shopping. How about a visit to the Hippo Capital of Texas? The World's Largest Oatmeal Box? A re-creation of Stonehenge? 'Cause they're all here. How about the birthplace of Dr Pepper? OK, you *can't* pass up Tom Landry's hat. Why not start with that and work your way back to the others?

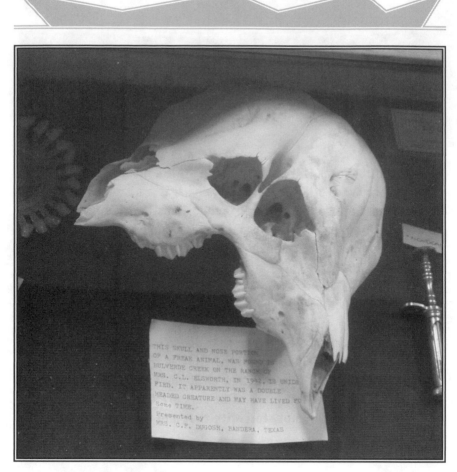

Are two heads better than one?
Photo by author, courtesy of the Frontier Times Museum.

Bandera
Frontier Times Museum

Long before there were stuffy, formal, *educational* museums, America was alive with "dime museums," private collections of anything and everything their owners found interesting, artifacts that were thrown together in no particular order. Visitors would pay 10¢ to gawk at freak animals in jars and trinkets from faraway lands. Sadly, there are very few dime museums left in the world, yet one of the best is still here in Bandera: the Frontier Times Museum, founded by J. Marvin Hunter in 1933.

The haphazard arrangement of the museum's artifacts is half its charm. In one display case you'll find a two-headed calf skull sitting beside a dentist's Novocain syringes. In another, Native American beadwork shares space with a serpent made from hundreds of English postage stamps. Over there is the "Shrunken Head of Zorro" from a doglike creature that lived in the jungles of Ecuador, which was unlucky enough to be captured by Jivaro headhunters. Another shrunken head, this one from a human, is back on display after being noggin-napped a few years ago; it was found abandoned in a plastic bag in a San Antonio parking lot, no doubt tossed aside when the thief was beset with a South American curse.

As its name implies, the Frontier Times Museum does have a western theme; it's got arrowheads, branding irons, pistols, a bottle from Judge Roy Bean's Saloon (see page 111), a "painting" of Texas made from rattlesnake rattles, and the mounted head of Big Tex, a longhorn whose horns measure 7 feet 6 inches from tip to tip—all very cool on their own. But then you stumble upon a pair of fleas dressed for a night on the town, or a stuffed lamb with two faces, and you wonder if you've been transported to oddball heaven. Take it from me: you have.

506 13th St., PO Box 1918, Bandera, TX 78003

(830) 796-3864

Hours: Monday–Saturday 10 A.M.–4:30 P.M., Sunday 1–4:30 P.M.

Cost: Adults $5, Seniors $3, Kids (6–17) $1

www.frontiertimesmuseum.com

Directions: One block north of the courthouse, on the northwest end of town.

BANDERA

Bandera claims to be the Cowboy Capital of the World, and they've got the monument to prove it. Standing outside the Bandera County Courthouse, an oversized belt buckle sculpture honors the seven national or world champion cowboys who hailed from this town. www.banderacowboycapital.com

Comfort
Yankee Memorial

Let's hear it for the freethinking German immigrants of Comfort. When faced with conscription into the Confederate Army in 1862, they knew the Southern cause was unjust, so they decided to enlist in the Union Army. Led by Fritz Teneger, 68 men took off for Mexico, first stop on a journey to the North. They were overtaken by a Southern posse on August 10, 1862; 19 were killed at the Massacre of the Nueces River, and nine more defenseless wounded were promptly executed by the Rebels. The survivors fled as far as the Rio Grande where, on October 18, 1862, they were attacked again. Twelve more died. Their bodies were abandoned for the vultures.

Still, the survivors were not deterred. They retrieved their compatriots' bones in 1865, and buried them beneath a limestone cairn back in Comfort. The 1866 Treue der Union (Loyalty to the Union) monument was the first Civil War memorial erected in Texas, and today is the only memorial to Yankee soldiers—or at least those who wanted to be—located in former Confederate Territory (except official burial grounds). The 36-star flag at the site is one of the few in the United States that is allowed to fly permanently at half-staff. The Treue der Union monument was vandalized so often over the years that it had to be restored in 1996.

350 High St., Comfort, TX 78013

(830) 995-3131

Hours: Always visible

Cost: Free

www.comfort-texas.com

Directions: Two blocks west of Rte. 27 (Front St.), between Third and Fourth Sts.

Crawford
GWB's "Ranch"

You've seen the footage hundreds of times, George Bush in jeans and a cowboy hat, standing in front of a bunch of hay bales or clearing brush. It makes for a nice backdrop, which is precisely the idea. It's almost easy to forget that Bush has never been a rancher, nor is he now, even with all the brush he's cleared. Oilman? Sure. Baseball team owner? In part. But rancher? Nope.

The Bush family purchased the 1,600-acre Prairie Chapel Ranch in 1999 following his reelection as Texas governor. Then after the 2000 presidential election it became known as the Western White House. Bush was here when he received the infamous August 6, 2001, PDB titled "Bin Laden Determined to Strike in U.S." Though the same memo might have alarmed lesser men, Bush seemed relaxed as he reported on how much he enjoyed "seeing the cows" that he claimed "talked to me, being the good listener that I am."

Now don't think you'll be able stop by and "set a spell" with the First Family; the ranch isn't even listed on maps. Nor is its entrance marked, though the half-dozen mobile trailers covered in antennas and satellite dishes across the road are a dead giveaway. Ask anyone in the shops along the main drag in Crawford for directions—they're a chatty bunch, they'll tell you all you need to know. If you want a photo with the president, nearly every shop in town has a cardboard cutout to pose with. Democrats are welcome, too, for not everybody in Crawford is in lockstep with the president. In 2004 both the mayor and Crawford's *Lone Star Iconoclast* endorsed John Kerry for president. A lot of good it did him. . . .

Greater Crawford Chamber of Commerce, 6775 N. Lone Star Pwy., Crawford, TX 76638

(254) 486-9626

Hours: Most stores 9 A.M.–5 P.M.

Cost: Free

www.crawfordchamberofcommerce.com

Directions: Most of the stores are along Lone Star Pwy./Ave. G (FM 317).

BRADY

Brady hosts the World Championship Barbecue Goat Cook-Off on Labor Day weekend each year.

CASTROVILLE

Castroville calls itself the Little Alsace of Texas and is the only Alsatian colony in the world. www.castroville.com

Could they be any more literal?

Dime Box
Dime Box

No offense to the current citizens of Dime Box, but their ancestors had to be the most unimaginative folks in all of Texas. Back in the early 1870s, settlers in the area would put dimes in a box at Joseph Brown's sawmill to fund mail delivery from nearby Giddings. When the town got a post office of its own in 1877, they decided to name it after their original postal system: Dime Box.

Now there are certainly towns in Texas with less imaginative names, but when a monument was erected years later in downtown Dime Box, well, it was hard to escape the conclusion that these folks just couldn't come up with an original thought. The erected a large, glass box on the main drag, and in it they hung a shiny 1917 Mercury dime the size of a manhole cover. It's still there today.

FM 141, Dime Box, TX 77853

No phone

Hours: Always visible

Cost: Free

Directions: Two blocks northwest of railroad tracks on FM 141.

ELGIN
Elgin has been named the Sausage Capital of Texas by the state legislature, as well as the Brick Capital of the Southwest. www.elgintx.com

Each October Elgin hosts a Hogeye Festival where a King Hog and a Sowpreme Queen are crowned and where plenty of sausage—called "hot guts" locally—is consumed.

FREDERICKSBURG
The first letters of the street names intersecting Main Street in Fredericksburg, reading east from Adams Street, spell "All Welcome." Heading west on Main from Adams, they spell out "Come Back."

Critters, critters everywhere.

Floresville
Concrete Zoo

Pink flamingos and lawn gnomes are a great way to dress up a home, but they're hardly original. But what Beatrice Jimenez has created in her front yard? *That's* unique. She calls her menagerie the Concrete Zoo, and it's populated with dozens of one-of-a-kind critters. Some look vaguely familiar—zebras and giraffes and ETs—but others are harder to figure out. Is that a monkey on the elephant's back? Why is that big-headed dinosaur wearing a tuxedo? What happened to that red baboon's arm that turned it into a directional arrow, welcoming you to stop in? Don't waste too much time trying to answer these questions, just soak in the beauty of this artistic visionary.

1205 Standish St., Floresville, TX 78114

Private phone

Hours: Always visible

Cost: Free

Directions: Just northeast of Fourth St. (Rte. 181) on FM 97 (Standish St.).

Fredericksburg
Bonfire Bunnies

If you believe the Fredericksburg travel brochures, this town's annual Easter Eve bonfires can be traced back to peace talks held in the area in 1847. Comanche warriors were camped in the hills around town during discussions with German settlers, led by John Meusebach. The negotiations just happened to fall on the night before Easter, and a local mother explained away the ominous glow of campfires surrounding the town as the Easter Bunny's egg-boiling operations.

A treaty was signed on Easter, and to this day Fredericksburg commemorates its good fortune by lighting bonfires on the night before Easter every year. The celebration starts at the Gillespie County Fairgrounds where a small fire is ignited by Mr. and Mrs. Easter Bunny (donning giant rabbit ears) in the middle of a makeshift Indian village. The flame is carried Olympic-style to 22 hilltops around town to light the main fires.

Too bad it's mostly bunk. Historians have pointed out that the treaty was actually signed a month *before* Easter in 1846, and that the fire tradition can be traced back to a pre-Christian pagan ritual brought over by German immigrants. This makes sense, because other elements of Easter are linked to the pagan celebration of the Spring Equinox. Geez, is no lie sacred?

Fredericksburg Convention and Visitors Bureau, 302 E. Austin St., Fredericksburg, TX 78624

(888) 997-3600 or (830) 997-6523

Hours: Saturday night before Easter Sunday

Cost: Free

www.gillespiefair.com

Directions: The main bonfire is located on Cross Mountain; the fairgrounds are two miles south of town on Rte. 16.

FREDERICKSBURG

Fredericksburg is the Polka Capital of Texas.

Enchanted Rock State Park

Enchanted Rock is impressive, jutting 425 feet out of the Texas Hill Country like a big, pink boil. Native Americans have long told stories of ghost fires appearing on the summit when the moon was full, and they feared the wrath of the gods if they ever set foot upon the rock outcropping. As was typical, the European settlers misinterpreted the legends and claimed the granite dome was the location of human sacrifices.

Though neither story seems to be true, there is one odd phenomenon that occurs here on hot summer evenings: after the sun goes down, the 640-acre rock cools, and as it contracts it emits strange, otherworldly sounds. No doubt the noises contributed to its mystique.

The rock itself is one of North America's oldest formations. During the August 16, 1987, Harmonic Convergence, hippies and New Age practitioners came to the park to celebrate . . . and were all sacrificed to the Gods of Harmony. Or so I've been told.

Enchanted Rock State Natural Area, 16710 RR 965, Mail Route 4, PO Box 170,
  Fredericksburg, TX 78624
(800) 792-1112 or (325) 247-3903
Hours: Daily 8 A.M.–5 P.M.; Overnight camping available
Cost: Adults $5, Kids (12 and under) Free
www.tpwd.state.tx.us/park/enchantd/enchantd.htm
Directions: Eighteen miles north of town on RR 965.

National Museum of the Pacific War

Fleet Admiral Chester Nimitz, commander of the Allied forces in the central Pacific during World War II, was born in Fredericksburg in 1885. He grew up in a steamboat-shaped hotel on Main Street. When veterans were looking for a place to build a museum commemorating the Pacific conflict, Nimitz's hometown was the perfect choice.

There are actually several buildings that make up the larger museum. The old hotel is dedicated to Nimitz's life and career. Behind the hotel, past the Japanese Peace Garden, the Veterans Walk of Honor, and the Plaza of the Presidents, is the George Bush Gallery. It traces the history of conflict, from Japan's first military conquests to its ultimate surrender. Along the way you'll see the only surviving midget-submarine used during the attack on Pearl Harbor, a hatch retrieved from the USS *Arizona*, a

re-creation of an island airfield, and a glob of New Mexico sand fused into glass by the first atomic bomb detonated at the Trinity site. The best part of the museum, however, is the Pacific Combat Zone two blocks away. A guide takes you on a walk though a Japanese-held atoll where Allied troops have just landed, as well as a PT boat base and a hangar deck with a TBM Avenger. War may be hell, but it can also be quite interesting.

340 E. Main St., Fredericksburg, TX 78624

(830) 997-4379

E-mail: nimitz@tpwd.state.tx.us

Hours: Daily 10 A.M.–5 P.M.

Cost: Adults $5, Students (with ID) $3, Kids (Under 12) Free

www.nimitz-museum.org

Directions: Two blocks east of Rte. 87 (Washington St.) on Rte. 290 (Main St.).

GROESBECK
Actor **Jo Don Baker** was born in Groesbeck on February 12, 1943.

HAMILTON
Each November 11 at 4 A.M., the town of Hamilton celebrates Armistice Day by blowing an anvil into the sky using a large quantity of black powder. The annual Anvil Shoot takes place in front of the American Legion Hall on Route 281, north of town.

HEWITT
Hewitt police busted **Willie Nelson** for marijuana possession in March 10, 1994, but because the search of his car was improperly conducted, Willie walked.

JARRELL
The town of Jarrell was leveled by a tornado on May 27, 1997, killing 27 residents. The same town had been hit eight years earlier by another twister. On May 17, 1989, a storm killed one and destroyed over 100 homes.

JOHNSON CITY
In early December each year Johnson City hosts a Pickup Truck Parade where decorated trucks ring in the holiday season.

See for yourself.

Gonzales
Out of Time

The four clocks on the county courthouse in Gonzalez have never kept proper time, at least not since March 18, 1921. On that day, convicted murderer Albert Howard awaited his fate in the county jail. Sentenced to hang by the neck until dead, dead, dead, Howard took out his anger on the only thing he could see from his prison cell: the courthouse clocks. He cursed the timepieces, "After I am dead, nobody will ever be able to synchronize their hands!" he shouted . . . or something to that effect. And you know what? *Maintenance crews have never been able to do it!*

Gonzales residents should count themselves lucky that Howard didn't throw a Carrie-like curse on them all, but settled instead on a minor inconvenience. You can still visit the cell where Albert Howard spent his final days; the old jail is now a museum. The structure was used as a pokey from 1887 to 1975, and today holds a small collection of incarceration-related artifacts. You'll see the "women and lunatics" cells and a faithful reproduction of the gallows used on Mr. Howard.

Old Jail Museum, 414 E. St. Lawrence St., Gonzales, TX 78629

(830) 672-6532

E-mail: info@gonzalestexas.com

Hours: Courthouse, always visible; Museum, Monday–Friday 8 A.M.–5 P.M., Saturday 8:30 A.M.–4 P.M., Sunday 1–4 P.M.

Cost: Free

www.gonzalestexas.com/attractions.htm

Directions: On Courthouse Square at St. Joseph St.

KERRVILLE

When novelist **Kinky Friedman** ran for Kerrville Justice of the Peace in 1986 he promised, "If you elect me the first Jewish justice of the peace, I'll reduce the speed limit to 54.95!" He lost.

Kerrville claims to be the Mohair Capital of the World. www.kerrvilletx.com

KILLEEN

Elvis Presley underwent basic training at Fort Hood from March to September 1958, before he was shipped off to Germany. He and his parents rented a home at 906 Oak Hill Drive in Killeen, starting that May. Before that he lived in the barracks.

Hico
Brushy Bill Roberts or Billy the Kid?

Imagine the surprise New Mexico Governor Thomas Mabry must have felt when, on November 30, 1950, a law-abiding citizen from Hico, Texas, showed up and asked for a pardon. The man carried with him a 17-page legal brief, 22 pieces of evidence, and a few gunshot scars proving that he, Ollie L. "Brushy Bill" Roberts, was none other than Billy the Kid. Though most believed Billy had been gunned down by Pat Garrett on July 14, 1881, in Fort Sumner, New Mexico, Roberts wanted to set the record straight: *he* was the Kid, and he was very much alive. And, since he was pushing 91 years of age, there was the little matter of an outstanding warrant for his arrest to be cleared up.

The governor refused to pardon him (or to believe he even needed pardoning), and Roberts returned to his home on Second Street in Hico a broken man. Less than a month later, two days after Christmas, Roberts dropped dead of a heart attack in front of the town's post office.

Bill, or Billy, might have died that day, but the controversy lives on. Today, the Billy the Kid Museum offers a $10,000 reward to anyone who can prove the two men were *not* the same. Here's what makes the money tough to collect: it's not as if anyone has accurate documentation of the lifetime whereabouts of either man, and both went by so many aliases their nicknames were bound to intersect at some point. Historians believe Billy the Kid was born William Bonney in New York City on November 23, 1860. He called himself Henry Roberts, Henry Antrim, Henry McCarty, the Kid, and Billy the Kid over his short life. But not so fast; Brushy Bill claimed to have been born on December 31, 1859, in Cranfills Gap, Texas, and was given the name William Henry Roberts. His mother died when he was three, and he was sent to live with his aunt in Oklahoma. Her name? Kathleen *Bonney*. During his lifetime he went by William Henry Bonney, Oliver Roberts, Ollie L. Roberts, O. L. Roberts, the Kid, the Texas Kid, the Hugo Kid, and Brushy Bill. Oh yeah, and Billy the Kid.

Are you getting any of this?

Maybe it would make more sense to explain how Brushy Bill cheated death in New Mexico. Pat Garrett apparently thought he had unloaded three bullets into the Kid, but the man he gunned down was the desperado's friend Billy Barlow. Billy the Kid was wounded, but escaped. Rather than admit his mistake, and face the legal consequences of shooting the wrong man, Garrett buried Billy Barlow and claimed he was the Kid.

Meanwhile, Bill was nursed back to health by sympathetic locals, then fled to Mexico to lay low for a while. He eventually returned and led a fairly productive adulthood before deciding to come clean in retirement. In the beginning he mostly bent the ears of locals, but he finally sought out the governor to spill the campfire beans. And then he died.

The Billy the Kid Museum, housed in an 1896 motel saloon, is mostly a collection of photocopied newspaper articles and faded photos. Still, it's worth a visit. Hico celebrates Billy the Kid Days on the first weekend in April each year. And in 1993, artist James Rice erected a statue of Billy the Kid firing a gun in front of the old post office (Second and Pecan Streets), on the very spot where Brush Bill left for that Great Roundup in the Sky.

Billy the Kid Museum, 105 N. Pecan St., Hico, TX 76457

(254) 796-4004

Hours: Daily 10 A.M.–5 P.M.

Cost: Adults $3, Students $2, Kids (12 and under) Free

www.hico-tx.com/billy/index.html

Directions: Just south of Second St. (Rte. 6), two blocks west of Cedar St. (Rte. 220).

LULING

Luling claims to be the Toughest Town in Texas.

Luling trailer-park residents were terrorized by "The Thing" during the 1970s. The creature came out of the nearby Ottine Swamp to shake their mobile homes.

This is Texas?

Hunt
Stonehenge II

The original Stonehenge in Salisbury Plain, England, took hundreds of druids 500 years to build. Stonehenge II, a few miles west of Hunt, took three men about nine months. Then again, this is *Texas*.

   The whole idea got started in 1989 when Doug Hill upended a limestone boulder in his neighbor Al Shepperd's field. After some consideration, Shepperd asked Hill if he could use the stone as the starting block for a Stonehenge replica. Shepperd would pay for it if Hill would do the work. So, basing his plans on the size of the original stone, Hill decided to make a ⅗ths replica. With the help of craftsmen Jose Navarro and Jesus Contrerras, Hill built the remaining triptychs and lintels using rebar, metal lathe, and cement. One thing they didn't take into consideration, however, was Stonehenge's purpose as a celestial guide. In other words, don't plan to set your sundial by the 13-foot "stones" you find here. And, just to confuse folks, Hill added two Easter Island heads to the site in 1991.

Al Shepperd died in 1994, and his ashes were scattered at the site. Otherwise, life at Stonehenge II was relatively uneventful until the Millennium when a rumor circulated that a band of San Antonio skinheads planned to loot the local Wal-Mart of weapons, then commit mass suicide in the center of the circle at midnight on December 31. They apparently never got their act together.

FM 1340, Hunt, TX 78024

No phone

E-mail: alfredshepperd@hotmail.com

Hours: Always visible

Cost: Free

www.alfredshepperd.com/stonehenge/untitled.html

Directions: Two miles west of town on FM 1340.

ANOTHER STONEHENGE

For all you Neolithic nuts, there's *another* Stonehenge replica in the Lone Star State. It's located on the campus of the University of Texas of the Permian Basin in Odessa (John Ben Sheppard Boulevard and E. 42nd Street, www.odessahistory.com/menusthg.htm). You won't find Easter Island heads at this one, though.

MARBLE FALLS

The town of Marble Falls was laid out in 1887 by Civil War General Adam Rankin Johnson . . . who was blind at the time. www.marblefalls.org

---

During the Civil War, 17 Union sympathizers were murdered and thrown down Dead Man's Hole (Route 401), a 155-foot-deep cave near Marble Falls.

MEDINA

Medina is the Apple Capital of Texas and hosts the International Apple Festival each July.

Hutto
Hutto Hippos

Though there probably isn't a single competitor for the honor, Hutto claims to be the Hippo Capital of Texas. Back in 1915 a hippopotamus escaped from a traveling circus and ended up in nearby Cottonwood Creek. The local high school was inspired to name its mascot after the freedom-loving creature. Then, in 1992, the town commissioned Double D Statuary to erect a town mascot, Henrietta Hippo. She's 10 feet long, concrete, and has a staircase allowing folks to climb on her back to pose for pictures.

Then, a few years ago, the Hutto mayor conjured up an even grander scheme that involved—big surprise—more hippos. Today there are 87 hippos in a town that is no larger than 50 square blocks. Some citizens have grumbled that hippo hysteria has gotten out of hand, but they should ask themselves, would Hutto be on a tourist's radar without them?

East and Farley Sts., Hutto, TX 78634

No phone

Hours: Always visible

Cost: Free

www.hutto.org

Directions: Between Farley St. and Rte. 79.

NEW BRAUNFELS
The 2.5-mile Comal River in New Braunfels, which connects Landa Park to the Guadalupe River, is the World's Shortest River.

New Braunfels brags that it is the Bratwurst Capital of the World and hosts Wurstfest from late October to early November each year. (800) 221-4369, www.wurstfest.com

ROUND ROCK
The farm house from *The Texas Chainsaw Massacre* once stood on Quick Hill Road in Round Rock but is now long gone.

SAN MARCOS
Actress **Lynda Day George** was born in San Marcos on December 11, 1946.

Corky, we need you!

Lockhart
Waiting for Guffman

"Hock your jewels! Use your money for stools!" implore the cast of *Red, White and Blaine* in the 1997 indie film *Waiting for Guffman*. It's one of the few scripted lines in the movie, a gut-busting comedy and masterpiece of on-screen improvisation directed by Christopher Guest.

The movie is set in Blaine, Missouri, the Stool Capital of the World. In honor of the town's upcoming sesquicentennial, the Blaine City Council hires the high school drama teacher, Corky St. Clair (Guest), to stage an original musical highlighting the town's historical milestones. Corky assembles a cast of local residents: Sheila and Ron Albertson, "The Lunts of Blaine" (Catherine O'Hara and Fred Willard), cross-eyed dentist Allan Pearl (Eugene Levy), Dairy Queen clerk/ingenue Libby Mae Brown (Parker Posey), narrator Clifford Wooley (Lewis Arquette), and hunky mechanic Johnny Savage (Matt Keeslar). Word of the production makes it back to the Oppenheimer Group, New York producers who dispatch partner Mort Guffman to evaluate *Red, White and Blaine* for Broadway. Do they make it to the Great White Way? Rent the movie and find out.

The movie's Blaine, Missouri, is actually Lockhart, Texas. With the exception of the final performance, most of the scenes were shot around town, including the high school (201 S. Colorado Street) and Corky's apartment off the courthouse square. The celebration shown during the opening reel was an actual street fair in Lockhart. The film's final musical production was filmed in Austin at the Doris Miller Auditorium (2300 Rosewood Avenue, (512) 476-4118).

Corky's Apartment, Main and San Antonio Sts., Lockhart, TX 78644

No phone

Hours: Always visible

Cost: Free

www.lockhart-tx.org/Templates/filmsmade.dwt

Directions: On the southwest corner of Rte. 142 (San Antonio St.) and Main St., two blocks west of Colorado St. (Rte. 183).

SAN SABA

Actor **Tommy Lee Jones** was born in San Saba on September 15, 1946.

San Saba claims to be the Pecan Capital of the World.

SANTA ANNA

Each October Santa Anna hosts the World Championship Bison Cook-Off.

TAYLOR

Cartoonist Frederick Bean **"Tex" Avery**, creator of Bugs Bunny, Daffy Duck, and more, was born in Taylor on February 26, 1908.

A perpetual moon-jumping machine.

Luling
Pump Jack Sculptures

Luling, like so many Texas communities, sits atop a huge underground oil reserve, this one discovered in 1922. But *unlike* so many Texas communities, Luling decided to dress up its pump jacks a bit. In 1986, William "Speedy" Thomas converted 16 local pump jacks into moving works of art. Holly Hobby picks flowers continuously, a quarterback pumps his arm looking for a receiver, a cow jumps over and over and over a moon, and a "thumpadillo" (armadillo) rides a bucking watermelon. There's also a grasshopper, a flamingo in a Chevy convertible, and a diving killer whale.

Rte. 183, Luling, TX 78648

No phone

Hours: Always visible

Cost: Free

www.lulingcc.org

Directions: All over town; most of the pump jacks can be found along Rte. 183, both north and east of town.

World's Largest Watermelon

Luling's wacky for watermelons. Every year since 1953 the town, which calls itself the Watermelon Capital of the World, has thrown a Watermelon Thump festival on the last full weekend in June. The highlight of the event is the Seed-Spitting Contest where folks compete to see who can spit a seed the farthest. Lulingans even built an official Thump Pavilion downtown to host the event. It was here that the long-standing Thump record of 68 feet, 9⅛ inches was recently bested by a 75-foot, 2-inch spit. Yes, there was much rejoicing in Lulingland. The super-spitter was honored by the town's Watermelon Thump Queen, who wears both a crown and a full-length, watermelon-print gown.

If you can't make to the festivities, you can always stop by the see the World's Largest Watermelon . . . the town's creatively painted water tower. Many of the town's decorated pump jacks also have watermelon themes.

Luling Watermelon Thump, 421 E. Davis St., PO Box 710, Luling, TX 78648

(830) 875-3214

E-mail: lulingcc@bsc.net

Hours: Always visible

Cost: Free

www.watermelonthump.com

Directions: Along Rte. 183 in the middle of town.

ANOTHER BIG WATERMELON

The town of Dilley claims to be the Watermelon Capital of Texas, which seems kind of preposterous considering that Luling, the Watermelon Capital of the *World*, is also located here. And what does Dilley do to back up its claim? It erects a puny statue, no more than four feet end-to-end, in the Dilley City Park (Main and Miller Streets). Kooky, yes, but kinda sad.

Mexia and Houston
Anna Nicole Smith, Fried Chicken to Serious Dough

Long before she was a cable TV nightmare, before she was Mrs. J. Howard Marshall, before she was even named Anna Nicole Smith, Vickie Lynn Hogan was shagging fried chicken at a diner in Mexia. But her prospects started looking up once she started taking her clothes off.

Hogan was born in Houston on November 28, 1967, but was not (as she's claimed) Marilyn Monroe's secret baby; Monroe had been dead five years before Hogan entered the world. She attended Houston's Durkee Elementary (7301 Nordling Road) and Aldine Intermediate (14908 Aldine–Westfield Road) before her mother shipped her off to live with her aunt, Kay Beall, and attend Mexia High School (1120 N. Ross Avenue). After getting into a fistfight with another student, Hogan was expelled, never to return. The 17-year-old dropout went to work at Jim's Krispy Fried Chicken where she met her future first husband, 16-year-old cook Billy Smith. The pair was married in April 1985 and had a son the following year.

Jim's Krispy Fried Chicken, 312 E. Milam St., Mexia, TX 76667

(254) 562-5035

Hours: Monday–Friday 9 A.M.–9 P.M., Saturday 9 A.M.–10 P.M., Sunday 2:30–9 P.M.

Cost: Free; Meals, $4–$8

Directions: One block east of McKinney St. on Rte. 84 (Milam St.).

The marriage didn't last, so Smith took her newborn baby and left for the bright lights of Houston, where she lived at 300 Woerner Road, Apartment 2117. She worked a variety of strip clubs in Houston, including a day gig at the "upscale" Rick's Cabaret (3113 Bering Drive, (713) 785-0444). Smith was able to save enough in tips for two breast augmentation surgeries at Baylor and tottered out with size 42DD breasts.

They were worth every penny. One night at Gigi's Cabaret billionaire J. Howard Marshall II spotted his future wife wrapped around a pole, and it was love at first sight. At least for Marshall it was, though he was married at the time. Over the next several years, he showered Smith with money and gifts. After Marshall's wife Bettye died in September 1991, the pair were even more open about their relationship, often dining at the River Oaks Country Club (1600 River Oaks Boulevard).

But Smith caught the attention of *Playboy* as well, which gave her a photo spread in its March 1992 issue. She was Miss May two months later and was voted the 1992 Playmate of the Year.

Gigi's Cabaret, 11150 Northwest Fwy., Houston, TX 77092

(713) 686-3401

Hours: Monday–Saturday 11 A.M.–2 A.M., Sunday 5 P.M.–2 A.M.

Cost: $5 cover after 6 P.M.

Directions: One block south of 34th St. on the east-side frontage road on Rte. 290.

The 26-year-old Smith and 89-year-old Marshall wed in a quickie ceremony on June 27, 1994, at Houston's White Dove Wedding Chapel. Marshall, confined to a wheelchair, presented Smith with a 22-carat diamond ring, then announced (according to Smith's 11 family members, the only guests/witnesses in attendance), "I'm a millionaire. I've done everything I want to do in my life. Now, if I can take my money and see her spend it and get some of the things out of life and I can see it while I'm still living, I'll be happy."

Marshall didn't get to see *too* much; Smith left him at the reception and flew off to a photo shoot in Greece with her bodyguard/boyfriend Pierre DeJean in tow. Two weeks later Marshall signed over most of his considerable assets to his son, E. Pierce Marshall, as well as power of attorney over his business affairs, thus beginning a protracted legal battle between his son and the free-spending Smith.

White Dove Wedding Chapel, 727 Pinemont Dr., Houston, TX 77022

(713) 868-5254

Hours: By appointment

Cost: Free; Weddings extra

Directions: Just west of Shepperd Dr., three blocks south of Tidwell Rd.

J. Howard Marshall II passed away on August 4, 1995, and received two funerals, one for the Marshalls and the other for Smith's entourage. Anna wore her almost-new wedding gown, and sang "Wind Beneath My Wings" for the mourners. Her lawyer gave the eulogy. Marshall's ashes were divided equally between E. Pierce Marshall and Smith.

After several years in court, Smith was awarded $475 million, half her husband's estate, in January 2001. On August 15, 2001, a Houston

judge threw out the settlement and ordered Smith to pay $562,000 in court costs, declaring E. Pierce Marshall the sole heir. Then, on appeal, a judge confirmed on December 30, 2004, that Nicole was not entitled to any of Marshall's estate. Smith vows to take her case all the way to the U.S. Supreme Court. Clarence Thomas, are you ready?

Geo. H. Lewis & Sons Funeral Home, 1010 Bering Dr., Houston, TX 77057

(713) 789-3005

Hours: Always visible

Cost: Free

Directions: One block north of San Felipe St., one block west of Chimney Rock Rd.

THRALL
On September 9–10, 1921, 38.2 inches of rain fell on Thrall, the most ever recorded in Texas during a 24-hour period.

WACO
If you throw banana peels on the streets of Waco, you're breaking the law.

Baylor University campus police have written tickets to students for farting loud enough for others to hear.

While training for the U.S. Army at Fort Hood, **Elvis Presley** spent many of his weekends at the home of Eddie Fadal in Waco, at 2807 Lasker Avenue. Fadal was a disc jockey who had built an addition onto his house just for the King. The oak tree in the back yard was planted by Presley in honor of his mother, Gladys, who died of hepatitis on August 14, 1958.

Just add oatmeal.

Oatmeal
World's Largest Oatmeal Box

What more logical place to erect the World's Largest Oatmeal Box than the town of Oatmeal? Well, perhaps a town named Oatmeal Box . . . if there was one . . . which there isn't . . . so Oatmeal will have to do. The box doesn't really hold oats but is, in fact, the town's water tank, painted red and yellow with the 3-Minute Brand logo.

Each Labor Day since 1978, the nearby town of Bertram hosts an annual Oatmeal Festival, which includes eating and cooking competitions. Older women (55+) can compete for the title of Miss Bag of Oats, should anyone choose to seek it. The festival's most popular event is the Oatmeal Sculpting Contest, which is not as simple as it sounds. And the whole shebang culminates with a plane dropping 1,000 pounds of oatmeal over the cheering crowd.

FM 243, PO Box 70, Oatmeal, TX 78605

(512) 355-2197

Hours: Always visible

Cost: Free

www.bertramchamber.com/Recreation/OatmealFestival.asp

Directions: Just north of town on Rte. 243.

WACO

Several twisters swept through Waco on May 11, 1953, killing 114 residents.

Students at Waco's Baylor University were allowed to dance for the first time in 1996. Three years earlier, art students were given the chance to draw nude figures in art class, but two days later the long-standing ban on the naked human form was reinstated.

Actor **Steve Martin** was born in Waco on August 14, 1948.

Three-fourths of the world's Snickers bars are manufactured at the Mars plant in Waco.

On with their heads!

San Marcos
Rooster Head House

Somebody in San Marcos sure loved roosters, or at least their heads.
Along the road to Wonder World you'll see it—a seemingly abandoned
white home with a collapsing porch and dozens of red, white, and yellow
rooster heads nailed everywhere. Not to worry, they're not *real* rooster

heads, but identical plywood cutouts that adorn the fence, the gate, a dead tree, several posts . . . anywhere and everywhere. What's the story? I have no cock-a-doodle idea.

1236 Hopkins St., San Marcos, TX 78867

No phone

Hours: Always visible

Cost: Free

Directions: South from downtown along Hopkins St. (Rte. 80), just before Bishop St.

Wonder World

Mother Nature can really get something accomplished when she applies herself. Most caves take millions of years to form, but the Wonder Cave took just three and a half *minutes*; about 30 million years ago a single massive earthquake opened this fissure in the earth.

Your 45-minute one-way tour through the gigantic crack starts at the gift shop and descends as deep as 160 feet. You will see fossils along the trail, but very few stalactites or stalagmites—this is not a "growing" cave. At the end of the rocky path you arrive at an elevator that brings you back to the surface . . . and higher . . . where the fun really begins!

Having just tested your claustrophobia, you exit the elevator at the top of the 110-foot Tejas Observation Tower. From the upper deck you can explore your fear of heights while looking down, wayyyyy down, at the Balcones Fault that created this tourist attraction so many years ago. Then, back down on the ground, you can visit Wonder World's Anti-Gravity House. Have no fear, you will not fly off into space upon entering—gravity still keeps your feet on the floor, but everything around you seems a little topsy-turvy. Finally, hop aboard the train for a trip through Mystery Mountain and Crystal Falls to the Wildlife Petting Park across the street. Nothing to fear there.

1000 Prospect St., PO Box 1369, San Marcos, TX 78867

(512) 392-3760

Hours: June–August, daily 8 A.M.–8 P.M., September–May, daily 9 A.M.–5 P.M.

Cost: Adults $15.95, Seniors $12.95, Kids (4–11) $11.95

www.wonderworldpark.com

Directions: South from downtown along Hopkins St. (Rte. 80), right on Bishop St. for
   three blocks, then right on Prospect St. for two more blocks.

UNDER THE TEXAS HILLS

Does the Wonder Cave leave you wondering what else is hidden beneath these hills? Well, there's more than one way to get really deep in the heart of Texas.

Cascade Caverns (226 Cascade Caverns Road, Boerne, (830) 755-8080, www.cascadecaverns.com): The 90-foot waterfall in Cascade Caverns is such a crowd-pleaser, they've hooked it up to a pump to make sure it still flows during the dry season. And while most caves are uncomfortably cool, this place is 68°F year-round. At the surface, check out the large fiberglass dinosaur from *Father Hood*, starring Patrick Swayze. Never saw the movie? Join the club.

Cave-Without-a-Name (325 Kreutzberg Road, Boerne, (830) 537-4212, www.cavewithoutaname.com): "It's too pretty to name," claimed a child during a 1939 contest to identify this roadside attraction. So, rewarding resignation instead of creativity, the owners titled their attraction the Cave-Without-a-Name. That kid might have been right: the formations are amazing, especially the four-inch-wide "bacon strip" formations. Mmmmmm . . . *bacon* . . .

Caverns of Sonora (RM 1989, Sonora, (325) 387-3105, www.caverns ofsonora.com): The Caverns of Sonora offer a variety of tours, from a short walk to the Horseshoe Lake to a two-mile hike through the Crystal Palace branch. For spelunkers they've even got cave excursions; the Level III Tour concludes with a 50-foot rappel into the Devil's Pit, which you will no doubt have to explain come Judgment Day. For over-the-top cave nuts, they even offer wedding ceremonies in the Cavern of Angels, where the stalactites and stalagmites are tastefully backlit to establish the proper mood.

Inner Space Cavern (4200 S. I-35 Frontage Road, Georgetown, (512) 931-CAVE, www.innerspace.com): Who says urban sprawl doesn't have an up side? While surveying the route for I-35 in 1963, crews uncovered Inner Space Cavern, right under the highway! It was 1963, and the Space Race was in full swing, which might explain the various formations' names: the Lake of the Moon, the Lunar Landscape, and the Flowing Stone of Time. The cave seems also to have been an Ice Age dining room for a saber-toothed tiger; crews have uncovered the bones of a giant sloth, a mammoth, and a human tooth, as well as the dead, no-longer-voracious tiger.

Longhorn Caverns State Park (6211 Park Road 4 South, Burnet, (830) 598-CAVE, www.longhorncaverns.com): These 11 miles of caves are easily accessible from the surface, which is why they were used by the Confederacy to manufacture gunpowder, and by drunks as a speakeasy during Prohibition. Some treasure hunters think Sam Bass hid $2 million back in there somewhere, but don't expect the folks here to let you go look for it.

Natural Bridge Caverns (26495 Natural Bridge Caverns Road, Natural Bridge Caverns, (210) 651-6101, www.naturalbridgecaverns.com; Wildlife Ranch, (830) 438-7400, www.nbwildlifechtx.com): The Castle of the White Giants, Sherwood Forest, Pluto's Anteroom, the Hall of the Mountain King—they're all part of this elaborate cave system, first opened in 1964. If you're willing to take the grueling Adventure Tour, they'll show you the longest soda straw formation in North America—it's 14 feet long! A drive-through Wildlife Ranch sits atop the cave for family members who'd rather not go below.

TALKIN' ABOUT TEXAS

"If I owned Texas and Hell, I would rent out Texas and live in Hell." —General Philip Sheridan

"Like most passionate nations Texas has its own private history based on, but not limited by, facts." —John Steinbeck

"Texas is heaven for men and dogs, but a hell for women and oxen." —Unknown settler

"Calling a taxi in Texas is like calling a rabbi in Iraq." —Fran Lebowitz

"Texas is the place where there are the most cows and the least milk and the most rivers and the least water in them, and where you can look the farthest and see the least." —H. L. Mencken

"Once you are in Texas it seems to take forever to get out, and some people never make it." —John Steinbeck

"The only thing that smells worse than an oil refinery is a feedlot. Texas has a lot of both." —Molly Ivins

Big pecans, standard . . .

Seguin
Big Pecans

You might never have heard of Cabeza de Vaca were it not for nuts—pecans specifically. The explorer was held captive in the New World for nine years, and while he was being dragged around the southwest he survived on pecans that grew along the River of Nuts, today known as the Potomac . . . no, excuse me . . . *Guadeloupe* River.

Why does this matter? In 1962 a Seguin dentist decided to honor both the explorer and the pecan (the official Texas State Health Nut), so he forged a giant pecan out of metal and placed it in front of the courthouse with a sign proclaiming it the World's Largest Pecan. The pecan was replaced with a new 1,000-pound nut in 1978, this one created with cement by Monroe Engbrock. A commemorative plaque was installed at the same time by the Texas Pecan Growers Association in honor of Cabeza de Vaca's "contribution to the pecan literature."

Though the big pecan still stands, it no longer holds the world record, or the town record for that matter. There's an even larger nut

and mobile . . .

outside Seguin's Pape Pecan House, and it's on wheels! The Pape Nut House also has a small Nutcracker Museum, which sounds to me like putting a Garlic Museum next to the World's Largest Dracula.

But not even Pape's mobile meganut can claim the world title; that honor goes to a 12-foot, 12,000-pound pecan outside the Nut Hut in Brunswick, Missouri.

Guadeloupe County Courthouse, 101 E. Court St., Seguin, TX 78155

(800) 580-PECAN or (830) 379-6382

Hours: Always visible

Cost: Free

www.visitseguin.com

Directions: On Rte. 90 Alt. (Court St.) at Rte. 123 Business (Austin St.).

Pape Pecan House, 101 S. Rte. 123 Bypass, Seguin, TX 78155

(830) 379-7442

Hours: Always visible

Cost: Free

Directions: At the east end of town on Rte. 90 Alt. (Court St.) and Rte. 123.

About all that's left.
Photo by author, courtesy of the Branch Davidians.

David Koresh: Up in Smoke

Virtually everyone who still dwells on the Branch Davidian tragedy comes at the story from an antigovernment mindset. But to fully understand what happened on April 19, 1993, you need to back up to the late 1980s. Did the ATF attack an innocent religious group, or did they have good reason to approach the Mount Carmel with guns drawn?

Ask yourself, have you ever heard about the *first* shoot-out at the compound? It started as a Resurrection Showdown between George Roden and David Koresh (born Vernon Howell). Roden, the group's then leader, had had a dead female cultist exhumed from a local cemetery on Halloween to show that he (Roden) was the Chosen One. Koresh, who was not living at Mount Carmel at the time, called the cops to report that a corpse was being abused. Police refused to respond unless they were given evidence that a body was in the coffin Roden had, so on November 3, 1987, Koresh and several followers tried to sneak into the compound with a camera. A fierce gunfight between the two factions erupted. Roden fought back with an Uzi but was wounded.

Police charged Koresh with attempted murder, but he was later released. Roden, on the other hand, was thrown in jail for contempt of court after he filed a bizarre threat/brief with the county against Koresh. During a later hearing, the exhumed casket was brought to the courtroom and Roden tried to raise the dead woman one last time. She didn't budge. (Roden spent the rest of his life in a Big Spring mental hospital and died of a heart attack during a failed escape attempt on December 7, 1998.)

With Roden in jail, Koresh took over as the leader of the Branch Davidians and grew increasingly unbalanced. Followers were often made to eat nothing but popcorn and peanuts, or certain fruits in special combinations (they were once forced to live on a diet of only bananas). Members were ejected from the compound for eating French fries or chocolate-chip ice cream. Koresh went around Waco handing out business cards that said "Messiah." Husbands and wives were separated into two dorms. He proclaimed that God said all the women in the world were his, and that he had the right to impregnate them to form a new army of God's children. However, he complained to his flock that he was suffering because few of the women were sufficiently attractive. And worst of all, he forced members to watch Jean-Claude Van Damme movies.

By the time the ATF showed up on February 28, 1993, Koresh and his followers were *already* referring to their enclave as Ranch Apocalypse. That day, the U.S. District Attorney was to serve papers on Koresh for child abuse, having sex with minors, and amassing an arsenal of illegal weapons. After 10,000 rounds of ammunition were exchanged, six Branch Davidians and four federal agents lay dead, and 16 more feds were wounded. Koresh was shot in the side and the hand, which made him very cranky during the 51-day standoff.

The scene outside the law enforcement perimeter became a zoo. Demonstrators, including a then-unknown Timothy McVeigh, protested the government's "Gestapo tactics." Several preachers tried to call out the demons in Koresh using loudspeakers, but were overpowered by the ATF, which was blasting recordings of Tibetan monks, rabbits being slaughtered, dentist drills, ticking clocks, and Nancy Sinatra's "These Boots Were Made for Walkin'" into the compound. Some visitors brought large wooden crosses, even one who claimed to be Christ's twin brother. During the stand-off, two men actually broke through the barricades, ran up to the compound, and were allowed in. One was named Jesse "Lord Lightning" Amen; Lord Lightning had his feet washed by Koresh but was later kicked out.

In the plus column, the local chamber of commerce estimated $1 million was being injected into the economy each week. Vendors sold Koresh Burgers and Koresh Hot Dogs to the gathered crowds. T-shirts proclaimed "WACO = Weird Asshole Come Out." Camera crews were everywhere.

Meanwhile, inside Mount Carmel, Koresh was decoding the book of Revelations' "Seven Seals." Radio station KRLD (AM 1080) broadcast his occasional rants. His followers survived on rations left over from Operation Desert Storm, which they had purchased with food stamps before the ATF raid.

Against the advice of local officials, the feds launched a final assault on the Mount Carmel compound on April 19. Tanks pumped CS nerve gas into the main building, but the Branch Davidians had gas masks. Members were spotted walking around, reading their Bibles, *and doing laundry*. Then three fires started almost simultaneously. Microphones reportedly caught Koresh saying "Well, you always wanted to be a charcoal briquette" to one of his followers. In all, 82 people perished in the siege, including two dozen children, many of whom were sired by Koresh. Evidence suggests that their leader was shot by his lieutenant, Steve Snyder, before he was incinerated. Seventeen other victims, including five kids, were also shot before the flame reached them.

Did the ATF start the fires, or did Koresh? Several books and movies point to a federal cover-up, but potential corroborating evidence was bulldozed under long ago. Ownership of the site has reverted to the Roden faction, the 90-something percent of Branch Davidians who never supported Koresh and his extreme theology. They've planted trees for each of the fire's victims, and erected markers to remember the fallen ATF agents and the victims of the Oklahoma City bombing. There's not a lot left to see except the compound's old swimming pool, a few concrete slabs, and Koresh's old motorcycle, run over by a tank. A conspiracy-friendly Loud Cry Museum was erected on the site, but an arsonist torched it in 1997; its replacement was ignited in 2000. The third museum is open sporadically.

Double EE Ranch Rd., Waco, TX 76705

Private phone

Hours: Daily 9 A.M.–5 P.M.

Cost: Free; donations appreciated

www.waco93.com

Directions: Head southeast on Loop 340 from Rte. 84, northeast of town, turn left on FM 2491 (Elk Rd.); turn left off FM 2491 onto Double EE Ranch Rd., just past the intersection with FM 2957.

Dr Pepper Museum and Free Enterprise Institute

Back in 1885, pharmacist Charles Alderton was experimenting with various syrups at the Old Corner Drug Store, which was located in the ground floor of Waco's McLelland Hotel (Fourth Street and Austin Avenue, since torn down). His goal was to create a "floral" taste, and the concoction he came up with was dubbed "The Waco." On the suggestion of the pharmacy's owner, Wade Morrison, the drink was renamed Dr Pepper's Phos-Ferrates. Dr. Charles Pepper was the father of the woman Morrison once hoped to marry. (Morrison's shameless last-ditch ploy to impress his sweetheart's dad didn't work; the pair never wed.)

One of Morrison's soda fountain patrons was a beverage chemist named Robert S. Lazenby. He studied Alderton's mixture for two years and patented the formula that is still used today. Early promotional campaigns played on the soft drink's medicinal name and suggested that you should drink a bottle at 10, 2, and 4 o'clock to get the full effects of its "rejuvenating powers." Many people swore that it kept them regular, which led to the myth that prune juice was the key ingredient. It isn't; *apricot* juice is. (Here's another interesting bit of trivia to spring on your friends: Dr Pepper does not use a period in "Dr".)

Today, the Dr Pepper Museum and Free Enterprise Institute is located in the building once used by the Artesian Manufacturing and Bottling Company, which began bottling Dr Pepper in 1906. The curators of this museum use the Dr Pepper story as a case study on the benefits of free-market capitalism, and since they aren't selling flammable pajamas or Ford Pintos, who's going to argue?

In addition to learning the history of the world's most popular non-cola soft drink, you can sip a genuine Waco at a turn-of-the-century soda fountain, like the one where it was first sold. There's also a large gift shop with all sorts of Dr Pepper trinkets.

300 S. Fifth St., Waco, TX 76701

(254) 757-1025

Hours: Monday–Saturday 10 A.M.–5 P.M., Sunday Noon–5 P.M.

Cost: Adults $5, Seniors (65+) $4, Kids (5–17) $3

www.drpeppermuseum.com

Directions: West of I-35 at the corner of Mary Ave. and Fifth St.

Secret Societies Open Their Doors

There might have been a time when secret societies like the Masons, the Odd Fellows, and the Improved Order of Red Men kept their doings to themselves, but no more. Faced with declining membership, they've thrown open their doors to anyone who wants to take a look around . . . and hopefully join. There are *three* such not-so-secret museums in Waco, and let me tell you, they've got some nifty doodads behind those oaken doors.

The best museum of the bunch is run by the Improved Order of Red Men. This fraternal organization started in New England as the Sons of Liberty, the guys who dressed as Indians and threw British tea into Boston Harbor. In addition to an extensive noncirculating library, the museum contains an eclectic mix of artifacts. There's a peace blanket from Geronimo, John Wayne's cavalry jacket from *Rio Lobo*, a bugle recovered from Gettysburg, Aaron Burr's 1815 writing desk and replica dueling pistols, Rudolph Valentino's ring from *The Sheik*, a first edition of *Frankenstein*, and a 1912 watercolor of flowers in a vase . . . painted by Adolf Hitler. Weapons lovers can check out a 700-year-old Scottish sword of Sir James Douglas, a pair of Bonnie and Clyde's guns, and one of Ranger Frank Hamer's engraved Colt .38 pistols.

Improved Order of Red Men Museum & Library, 4521 Speight Ave., Waco, TX 76711

(254) 756-1221

Hours: Monday–Friday 9 A.M.–4 P.M., Saturday–Sunday by appointment

Cost: Free

www.redmen.org

Directions: One block northeast of New Rd./Government Dr., one block northwest of Bagby Ave.

The Scottish Rite Foundation of Texas is housed in an impressive mausoleum-like structure southwest of downtown. As a division of the Freemasons, its museum is filled with aprons and trowels and robes and breast jewels and ceremonial collars—all those things that you'd expect to find. But they've also got sculptures, banners, and books. The museum is scattered in display cases from one end of this temple to another, on all three floors, so feel free to explore!

The Scottish Rite Foundation of Texas, 2801 W. Waco Dr., PO Box 3080, Waco, TX 76707

(254) 754-3942

Hours: Monday–Friday 9–11:30 A.M. and 1–3:30 P.M.

Cost: Free

www.scottishritefoundationoftexas.org

Directions: Two blocks southwest of 26th St. on Rte. 84 (Waco Dr.).

The Masonic Grand Lodge of Texas near downtown has a large library for anyone who wants to learn more about this ancient society. They've got a museum as well, flanked by statues of Sam Houston and Dr. Anson Jones, both former Texas Freemasons. The library is home to the complete writings of Sam Houston and his ceremonial gavel.

This particular lodge is also responsible for establishing Tranquility Lodge No. 2000 (www.tranquilitylodge2000.org), officially known as The Most Worshipful Grand Lodge of Texas, Ancient Free and Accepted Masons, on the Moon. That's right, when Buzz Aldrin set foot on the moon on July 20, 1969, he exercised his Special Deputation to form a lunar lodge. (He also took communion on the moon.) Though membership is not restricted to astronauts or aliens, only Masons in good standing, the lodge's mission is clearly out of this world; its brochure reads like a James Bond script: "The Moon is the first step to expanding our Fraternity throughout the Universe!"

The Masonic Grand Lodge of Texas, 715 Columbus Ave., PO Box 446, Waco, TX 76703

(254) 753-7395

Hours: Monday–Friday 8:30 A.M.–4 P.M.

Cost: Free

www.grandlodgeoftexas.org

Directions: Two blocks southeast of Rte. 84 (Waco Dr.), two blocks southwest of Fifth St.

Texas Ranger Hall of Fame

The Texas Rangers were established on August 5, 1823, as an elite mercenary corps to defend settlers against Native American attacks and to keep the peace for the citizens of Texas. Their motto? "One riot, one Ranger." Though originally chartered to have no more than 20 to 30 members, they've ballooned to 103 members today. The Rangers' Company F operates out of this post, which was built to look like an 1837 fort.

Step on in to the Hall of Fame and you'll see just how they do it: with *guns*. Guns, guns, and more guns—the display cases are literally crammed with firearms, and not all of them from Rangers; they've also got 10 of Bonnie and Clyde's weapons, right beside the expense report Officer Frank Hamer turned in while he hunted down the dastardly duo. You'll learn that the Rangers have not only been interested in bringing cold-blooded killers to justice, but have been killjoys-for-hire who have cracked down on vice. Just check out the confiscated craps tables, playing cards, copper stills, and pot pipes. They've also been instrumental in busting a labor strike or two.

The Pop Culture Gallery is the last room you'll get to, which shows how the Rangers have been portrayed in books, radio, film, and television over the years. They've got Walker's (Chuck Norris's) signature hat, shirt, and plastic gun. Wait a second—*plastic* gun? No wonder he has to fall back on karate chops!

Fort Fisher Park, 100 Texas Ranger Tr., PO Box 2570, Waco, TX 76702

(254) 750-8631

Hours: Daily 9 A.M.–5 P.M.

Cost: Adults $5, Seniors $2.50, Kids (6–12) $2.50

www.texasranger.org

Directions: Just east of the University Parks Dr. Exit (334B) from I-35, at the Brazos River.

Tom Landry's Hat

Not since Davy Crockett wore a coonskin cap did one man's chapeau inspire such universal awe in the hearts of Texans . . . until Tom Landry came along. True, nobody would have much cared what he wore had his Dallas Cowboys not brought home so many championship seasons and Super Bowl trophies. Landry's hat was almost as recognizable as the man

himself, and now that he's finally hit the showers in that Big Locker Room in the Sky, it's all we have left. All the Texas Sports Hall of Fame has left, that is. You can see it in a special display case in the Tom Landry Theater at the center of the museum.

Not a Cowboys fan? Wonder what else there is to see here? How about hundreds of pieces of equipment from this organization's 350+ inductees? They've got Carl Lewis's track shoes, Byron Nelson's golf bag, George Foreman's gold shoes and grill, Johnny Rutherford's charred racing jumpsuit, Payne Stewart's knickers, Willie Shoemaker's racing silks, a Nolan Ryan baseball, Bum Phillips's cowboy boots, Martina Navratilova's Wimbledon jacket, Bill Tilden's tennis sweater, and Troy Aikman's helmet, shoes, and Wheaties box. They've even got a display tracing the evolution of the tennis ball machine, invented in Dallas, including a working 1959 Strokemaster.

Texas Sports Hall of Fame, 1108 S. University Parks Dr., Waco, TX 76706

(800) 567-9561 or (254) 756-1633

Hours: Monday–Saturday 9 A.M.–5 P.M., Sunday Noon–5 P.M.

Cost: Adults $5, Seniors (60+) $4, Kids $2

www.tshof.org

Directions: East of I-35 two blocks on University Parks Dr.

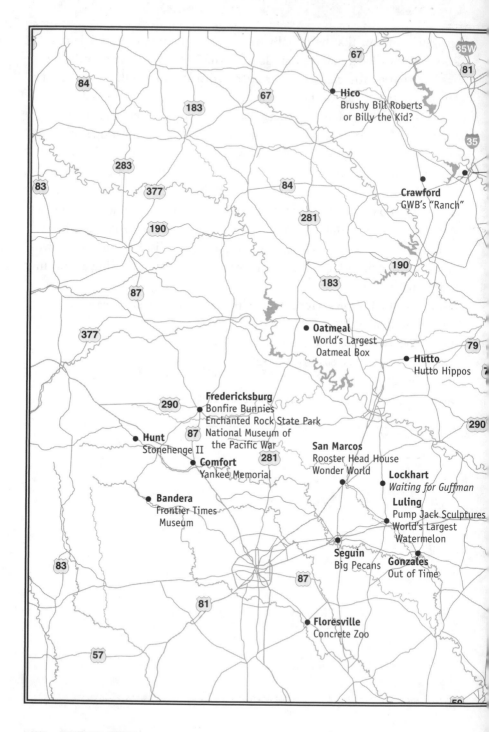

67

84

183

67

● **Hico**
Brushy Bill Roberts
or Billy the Kid?

35W

81

35

283

83

377

84

281

● **Crawford**
GWB's "Ranch"

190

190

183

87

377

● **Oatmeal**
World's Largest
Oatmeal Box

79

● **Hutto**
Hutto Hippos

290

Fredericksburg
Bonfire Bunnies
Enchanted Rock State Park
87 National Museum of
the Pacific War

290

● **Hunt**
Stonehenge II

San Marcos
Rooster Head House
Wonder World

● **Comfort**
Yankee Memorial

281

Lockhart
Waiting for Guffman

Luling
Pump Jack Sculptures
World's Largest
Watermelon

● **Bandera**
Frontier Times
Museum

83

Seguin
Big Pecans

Gonzales
Out of Time

87

81

● **Floresville**
Concrete Zoo

57

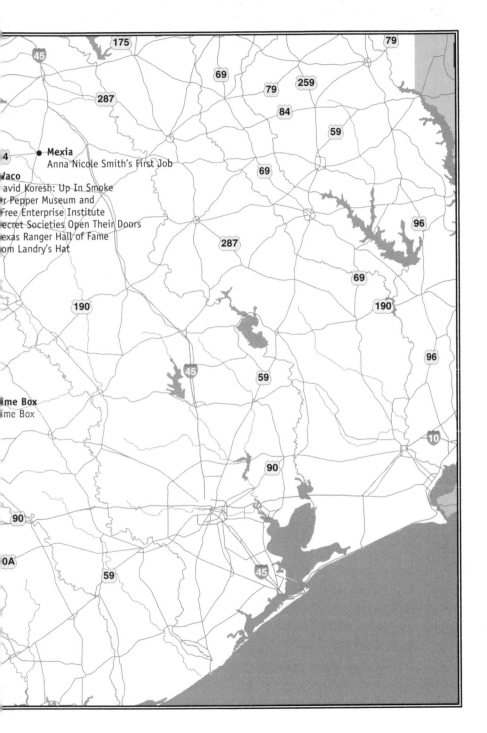

175

45

69

79

79 259

287

84

59

4 • **Mexia**
Anna Nicole Smith's First Job

69

Waco
avid Koresh: Up In Smoke
r Pepper Museum and
Free Enterprise Institute
ecret Societies Open Their Doors
exas Ranger Hall of Fame
om Landry's Hat

96

287

69

190

190

96

45

ime Box
ime Box

59

45

10

90

90

0A

59

45

6

AUStiN AREA

*I*t's no secret that the weirdest people in Texas live in Austin, even when you factor out the state legislature. Take a sampling of Austin's annual festivals. On the last Saturday in April each year, Austin celebrates Eeyore's birthday (www.sexton.com/eeyores). You know Eeyore, the donkey from *Winnie-the-Pooh* who complains that nobody remembers his birthday? Here in Austin they remember . . . by crowning a Hippie Queen. If you can't figure that one out, try the Pandemonious Potted Pork Festival—dubbed Spamarama (www. spamarama.com)—Austin's annual salute to canned meat. In addition to a Spam Cook-Off, they've got a Spam Toss, a Spam Carving Contest, a Spam Call, and a gut-busting Spam Cram. The big event takes place around April Fools Day each year.

You get the picture? *There's something wrong with these folks.* Seriously wrong . . . and seriously right, I might add. If you go anywhere in the Lone Star State, I say go to Austin where oddness is a virtue.

Austin
The Bush Twins: Party Animals!

On May 29, 2001, the manager at Chuy's restaurant called 911 and reported that several minors were trying to buy alcohol with fake IDs. Police arrived to discover that two of the kids were the nation's new First Daughters, Jenna and Barbara Bush. Jenna was charged with a Class C misdemeanor for trying to pass off somebody else's license as her own; the bartender had refused her order after seeing the ID. Barbara, who was not asked to show an ID, was more successful; she was sipping a margarita when police arrived. The cops wrote her a ticket for underage possession of alcohol, another Class C misdemeanor. Interestingly, the Secret Service detail assigned to the 19-year-old First Twins did nothing to stop the pair. Both young women were packed off to the First Woodshed at Camp David. Grandma Babs chuckled that her son George was finally getting some payback for the grief she'd endured.

It wasn't Jenna's first brush with the law. On April 27, 2001, she was busted for having a beer in another Austin bar (Cheers Shot Bar), 416 E. Sixth Street, (512) 499-0093) by two off-duty cops. She pleaded no contest and was ordered to pay $51.25 in court costs, attend alcohol-awareness classes (oh, she's *aware*), and perform eight hours of community service; she did clerical work for Austin's Mexic-Arte Museum (419 Congress Avenue, (512) 480-9373).

For the Chuy's bust, Barbara pleaded no contest and got three months, probation, alcohol-awareness classes, and community service. Jenna pleaded not guilty, but the judge found otherwise; she got a $100 fine, lost *her* driver's license for 30 days, and was ordered to perform 36 hours of community service. Oh, and because she was still on probation for the earlier offense, she had to pay an additional $500.

Anyone who read George Bush's *A Charge to Keep* (HarperCollins, 1999) could have seen this coming a mile away. In it Bush recounted an amusing tale: "I may have been a candidate for governor, but I didn't have much status at my house. I will never forget one night in 1994. After a long day on the campaign trail, I went to pick the girls up at a party at 11 P.M., well past my bedtime. They had ordered me, 'Do not come in,' so I sat outside waiting and waiting as other parents walk in and out to retrieve their children, until mine finally came out to the car 30 minutes later."

The girls had just turned 13.

Chuy's, 1728 Barton Springs Rd., Austin, TX 78704

(512) 474-4452

E-mail: hey@chuys.com

Hours: Sunday–Thursday 11 A.M.–10:30 P.M., Friday–Saturday 11 A.M.–11 P.M.

Cost: Free; Meals, $7–$15

www.chuys.com

Directions: Four blocks west of Lamar Blvd., two blocks south of Town Lake.

Cathedral of Junk

Though it's hardly uncommon to find a Texas yard strewn with junk, Vince Hannemann's place has definitely raised the bar. About 30 feet . . . and growing. Since 1989, he's collected more than 60 *tons* of discarded stuff and shoehorned it into his backyard in a chaotic yet purposeful way. He named his creation *Yard Space 11*, but it's better known as the Cathedral of Junk.

Why a cathedral? The structure is divided into many churchlike rooms—the Choir Loft, the Doll Niche, the Prayer Tower, the Nave, and two Throne Rooms. In 1999 he sanctified it by marrying a very understanding woman, Jo Rabern, in the central Throne Room.

But really, what is the Cathedral of Junk? It's bikes and baby carriages and wrought iron fences and car bumpers and televisions and hubcaps and crutches and . . . well, anything you can think of, all arranged into passageways and platforms and stairwells in the trees. The entire structure is wired for electricity and is best experienced after sunset. It's open every Saturday, and you're welcome to check it out for yourself.

Now before you go and feel sorry for Hannemann's neighbors, you should realize that you can barely see the cathedral when you're standing in front of his house. It's not like a Chevy up on blocks in the driveway, thank you very much.

4422 Lareina Dr., Austin, TX 78745

(512) 441-6906

E-mail: wildyard@swbell.net

Hours: Saturdays only, 6–9 P.M.

Cost: Free; donations accepted

www.austinamericana.com/photos/junk/

Directions: Two blocks south of Rte. 290 on Congress Ave., then two blocks west on St. Elmo Rd. to Larenina Dr., then left.

Charles Whitman, Sharpshooper

Looking back, it's easy to say that the folks who discovered Charles Whitman dressing out a deer in the bathroom of a University of Texas dormitory should have warned authorities, but the profile of the modern mass murderer had yet to enter the nation's consciousness. Harder to explain was the psychologist who jotted down a statement made by the future killer during a therapy session (Whitman had gone to the doctor because of headaches and violent thoughts): "I am thinking about going up on the tower with a deer rifle and start shooting people." Okey-dokey, the doctor noted, and prescribed Valium.

Whitman, a clean-cut former altar boy, Eagle Scout, and Marine sharpshooter, made good on his word on August 1, 1966. The night before his rampage, he strangled and shot his mother at the Penthouse Apartments (1212 Guadalupe Street, Apartment 505), then stabbed his wife to death at their home (906 Jewell Street). He attached confessional notes to both of their bodies. In the morning he purchased several guns around town, at Sears and Roebuck, Charles Davis Hardware, and Chuck's Gun Shop—no Brady Bill waiting period in those days!— then carted his arsenal over to the UT Main Tower in a trunk on a rented dolly.

When he reached the 28th-floor observation deck, Whitman killed the receptionist. Four sightseers had the misfortune of running into him there; two were murdered and the other two were wounded. After barricading himself on the deck, this 25-year-old on-again, off-again mechanical engineering student began picking off people on the quad below. During the next 96 minutes, he killed 11 more bystanders and wounded 31 others. About a hundred law enforcement officials and a few zealous citizens participated in the shoot-out, but it was patrolman Ramiro Martinez who killed Whitman as policemen stormed the deck.

A non-malignant brain tumor was found on Whitman's hypo-thalamus during his autopsy, though today few believe it was a contributing factor in his strange behavior. The observation deck was closed to visitors in 1974, not because of the shooting but due to a rash of student suicides. Rumor has it that you can still see a bullet hole on the base of the Jefferson Davis statue (south of the tower), but there are so many

chips on the pedestal it's difficult to tell. You can visit the observation deck today, but only as part of a tour organized by the student union.

Main Building/Clock Tower, University of Texas, Austin, TX 78712

(512) 475-6633

Hours: Always visible; Tower Tours by appointment only

Cost: Free; Tower Tours, $5

www.utexas.edu/student/txunion/ae/towertours/

Directions: East of Guadalupe St. on 24th St.; Tower is on the south side of 24th before Speedway.

AUSTIN

First Lady **Laura Bush** was the school librarian at Austin's Dawson Elementary (3001 S. First Street) from 1974 to 1977.

Austin is the Live Music Capital of the World.

The ghost of a jilted bride is said to walk the halls of Austin's Driskill Hotel (604 Brazos Street, (512) 391-7222, www.driskillhotel.com), still wearing her wedding dress, carrying a pistol. She shot herself in Room 29 after being left at the altar.

In 1989 a vandal poisoned Austin's Treaty Oak (503 Baylor Street), and half of the tree had to be removed. During its recovery, folks left get-well cards at its base.

In case you get lost.

Concrete Map

Ira Poole is proud to be an American—so proud that in 1965 he built a large concrete map of the United State (minus Alaska and Hawaii) in his front yard. And he didn't stop there. Poole added Texas star–shaped planters, which he embellished with miniature oil derricks and prairie windmills, and a flag pole, and a few sphinxes, and a bald eagle or two. Then, in 1987, he added a Statue of Liberty to raise her torch high above it all. The concrete map and statues are illuminated at night, so anytime's a good time to see it.

2400 E. Martin Luther King Jr. Blvd., Austin, TX 78702

Private phone

Hours: Always visible

Cost: Free

Directions: One block east of Chestnut Ave. on FM 969 (Martin Luther King Jr. Blvd.).

Held for the Ransom Center

There was a time when the contents of the vaults at the Harry Ransom Center were off limits to the general public, but no more. This UT institution is the repository for hundreds of thousands of artifacts, and millions of books, encompassing everything from an original Gutenberg Bible to the serial killer's mask from *The Texas Chainsaw Massacre*. Objects are rotated through their display areas, so you'll never know what you'll see when you visit. The Ransom has Jack Kerouac's *On the Road* notebook, Gloria Swanson's sunglasses, Sir Arthur Conan Doyle's death socks, Carson McCullers's cigarette lighter, Robert Frost's desk lamp, Charles Lindbergh's compass, and the world's first photograph, taken by Joseph Niépce in 1826.

Movie fans will enjoy seeing items from the David O. Selznick Collection, including Scarlett O'Hara's green drape dress and the original screen tests from *Gone With the Wind*. Magic lovers can find an impressive Houdini memorabilia collection. And political junkies will find Woodward and Bernstein's Watergate papers here, not quite as interesting now that we know who Deep Throat is.

Harry Ransom Humanities Research Center, 21st and Guadalupe Sts., PO Box 7219, Austin, TX 78713

(512) 471-8944

Hours: Tuesday–Wednesday and Friday 10 A.M.–5 P.M., Thursday 10 A.M.–7 P.M., Saturday–Sunday Noon–5 P.M.

Cost: Free

www.hrc.utexas.edu

Directions: Just east of Guadalupe St., two blocks north of Martin Luther King Jr. Blvd.

AUSTIN

Author **James Michener** is buried in Austin Memorial Park (Bull Creek Road at Hancock Drive).

Linklater Locations

Richard Linklater burst onto the independent film scene in 1991 with *Slacker*, a character-driven homage to the eccentric, and more than a little lazy, slacker subculture of Austin. The movie follows one or two characters at a time as they pass the story—a digression, really—from one person to another. Along the way there are discussions of the faked moon landing, anarchism, love gone awry, alternate realities, the Kennedy assassination, and Madonna's pap smear.

Most of the locations used for the low-budget film have since been replaced by businesses of the TGIFridays ilk, but if you look closely enough, the sites will look vaguely familiar. The hit-and-run scene was filmed at the corner of 24th and Nueces Streets. Quackenbush's (officially Captain Quackenbush's Intergalactic Dessert Company and Espresso Café) served as the film's coffeehouse; though there's a new Quackenbush's at 411 E. 43rd Street, the original was located at 2120 Guadalupe Street, but no more. *Slacker*'s party house (809 W. Martin Luther King Jr. Boulevard) has been made into the oh-so-quaint Inn at Pearl Street Bed & Breakfast—the horror!—and the Les Amis Café, where two very drunk burnouts delve into the hidden agendas of Scooby Doo and the Smurfs, is now . . . brace yourself . . . a Starbucks (504 W. 24th Street). It's enough to make you want to throw yourself off Mount Bonnell. As it turns out, that's precisely where the movie ended, but a camera was tossed over the precipice, not a movie fan.

Mount Bonnell, 3800 Mount Bonnell Dr., Austin, TX 78703

No phone

Hours: Always visible

Cost: Free

Directions: Head west on 35th St. from the Mopac Expressway, turn left on Old Bull Creek Rd., then right on Mount Bonnell Dr.

In 1993 Linklater followed *Slacker* with another Austin-based film, *Dazed and Confused*. The movie takes place on the last day of school, and the first early morning of summer vacation, in 1976. The soon-to-be-seniors from Robert E. Lee High (in reality Bedichek Middle School) descend on the soon-to-be-freshmen at the nearby junior high (in reality Williams Elementary, 507 E. University Avenue, Georgetown) for some good old-fashioned sadistic hazing. After hours of driving aimlessly around town, stopping for burgers (at the Top Notch Restaurant, 7525 Burnet Road, (512) 452-2181) and booze, it ends with a kegger at Zilker Park.

The film has been described as a 1970s *American Graffiti* because of its large cast of just-discovered talent: Parker Posey, Jason London, Milla Jovovich, Ben Affleck, and more. The cast's only non-teen breakout performance came from Matthew McConaughey as Wooderson, who drives a 1970 Chevelle named Melba Toast and still hangs with the high school crowd. Wooderson explains why in the film's most memorable line: "That's what I love about these high school girls, man. I get older, they stay the same age."

Zilker Park, 2100 Barton Springs Rd., Austin, TX 78746

(512) 974-6700

Hours: Always visible

Cost: Free

www.ci.austin.tx.us/zilker

Fan site: www.dazed-and-confused.net

Directions: Six blocks west of Lamar Blvd. on Barton Springs Rd., at Town Lake.

AUSTIN

Austin is home of the O. Henry Pun-Off, held the first weekend in May each year. William Sydney Porter—**O. Henry**—lived at 409 E. Fifth Street from 1884 to 1895, where he published *The Rolling Stone* from 1894 to 1895. (Home, (512) 472-1903, www.ci.austin.tx.us/parks /ohenry.htm; Pun-Off, (512) 973-9929, www.punpunpun.com)

Austin was once named Waterloo.

Stephen Austin, Congresswoman Barbara Jordan, and **Governor John Connally** are all buried in Austin's Texas State Cemetery (907 Navasota Street). Part of the Magic Bullet (see page 320) was still in Connally's body when he was laid to rest.

He's a robot!!!!
Photo by author, courtesy of the LBJ Library and Museum.

Lyndon Baines Johnson Library and Museum

Lyndon Baines Johnson was as big as Texas itself, so when he had his presidential library built in Austin he asked that the replica of his Oval Office be done on a ⅞ths scale, so that punier folk—folk like you—could appreciate it as he did at his size. Wow, even in death he's playing macho head games. As you gaze upon the shrunken room and its authentic furniture, reflect on the stories of how Johnson apparently bragged to aides that he'd had sex with his secretary on his Oval Office desk. *This* desk. Adjacent to the Oval Office, you'll see Lady Bird's '60s-mod office where her bowling ball and shoes have been given a display case of their own.

The library's most interesting artifacts, however, are on its bottom two floors: his fourth-grade report card showing a C in deportment, the Bible used to swear him in on Air Force One in Dallas (see page 318), a moon rock from Apollo 15, his 1968 Lincoln Continental stretch limousine, and a diffused bomb from Rolling Thunder. There are two long rows of gifts from heads of state, but they're not as interesting as the shelves crammed with homemade crafts from the American people: painted rocks and long-eared beagles made from egg cartons and felt, a wood carving of LBJ on the phone and a portrait of a rooster made of buttons, an ostrich egg music box and a branding iron made bearing his initials. Cool stuff. And if you'd like to visit with the former president, have a seat near the LBJ robot leaning on a fence; he'll tell you several animated jokes with the president's own voice.

It's hard not to admire the LBJ Library and Museum. While so many other presidential libraries focus almost exclusively on their subjects' triumphs, this library isn't shy about exploring Johnson's mistakes and the turbulent times in which he governed, and in many ways helped create.

2313 Red River St., Austin, TX 78705

(512) 721-0200

Hours: Daily 9 A.M.–5 P.M.

Cost: Free

www.lbjlib.utexas.edu

Directions: Just west of I-35, one block south of 26th St., on the northeast end the University of Texas campus.

BORN IN AUSTIN

Dabney Coleman—January 3, 1932

Ethan Hawke—November 6, 1970

Madalyn Murray O'Hair Meets Her Maker

On August 27, 1995, America's favorite atheist, Madalyn Murray O'Hair, disappeared from her Austin home (3702 Greystone Drive), along with her son, Jon Garth Murray, and granddaughter, Robin Murray O'Hair. A handwritten note was taped to the door of the American Atheist General Headquarters (8101 Cameron Road) announcing that the offices would be closed until further notice. The staff, volunteers mostly, had come to

expect such eccentric behavior from the trio, so they paid it little mind.

At first authorities suspected they'd fled the country, as O'Hair had recently moved $750,000 to a bank account in New Zealand. But then police learned that on September 29 Jon Murray had picked up $500,000 in gold coins from a San Antonio jeweler, purchased with funds from the New Zealand account, and that he had been accompanied by an unknown man. Even more curious, another $125,000 in gold coins was ordered but never retrieved.

In actuality the trio had been kidnapped by David Waters, their former office manager, and a man named Gary Karr. Waters had been fired by O'Hair in 1994 for embezzling $54,000 from the American Atheists. Waters had worked out a restitution plan with O'Hair through the courts before being placed on 10 years, probation. Had police bothered to check Waters's prior criminal history, which included a murder and assaults on his mother and former fiancée, he might have been locked up for the theft.

O'Hair and her family were held hostage in a second-floor suite at the Warren Inn in San Antonio (5050 Fredericksburg Road, (210) 342-1179). They had been told that as soon as Murray retrieved the gold they would be released. Three days before the coins arrived the trio was moved to the nearby La Quinta Inn (7134 NW Loop 410, (210) 680-8883) where, with the help of drifter Danny Fry, they were strangled the night of September 29. Their bodies were taken to an Austin storage unit where Fry cut them up and placed them in three 55-gallon barrels. With the dirty work done, Waters and Karr murdered Fry on October 2 and dumped his headless and handless torso on the banks of the Trinity River in southeast Dallas. Three days later they buried the three in drums on the Cooksey Ranch, a 5,000-acre spread south of Camp Wood. Fry's head and hands were placed in one of the barrels.

Back in Austin, Waters and Karr spent about $80,000 in just a few days but had put the remaining $420,000 in a suitcase back at the storage unit. By the time they returned for more, the gold was gone. It had been stolen by three very lucky San Antonio gang members who'd found a Master Lock skeleton key and were opening units at random. The burglars blew all but one Canadian Maple Leaf on a two-year, stripper-filled spending spree.

It took five years, but thanks to John MacCormack, an investigative reporter at the *San Antonio Express-News*, authorities started putting all the pieces together. Waters and Karr were arrested on parole violations, and they eventually cut deals to tell where the bodies were. The O'Hairs (and Fry's head) were unearthed on January 27, 2001.

Burnet Road Self Storage, Storage Unit #1640, 6400 Burnet Rd., Austin, TX 78757

(512) 453-6302

Hours: Always visible; view from street

Cost: Free

Directions: Two blocks north of Allandale Rd./Koenig Ln. (FM 2222) on Burnet Rd.

Naked in Austin

If you like to get naked—and let's face it, who doesn't?—Austin's your place. Here you'll find Canyon Villa, America's premier nudist apartment complex. The apartments are shielded so that residents may walk around nude in the halls, or down to get their mail, or out to the pool, or even over to their laundry, assuming they have any. (Ah, what a life!) The waiting list for Canyon Villa units is long.

Austin is also home to the Naked Motorcycle Club. The group's membership is secret, but they have very little to hide when they're out touring. To avoid being arrested, riders usually cruise the local highways at night, so if you see them, it'll be quick. And they'll be naked.

But Austin's best-known nuditarium is Hippie Hollow. While nudity is not technically legal at the clothing-optional swimming hole, police don't seem to mind. Visitors are welcome, but don't be surprised if the regulars refer to you as a "cottontail." And if you just come to gawk, beware: in 2004 a 60-person, double-decker craft capsized on Lake Travis after the rubbernecking passengers all rushed to the Hippie Hollow side of the boat. Two people were injured. Lesson? Nudity doesn't hurt people; people who stare at nudists do.

Hippie Hollow, 7000 Comanche Tr., Austin, TX 78732

(512) 854-7275

Hours: Daylight

Cost: By car, Adults $8 + $2/car; Pedestrians and bikes, Adults $3 + $2/bike

http://hippiehollow.noclothes.com and www.co.travis.tx.us/tnr/parks/hippie_hollow.asp

Directions: Take Comanche Tr. North from RR 620, toward Bob Went Windy Point County Park.

Now before you go and let everything hang out, at least listen to this cautionary tale. On October 25, 1999, Austin police responded to a loud music complaint on swanky Meadowbrook Drive. As they walked around the back of the home they spotted a nude, drunken man dancing around the living room banging on a pair of bongo drums. Another man, also drunk, though not naked, was clapping along to the music. Officers noticed a bong on a coffee table and decided to take the stoned, inebriated revelers into custody. The clothed man did not put up a fight, but the bongo player cursed and struggled against the handcuffs. Once a driver's license was pulled from a pair of cast-off pants, police realized who they had in custody: actor Matthew McConaughey. Fans forgave the pot, the nudity, and even the unruly behavior. But *bongo drums*? That took a while.

2004 Meadowbrook Dr., Austin, TX 78703

Private phone

Hours: Always visible; view from street

Cost: Free

Directions: Two blocks west of Exposition Blvd., between Clearview Dr. and Gilbert St.

That Wacky Texas Legislature

University of Texas professor and well-known folklorist James Frank Dobie once observed, "When I get ready to explain homemade Fascism in America, I can take my example from the State Capitol in Texas." In fairness, the state legislature is every bit as incompetent and corrupt as it is Fascist. Here are a few examples of what I'm talking about:

➡ In 1971 a Waco legislator wanted to highlight his colleagues' attention to the bills they signed. He drafted a resolution to honor Albert DeSalvo for service to "his country, his state, and his community. This compassionate gentleman's dedication and devotion to his work has enabled the weak and the lonely throughout the nation to achieve a new degree of concern for their future. He has been officially recognized by the State of Massachusetts for his noted activities and unconventional techniques involving population control and applied psychology." DeSalvo, it should be noted, was the Boston Strangler. The resolution passed. *Unanimously.*

➡ Democrat John Wilson was reelected to the legislature in 1982 with 66 percent of the vote, even though he was two months dead.

➡ State Senator Drew Nixon (R) was busted for soliciting oral sex in 1997, and, after his sentencing, became the first state legislator to serve in the Senate while spending weekends in jail.

➡ Speaker of the House Gib Lewis (D) introduced a group of wheel-chair-bound activists who had come to the capitol on Disability Day by requesting, "Will y'all stand and be recognized?"

➡ When explaining why he didn't want an asbestos factory closed in his district in 1972, Representative Billy Williamson remarked, "I think we are all willing to have a little crud in our lungs and a full stomach rather than a whole lot of clean air and nothing to eat."

➡ Democratic Congressman Charles Wilson bounced more than 80 checks from the capitol bank, including a $6,500 payment to the IRS. "It's not like molesting young girls or young boys," he dismissed.

➡ Legislator Larry Evans was found to have voted on a bill in 1991, even though at the time he was dead in his Austin apartment.

➡ The Texas House once approved a bill to establish "Speeding Coupons" to pay troopers on the spot.

All those shenanigans took place under the dome of the tallest state capitol in the nation. The building tops out at 309 feet, 8 inches, about seven feet taller than the U.S. Capitol in Washington, D.C. The Texas Capitol was built between 1882 and 1888 in exchange for three million acres of land in the Panhandle. The structure is topped by a statue of the Goddess of Liberty.

State Capitol Building, 112 E. Eleventh St., Austin, TX 78703

(512) 463-0063

Hours: Monday-Friday, 8:30 A.M.–4:30 P.M., Saturday 9:30 A.M.–4:30 P.M., Sunday 12:30–4:30 P.M.

Cost: Free

www.capitol.state.tx.us

Directions: Five blocks north of Sixth St. on Congress St.

AUSTIN

Colonel R. M. Love, the Texas Comptroller of Public Accounts, was gunned down in the State Capitol in Austin on June 30, 1903. W. G. Hill, a disgruntled former employee, was charged in the crime.

TEXAS LAWS

So what kinds of laws has the Texas legislature passed? Here are a few doozies:

★ All criminals must give their victims 24-hour advance warning, either verbally or in writing.

★ Peeping Toms are exempt from prosecution if they have one eye, are over 50 years old, or are a member of the Texas legislature.

★ It is against the law to carry concealed pliers, though concealed guns are OK.

★ You may not shoot a buffalo from the second floor of a Texas hotel.

★ If two trains meet at a crossing, both must stop, and neither can proceed before the other has moved.

★ You cannot carry a spear or sword into a voting booth.

★ By law you must believe in a Supreme Being to be elected to office in Texas.

★ You cannot use a feather duster in a state building.

★ It is illegal to milk another person's cow in the Lone Star State.

★ Voting in Texas was long off limits to "idiots, imbeciles, aliens, the insane, and women."

★ It is illegal to sell your eyes.

★ Any man caught wearing a suit in public after midnight can be arrested for vagrancy.

★ You cannot swear in front of a corpse.

To the Bat Bridge!

Just south of downtown Austin is the largest urban bat colony in North America: the Congress Avenue Bridge over the Colorado River. You wouldn't know it to drive over the structure in the middle of the day, but around sunset the bridge erupts with 1.5 million Mexican free-tailed bats. Actually, there are only about 750,000 in early summer, but by July the females give birth to another 750,000. So many bats emerge from under the bridge that they can be tracked on weather radar.

You've got nothing to fear from these flying mammals, unless you're an insect; this colony alone consumes 10,000–30,000 pounds of bugs *each night*. In thanks for keeping the mosquito population in check, the Texas Legislature has named the Mexican free-tailed bat the State Flying Mammal.

Congress Avenue Bridge, Cesar Chavez St. and Congress Ave., Austin, TX 78701

(512) 416-5700

Hours: April–October, Sunset

Cost: Free

Directions: Just south of Cesar Chavez St. (First St.) on Rte. 275 (Congress Ave.); best viewed from the middle of the bridge.

Contact: Bat Conservation International, PO Box 162603, Austin, TX 78716

(800) 538-BATS or (512) 327-9721

www.batcon.org

LOOKING FOR *MORE* BATS?

If you're interested in bats, but would like to get a little closer than you can at the Congress Avenue Bridge, head to Mineral Wells, home of the Bat World Sanctuary (217 N. Oak Avenue, (940) 325-3404, www.batworld.com). Amanda Lollar founded a home to rehabilitate injured bats in 1987, and she now has affiliates across the country. Though the original sanctuary is not open for walk-ins, you can call ahead and arrange a personal tour. Lollar uses the donations she receives to erect bat houses around town, and to educate humans about the beneficial aspects of these flying mammals.

7

East Texas

Without East Texas, there would be no Texas. It was here, at Washington-on-the-Brazos, that the Texas Declaration of Independence was signed on March 2, 1836. It was here, at the Battle of San Jacinto, that Sam Houston's outnumbered troops routed the Mexican Army under the command of Santa Anna, ensuring the new republic's independence. And it was here, at Spindletop in Beaumont, that the Lucas Gusher blew on January 10, 1901, ushering in the state's first oil boom.

But you've probably already heard enough about all *that*. So instead, this chapter will tell you about those places left out of most travel guides, such as where to find dinosaur statues and giant crustaceans, spook lights and offbeat museums. Here you'll find everything from Dan Rather's birthplace to Old Sparky, Texas's retired electric chair. And for those of you traveling with a pooch, you can even visit the World's Largest Fire Hydrant.

Beaumont
Babe Didrikson Zaharias Museum

Mildred "Babe" Didrikson was born in Port Arthur on June 26, 1911, but her family moved to 850 Doucette Avenue (still standing, private) in Beaumont when she was four. She always considered Beaumont her hometown, and Beaumont, in return, has always considered her its Native Daughter. It even built her a museum in 1976.

Babe Didrikson is widely regarded as America's greatest female athlete, having been named Woman Athlete of the Year by the Associated Press. *Six times.* She once observed, "You can't win them all, but you can try," which was more of a threat to her competitors than a personal motto. Truth was, Didrikson *could* win them all. She took home two golds and a silver medal in track and field from the 1932 Olympics, and probably would have won more had the Olympic Committee allowed her to participate in more events—they were concerned she would walk away with everything.

Didrikson conquered every sport she tried, including boxing, roller skating, diving, basketball, tennis, baseball, billiards, volleyball, fencing, bowling, handball, and golf, where she was one of the founders of the LPGA. She earned the nickname Babe after hitting so many home runs that fans crowned her the female Babe Ruth.

Even after being diagnosed with colon cancer, Didrikson went on to win five golf tournaments in 1954. She died at the age of 45 on September 27, 1956, at John Sealy Hospital (404 Eighth Street) in Galveston, and was buried in Beaumont's Forest Lawn Memorial Park (4955 Pine Street, (409) 892-5912). J. P. "The Big Bopper" Richardson, who perished with Buddy Holly and Richie Valens in Clear Lake, Iowa, is also buried at Forest Lawn.

A small fraction of her gazillion trophies, medals, and awards are on display in this small shrine/museum, as well as personal items from her childhood to her professional sports careers, including her much-used personalized golf bag.

1750 I-10 East, Beaumont, TX 77703

Contact: Babe Didrikson Zaharias Foundation, PO Box 1310, Beaumont, TX 77704

(800) 392-4401 or (409) 833-4622

Hours: Daily 9 A.M.–5 P.M.

Cost: Free

Directions: Take the Martin Luther King Pwy. Exit north from I-10, then head west on the north-side frontage road.

Edison Museum

With 1,093 patents to his name, Thomas Edison revolutionized modern life, from recorded sound, movies, and incandescent light to talking dolls and the electric chair. Yet there is only one museum west of the Mississippi that is dedicated to him, and this is it.

Housed in Beaumont's old Travis Street substation, the first electric substation in East Texas, the Edison Museum tells the story of this inventor's prolific career. Listen to the first recording of "Mary Had a Little Lamb" through a rubber phonograph tube. Pull a main switch and hear the cheers as his Pearl Street station lights up lower Manhattan for the first time. And watch an early silent movie titled *Searching Ruins on Broadway for Dead Bodies, Galveston 1900* (see page 211).

Some of the museums 2,000+ artifacts can be traced back to Edison himself, including a few of his first Japanese bamboo light bulb filaments, one of his notebooks, and a copper nail and floorboard from his laboratory in West Orange, New Jersey.

Travis Street Station, 350 Pine St., Beaumont, TX 77701

(409) 981-3089

Hours: Monday–Friday 9 A.M.–5 P.M.

Cost: Free

www.edisonmuseum.org

Directions: One block east of Main St. on Crockett St., then north one block on Pine St.

ANAHUAC

Anahuac has more alligators than citizens, by a three-to-one margin, and calls itself the Alligator Capital of Texas. The town celebrates Texas Gatorfest in Anahuac Park each September. (409) 267-4190, www.texasgatorfest.com

---

The Eye of the World

For a quarter-century, from 1923 to 1948, Greek immigrant John Gavrelos sculpted a monument to the people, events, and locations he felt were integral to world history. Most of the pieces in his miniature wooden wonderland were carved out of tomato crates. The scenes were roughly divided into patriotic subjects—the Statue of Liberty, Betsy Ross sewing the first flag, and the Founding Fathers signing the Declaration of Independence—and Biblical scenes—Adam and Eve, Cain killing Abel, and the Tower of Babel. Throw in a Parthenon, a few busts of composers and authors, the Alamo (of course), and there you have it: the Eye of the World!

Gavrelos has long since passed away, but his creation lives on in a side room attached to a Texas steakhouse. You don't have to eat there to take a look at it, but considering that the restaurant is keeping this folk art treasure alive, couldn't you at least spring for a T-bone?

Lone Star Steakhouse Seafood & Grill, 6685 N. Eastex Fwy., Beaumont, TX 77706

(409) 898-0801

Hours: Monday–Friday 11 A.M.–9 P.M., Saturday–Saturday 11 A.M.–10 P.M.

Cost: Free; Meals, $6–$20

Directions: On the southwest-side frontage road of Rte. 69/96/287 (Eastex Fwy.), two blocks south of the FM 105 Exit, on the north end of Beaumont.

ANGLETON

A ghost light is sometimes seen near the Angleton grave of Brit Bailey, five miles west of town on Route 35. Bailey was a drunken cowboy who asked to be buried in a standing position and was in December 1832. Many others claim to have seen Bailey's ghost walking the surrounding countryside, staring in windows, looking for booze.

BATSON

The town of Batson held a Batson Round-Up in 1903 when all unmarried women were brought to the town square and auctioned off as wives.

BRYAN

Newscaster **Linda Ellerbee** was born Linda Jane Smith in Bryan on August 15, 1944.

World's Largest Fire Hydrant

From the looks of it, businesses that catch fire in downtown Beaumont have to worry less about burning down than they do being washed away—the fire hydrant at the corner of Walnut and Mulberry is 24 feet tall!

But looks can be deceiving; this isn't a working fire hydrant, and even if it were, the Beaumont Fire Department doesn't have a humongous hose to fit it. The Disney Studios built the World's Largest Fire Hydrant in 1999 to promote the rerelease of the original *101 Dalmatians*, and later donated it to the museum. This explains the white-with-black-spots paint job. The hydrant *is* hooked up to the city's water supply, but only to a sprinkler mounted on top.

The World's Largest Fire Hydrant sits beside a 1927 firehouse that today houses both the Fire Museum of Texas and the headquarters of the Beaumont Fire Department. They've got hoses and axes and engines, including a 1931 Light Truck that worked both the 1937 New London school explosion and the 1947 Texas City disaster (see page 229). You'll also find the headstones of three long-gone station mascots: Spot, Bob, and Major. And for the little ones, there are how-to exhibits (as in "How to survive a fire") and how-not-to displays (as in "How not to start a fire"). Both are good for kids to know.

Fire Museum of Texas, Central Fire Station, 400 Walnut, PO Box 3827, Beaumont, TX 77704

(409) 880-3927

E-mail: firemuseum@ci.beaumont.tx.us

Hours: Monday–Friday 8 A.M.–4:30 P.M., Saturday by appointment

Cost: Free; donations accepted

www.firemuseumoftexas.org

Directions: One block northeast o Main St. (Rte. 90), at Mulberry St.

CLUTE

Clute hosts the Great Texas Mosquito Festival on the last weekend in July each year. Willie Manchew, the World's Largest Mosquito, is the festival's mascot. Events include a Ms. Quito beauty pageant, a Mosquito Calling Contest, a Mosquito Chase (run), and a Mr. and Mrs. Mosquito Legs Contest. (800) 371-2971, www.mosquitofestival.com

You can't change a leopard's spots . . . or this house's.

Buna
Polka Dot, Like It or Not

Years ago an owner of a small house on Main Street in Buna painted polka dots on the structure's outer walls. Neighbors took a shine to the dots and weren't pleased when they were painted over years later. So they decided to take action. When the owner returned from being out of town, the polka dots had magically reappeared. As many times as they were painted over they returned, like a bad rash, sometimes in the middle of the night.

The building was eventually sold to the Buna Chamber of Commerce, which wouldn't dream of covering up the big blue dots . . . not that it has any real choice in the matter.

Main St., PO Box 1739, Buna, TX 77612

(409) 994-5586

Hours: Always visible

Cost: Free

Directions: Just south of the Volunteer Fire Department on Main St. (Rte. 62), three blocks north of the railroad tracks, on the west side of the road.

Something to celebrate.

Burton
The Granite Block

When life gives you lemons, make lemonade. And when the railroad gives you a granite boulder, make a monument. Of course, there's no need to *rush* things, at least not in Burton. The memorial plaque downtown says it all:

> This Texas pink granite rock was one of many such rocks that shook off the flat cars of the H&TC Railroad when they were being transported from Granite Mountain in Burnet County through Burton en route to be used in the building of the Galveston Seawall which was started in 1902 and finished in 1904. This was the same stone that was used in the building of the State Capitol of Texas. This rock has been on the railroad right of way near Burton these many years and was moved to this site on May 27, 1987.

Main St. and FM 390, Burton, TX 77835
No phone
Hours: Always visible
Cost: Free
Directions: At the intersection of FM 1697 (Main St.) and FM 390.

Caldwell
Sculpture Yard

When family physician Joe C. Smith retired, he wanted to keep his hands busy, so he took up sculpture. Working mostly in cast-off stone and steel, Smith created dozens of unique pieces for his front lawn. *Big* pieces. Some as tall as his home. Most seem to focus on the human body— about what you'd expect from a doctor—including many bodyless heads and a twisted tube titled "Ode to Excretion."

You're welcome to stop and take a look around, but if you write him in advance, Smith will give you a personal tour. If you don't get a chance to meet Smith, he's done a self-portrait titled "The Impossible Dream," a one-footed winged man with a yellow baseball cap. It bears *some* resemblance.

501 N. Stone St., Caldwell, TX 77836

Private phone

Hours: Always visible

Cost: Free

Directions: Along Rte. 21, one block north of the railroad overpass.

College Station
George Bush Presidential Library and Museum

As you know, before there was Bush 43, there was Bush 41. After being defeated for reelection in 1992, Bush 41 got to work planning his presidential library. Plenty of people, countries, and corporations chipped in; you can see them on the Donors Wall in the grand Rotunda. Most of the names look familiar—Amoco, Shell Oil, Chevron, Conoco, Halliburton, Enron, Amway, the Sultan of Oman, Prince Bandar bin Sultan, the United Arab Emirates, and the *Washington Times* Foundation—but there are a few surprises, such as Ariana Huffington and the Teresa & John H. Heinz III Foundation. Oddly, the $1 million donation from the Reverend Sun Myung Moon is *not* listed, at least not under his name.

Well, wherever the money came from, it was well spent—it's a fantastic museum! The exhibits are arranged in roughly chronological order, from Bush's birth into a family of Connecticut bluebloods to his current retirement in Kennebunkport, Maine. Along the way you'll see a 1944 TBM Avenger like the one he piloted in World War II (see page 116), his Yale baseball mitt, Babs's wedding dress, a restored 1947 Studebaker (see

page 124), and mementos from his careers as a Texas Representative to the U.S. Congress, Chairman of the Republican National Committee, Ambassador to China, Director of the CIA, and Vice-President.

After passing under a replica of the White House, you'll find gowns worn by Barbara to state dinners, a genuine chunk of the now-demolished Berlin Wall, a gallery of gold-plated and jewel-encrusted gifts from foreign leaders, a replica of the Presidential Cabin on Air Force One, a firing range target recovered from Manuel Noriega's Panamanian palace with Bush's name on it, and a full-scale reproduction of his Laurel Office at Camp David, including paper clips from the original. Even the world's most powerful man snags office supplies—who knew?

Finally, the Gulf War exhibit begins with an hourglass that turns over at the push of a button, giving Saddam Hussein a deadline to get out of Kuwait. (Did curators draw inspiration from *The Wizard of Oz*?) The gallery contains Desert Storm artifacts, including a captured Iraqi missile launcher and an ornate wooden door given to Bush by the Kuwaiti government following the conflict, indicating that Bush is a member of the Kuwaiti family for life.

George and Babs will be buried at the Bush Library when the time comes; their daughter Robin, who died at age three of leukemia, is already there. The former president's papers are also located at the library, but due to an executive order signed by his son in November 2001, they don't have to be released to the taxpaying public. *Ever.* Bush 43's papers as Texas governor are also archived here, until they are moved to his own library in 2010, or so.

1000 W. George Bush Dr. West, College Station, TX 77845

(979) 691-4000 or (979) 260-9552

Hours: Monday–Saturday 9:30 A.M.–5 P.M., Sunday Noon–5 P.M.

Cost: Adults $7, Seniors (62+) $5, Kids (6–17) $2

http://bushlibrary.tamu.edu

Directions: Northeast of the West Loop (FM 2818) on George Bush Dr. (FM 2347).

CUERO
Cuero calls itself the Turkey Capital of the World and has had a Turkey Trot Parade every year since 1912.

Columbus
Grave of the Infidel

Ike Towell was an ornery, freethinking cuss, not only when he walked this earth, but now in death. His tombstone says it all:

> Here rests Ike Towell, an Infidel who had no hope of Heaven or fear of Hell, was free of superstition to do right and love. Justice was his religion.

Towell was once the Columbus town marshal who had little use for organized religion. Today he feeds the worms in a cemetery on the west side of town.

Odd Fellows Cemetery, Montezuma St., Columbus, TX 78934

No phone

Hours: Always visible

Cost: Free

Directions: Exit I-10 heading north on Rte. 71 Business, then left (west) on Montezuma St.; the cemetery is on the right side of the road just outside of town.

Mary Elizabeth Hopkins Santa Claus Museum

Mary Elizabeth Hopkins must have had a one-way chimney, because more than 2,500 Santas entered her home . . . *but they never left.* Well, their loss is your gain, because she opened a museum dedicated to these jolly, happy, captive old men.

You'll see not only every cultural variation of Santa in this private collection—St. Nicholas, Kris Kringl, Sinterklaas, and more—but every commercial item that has ever used his image. Hopkins has collected Santa statues, Santa earrings, Santa dolls, Santa teapots, Santa mugs, Santa toys, Santa postage stamps, Santa piggy banks, Santa pop-up books . . . so many jolly, red-and-white items that you'll reach one inescapable conclusion: when it comes to self-promotion, this guy is a ho, ho, ho.

604 Washington St., Columbus, TX 78934

(979) 732-8385

Hours: Monday and Thursday 10 A.M.–4 P.M.

Cost: Adults $2, Kids (6–11) $1

www.columbustexas.org/attractions.htm

Directions: Two blocks south of Walnut St. (Rte. 90 Bus.), four blocks east of Fanin St. (Rte. 71).

Galveston
The Great Storm

In an age before weather satellites and modern communication, it was difficult to plot or predict hurricanes, as the residents of Galveston learned the hard way in 1900. In retrospect, it might not have been the best idea to build a city on a glorified sandbar that didn't rise more than nine feet above sea level. Still, Dr. Isaac Cline of the Galveston Weather Bureau told city officials for years that the threat of a Galveston hurricane was remote, if not impossible. Cline was proven wrong on September 8, 1900.

Galveston residents were cut off from the mainland before they knew what was coming. The barometer dropped to 28.53 inches and wind speeds reached 120 mph before Cline's anemometer blew away. A 20-foot storm surge swept over the island and took more than 6,000 people and 3,600 homes with it—one third of the city—making it the deadliest natural disaster in American history.

During the storm 10 nuns at St. Mary's Orphanage tied their 93 children together with clothesline to keep them from blowing away. When the building collapsed, three orphans untied themselves and survived, but the remaining 90 were found dead after the storm, still lashed together with the sisters. All were buried on the site. To speed up the cleanup, about 700 victims were loaded onto barges and buried at sea. Many later washed up on the beaches and had to be cremated in funeral pyres.

Galveston decided it would raise the grade of the city as it rebuilt, and add a 17-foot, 4.5-mile seawall along the southern shore. (It was later extended the entire length of the island.) Despite his poor prognostication effort in 1900, Cline was later *promoted* to chief of the New Orleans Weather Bureau, where Clinie did a heckuva job.

The story of the hurricane is hold in harrowing detail in a 30-minute documentary called *The Great Storm* on Pier 21, and in the book *Isaac's Storm* by Erik Larson.

The Great Storm Theater, Pier 21, Harborside Dr., Second Floor, Galveston, TX 77550

(409) 763-8808

Hours: Sunday–Thursday, 11 A.M.–6 P.M., Friday–Saturday, 11 A.M.–8 P.M.

Cost: Adults $3.50, Kids (7–18) $2.50

www.galvestonhistory.org/plc-pier21.htm

Directions: At the north end of 21st St., along the north side of the island.

It Sank Like Concrete

With steel in short supply during World War II, the U.S. Navy experimented with other materials to build its fleet, including a few ships outfitted with concrete hulls. One such vessel, the USS *Selma*, ran aground off the northeast shore of Galveston's Pelican Island. The navy soon learned that concrete doesn't float nearly as well as one might think; the *Selma*'s still there. Look north from Seawolf Park and you can make out the bow, the only part of the ship still above water.

As long as you're at Seawolf Park, stop and check out the USS *Cavalla*, the only submarine still around that can brag it sunk an aircraft carrier: the *Shokaku*, used by Japan in the attack on Pearl Harbor. You can also visit the decommissioned USS *Stewart*, an Edsall Class Destroyer Escort. This ship guarded FDR as he sailed down the Potomac out of Washington, headed for the 1943 Yalta Conference.

Pelican Island, Seawolf Pwy., Galveston, TX 77554

No phone

Hours: Always visible

Cost: Free; Parking $5

Directions: Take 51st St. north from Harborside Dr. or Broadway, then drive until it ends at the USS *Cavalla*.

DANEVANG
Danevang calls itself the Danish Capital of Texas.

EAGLE LAKE
Eagle Lake is the Goose Hunting Capital of the World.

EDNA
Edna was originally called Macaroni Station because of its large population of Italian immigrants.

FAYETTEVILLE
Fayetteville was once named Alexander's Voting Place and Lick Skillet.

A couple of colossal crustaceans.

King Crab and Jumbo Shrimp

You think you've got problems? Gaido's has the biggest case of crabs any-where . . . or should I say *crab*? Though the sign on the roof of this restaurant claims the crab was caught in Galveston Bay, I suspect they picked it up somewhere else. Until they find a pot big enough to boil it in, this crab will remain over the entryway.

And there's more: look to the east and you'll see another colossal crustacean, this one a jumbo shrimp. Casey's Seaside Café makes none of the bold claims that Gaido's does, but lets its enormous pink mascot speak for itself.

King Crab, Gaido's Famous Seafood Restaurant, 3900 Seawall Blvd., Galveston, TX 77550

(409) 762-9625

Jumbo Shrimp, Casey's Seaside Café, 3828 Seawall Blvd., Galveston, TX 77550

(409) 762-9625

Hours: Always visible

Cost: Free

www.galveston.com/gaidos/

Directions: Along the southern seawall, just west of 37th St.

FLATONIA
Flatonia celebrates a mix of Czech culture and Texas cuisine with Czhilispiel each October.

GALVESTON
Camels may not, by law, roam free in Galveston.

Blow this.

World's Largest Cornet

If the 26-foot-long cornet in downtown Galveston looks out of place, that's because it is. The 1986 sculpture was created by David Adickes for the New Orleans World's Fair. When that event wrapped, the colossal cornet was crated, and carted down the coast. Galveston hosts the nation's second largest Mardi Gras celebration each year, so it seemed like the right place for a Crescent City refugee. Should a hurricane like the Storm of 1900 ever blow through, residents might someday hear what it sounds like.

23rd St. and The Strand, Galveston, TX 77550

(888) GAL-ISLE

Hours: Always visible

Cost: Free

Directions: One block south of Harborside Dr./Ave. A, two blocks east of Rosenberg St./25th St.

Huntsville
Big Sam

Sam Houston was a big man, six feet, six inches of man, so it is only fitting that a monument in his honor be Texas-sized. Dedicated in 1994, *Tribute to Courage* (or "Big Sam," as locals know it) is the World's Largest Freestanding Statue of an American Hero. This Sam is 67 feet tall, weighs 60,000 pounds, and stands atop a 10-foot-tall pedestal. Since you can't take an elevator up into his head, they've got another Big Sam face in the Visitors Center, cast from the same mold artist David Adickes used for the original.

Sam Houston Statue Visitors Center, 7600 Highway 75 South, Huntsville, TX 77340
(800) 289-0389 or (936) 291-9-SAM

Hours: Statue always visible; Visitors Center, Monday–Saturday 10 A.M.–5 P.M., Sunday 11 A.M.–5 P.M.

Cost: Free

Directions: Two miles south of town off I-45; Exit 112 heading south, Exit 109 heading north.

If Big Sam doesn't satisfy your hunger for all things Houstonian, head on into town, to the Sam Houston Memorial Museum, located adjacent to Woodland Home, a replica of Houston's former 1847 residence. There you'll find artifacts from this former president of the Republic of Texas, and former governor, and former senator, including his letter opener and leopard skin vest, and the chamber pot he captured from Santa Anna at San Jacinto. The museum also has an impressive collection of items related to the Cherokees, who referred to Houston as Oo-loo-te-ka: the Raven. That was later changed (affectionately) to Big Drunk.

On the grounds of the museum complex, you'll also find the Steamboat House where Big Sam drew his last breath on July 26, 1863. Houston was buried in Oakwood Cemetery (Ninth Street and Avenue I) beneath a marker bearing a quote from Andrew Jackson: "The world will take care of Houston's fame."

Sam Houston Memorial Museum Complex, 1836 Sam Houston Ave., Huntsville, TX 77341
(936) 294-1832

Hours: Tuesday–Saturday 9 A.M.–4:30 P.M., Sunday Noon–4:30 P.M.

Cost: Free

www.SamHouston.org

Directions: South of downtown on Sam Houston Ave., at 18th St.

BESTED BY A GIRAFFE

Big Sam got a big slap in the face when the Dallas Zoo unveiled a new giraffe statue following renovations in 1997. Located at the entrance to the park is a 67½-foot giraffe, its tongue extended upward as if to pull down a leaf from a nonexistent tree, besting Big Sam's record-holding height by a mere six inches. (621 E. Clarendon Street, (214) 670-5656, www.dallas-zoo.org)

GALVESTON

The American Institute of Architects hosts its Sandcastle Competition in Galveston each June. www.aiasandcastle.com.

You may not, by law, land an airplane on any Galveston beach.

If you ride a bicycle in Galveston, by law you must do so at a "reasonable speed."

BORN IN GALVESTON

Jack Johnson—March 31, 1878

Valerie Perrine—September 3, 1943

Barry White—September 12, 1944

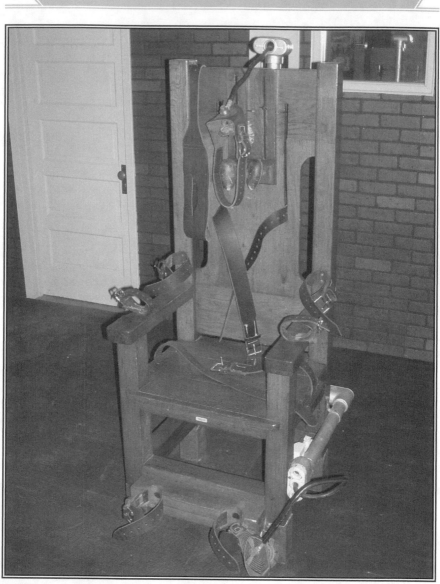

Seating is available, but not recommended.
Photo by author, courtesy of the Texas Prison Museum.

Old Sparky

The Lone Star State's former electric chair, Old Sparky, is the most popular exhibit in Huntsville's Texas Prison Museum. Big shocker, huh? It was used to fry 361 criminals between 1924 and 1964. Though the state has switched to lethal injection (see page 220), it still makes for a sobering display for those of you with young 'uns who have been acting up on the trip.

But Old Sparky—sometimes called the Texas Thunderbolt—is only part of this celebration of Huntville's biggest industry: locking folks behind bars. They've also got displays on inmate contraband (including a nasty shiv that folds out of an innocent-looking blue flip-flop), prison arts and crafts, death penalty protest signs, ball-and-chains, guard uniforms, relics from the 1974 Carrasco prison siege, famous criminals' weapons (such as Bonnie and Clyde's rifles and nickel-plated pistol), and leftover artifacts from the now-defunct Texas Prison Rodeo. And be sure to get your picture taken in the nine-by-six-foot replica cell. This brand-new museum also has conference facilities for corporate events or weddings, if you're planning something special. Or creepy.

Those of you who are interested in the complete Huntsville prison experience, but don't want to commit a crime to get it, pick up a copy of the Prison Driving Tour of 14 sites around town, from the old Walls Unit to the Peckerwood Hill Cemetery.

Texas Prison Museum, 491 State Highway 75 N, Huntsville, TX 77340
(800) 289-0389 or (936) 295-2155
Hours: Tuesday–Friday and Sunday, Noon–5 P.M., Saturday 10 A.M.–5 P.M.
Cost: Adults $4; Seniors (60+) $3, Kids (6–17) $2
www.txprisonmuseum.org
Directions: Just southeast of I-45 on Rte. 75, on the northwest side of town.

GOLIAD

Each June Goliad commemorates a 1976 cattle drive through town, which turned into a 100-beast stampede. The celebration is called the Goliad Longhorn Stampede. (409) 962-3631

GROVES

Groves is home of the Texas Pecan Festival each September.

HALLETTSVILLE

Hallettsville hosts the State Championship Domino Tournament on the Sunday before the Super Bowl each year.

FUN WITH CAPITAL PUNISHMENT

The Walls Unit in Huntsville has the dubious distinction of being the nation's first penal institution to utilize lethal injection for capital punishment. On December 6, 1982, convicted murderer Charles Brooks was strapped to a gurney and injected with an IV cocktail formulated to knock him out, paralyze his lungs, and give him a heart attack. It worked.

But that's not all. Did you know . . .

★ Death Row inmates in Texas are not allowed to smoke, for "health reasons"?

★ Old Sparky was built by a death row inmate in 1914 (the craftsman's sentence was later commuted)?

★ Judge Charles J. Hearn signed murderer Robert Nelson Drew's 1993 death warrant with a smiley face?

★ The guy who prepares the prisoners' last meals, convict Brian Price, recently published his popular recipe for Old Sparky's Genuine Convict Chili?

★ In 1997, 37 criminals were executed in Texas—a new state record!

★ The Visible Man (www.nlm.nih.gov/research/visible), a medical cadaver that was sliced deli-style and photographed, was the body of convicted murderer Joseph Jernigan, executed by lethal injection at the Huntsville Prison on August 5, 1993?

HEARNE

Hearne is the Sunflower Capital of Texas.

INDIANOLA

The Gulf Coast town of Indianola was swept into the ocean by a hurricane on September 17, 1875, killing more than 900 residents.

KATY

Actress **Renee Zellweger** was born in Katy on April 25, 1969.

LA GRANGE

Texas's first brewery was built in La Grange.

KARLA FAYE GETS HER DAY

Karla Faye Tucker was no angel. The former Allman Brothers Band groupie was sentenced to death by lethal injection for helping her boyfriend, Danny Garrett, kill Houston residents Jerry Lynn Dean and Deborah Thornton with a pickax on June 13, 1983. But in the months leading up to her execution, Tucker was the focus of worldwide media attention. Reverend Pat Robertson of *The 700 Club* begged Governor George W. Bush to commute her death sentence. Why? Because of her jailhouse conversion to Christianity. (Would Robertson have done the same had she converted to Islam? Just askin'. . . .)

Bush, known to many as "The Texecutioner," was not particularly interested in sparing Tucker's life, but he didn't announce his decision until February 3, 1998, when Tucker was already strapped to the gurney, awaiting his call. Why the delay? Bush's announcement was timed to coincide with the six o'clock news, where the as-yet-undeclared presidential candidate could reach the widest national audience. Tucker was dead by 6:45. Bush later gave a dead-on impersonation of Karla Faye Tucker's earlier appearance on *Larry King Live*. "Please don't kill me!" he mimicked for Tucker Carlson, who was writing an article for *Talk* magazine.

Oddly enough, later in 1998 Governor Bush *did* commute the death sentence of Henry Lee Lucas, perhaps America's most prolific serial killer. Lucas had a habit of confessing to so many killings that Bush didn't feel *any* of his confessions could be believed. The Texas Board of Pardons and Paroles concurred, and Lucas's sentence was changed to life without parole, which turned out to be a little more than two years. Lucas died of a heart attack on March 15, 2001, and was buried in the prison's Peckerwood Hill Cemetery.

LIBERTY

Liberty's full name is Villa de la Santissima Trinidad de la Libertad.

MADISONVILLE

It is illegal to tuck your pants into your cowboy boots in Madisonville unless you own at least two cows.

Talk about overkill.
Photo by author, courtesy of Forbidden Gardens.

Katy
The Not-so-Forbidden City

It might be forbidden in China, but not in Texas. Of course, the Forbidden City in Katy isn't quite as impressive as the original—it's only 1/20th the size. (How very un-Texan!) The original Forbidden City was built in the 15th century during the Ming Dynasty, and covers roughly 16 square miles of central Beijing. This detailed replica of its palaces is all housed beneath a large pavilion, protected from the elements and miniature Mongol hordes. Though most of the palaces and buildings are tiny, there are a few full-size replicas surrounding the layout, including the Emperor's dragon throne, the Empress's sedan chair, and a big room full of weapons.

But that's not all! You can also see a 1/3-scale re-creation of the terra cotta army of Emperor Qin. The pottery army was uncovered outside his tomb in 1974, and contains 6,000+ life-sized soldiers, each with unique facial features, uniforms, and weaponry. Thirty years after being discovered,

the entire army has yet to be completely excavated. But not in Texas. And as long as nobody wanders into your camera's viewfinder, a photograph of the army in Katy should be almost indistinguishable from the original.

Forbidden Gardens, 23500 Franz Rd., Katy, TX 77493

(281) 347-8000

E-mail: fgarden@btc.net

Hours: Friday–Sunday 10 A.M.–5 P.M.

Cost: Adults $10, Seniors (60+) $5, Kids (6–18) $5

www.forbidden-gardens.com

Directions: Take the Grand Parkway Exit north from I-10, then left on Franz Rd.

La Grange
Best Little Whorehouse No Longer in Texas

Houston TV personality Marvin Zindler is living proof that one person can make a difference . . . though probably shouldn't. For years the Chicken Ranch, the best-known whorehouse in Texas, operated with very few complaints in the town of La Grange. But Zindler, with mock piety and a camera crew, went and ruined it all.

This story starts in 1844, five years after La Grange was founded. The town's first brothel opened in a small hotel, and though it changed location, management, and ownership many times, it offered its services to the local community without interruption for the next 129 years. Miss Jessie [Williams] was madam in 1905 when the Chicken Ranch moved to its final location along the banks of the Colorado River west of town. It was here, during the Great Depression, that the whorehouse got its nickname; down-on-their-luck farmers (and more than a few coop-raiders) switched to the "poultry standard": one chicken for one 15-minute roll in the hay.

The folks of La Grange appreciated the Chicken Ranch's civic contributions. Miss Jessie made sure her girls supported locally owned businesses, carting them to town to do their shopping, displaying more civic responsibility than any modern Wal-Mart. The Chicken Ranch also established a direct phone line to the sheriff's department and acted as an informal La Grange Bureau of Investigation, passing along words uttered in flagrante delicto that might be of interest to authorities.

Miss Edna [Milton], the Chicken Ranch's final madam, took over in 1952. She expanded the operation to 16 rooms, and even arranged a shuttle (a cattle truck, actually) between the La Grange airport and the ranch for servicemen who flew in from Bergstrom AFB on taxpayer-funded helicopters. Miss Edna paid her taxes, donated $10,000 to help build a local hospital, was the town's biggest sponsor of Little League, and pitched in $1,000 for a new public swimming pool. Sheriff Jim Flournoy had no problem with the Chicken Ranch because the Chicken Ranch gave him no problems.

Enter Marvin Zindler. This flamboyant consumer affairs reporter from Houston's KTRK-TV (Channel 13) decided the hookers in his hometown weren't nearly as interesting as those at the Chicken Ranch, and set out to destroy the La Grange operation. His reports in 1973 made unproven allegations of Mexican bank accounts and Mob connections, and proven allegations of (shocking!) prostitution. Zindler challenged Texas Governor Dolph Briscoe to do something about it. The uproar eventually forced Sheriff Flournoy's hand, and he delivered the bad news to Miss Edna that she had to close the ranch. When all the "girls" had flown the coop, Miss Edna hung a sign on the front gate that read, "Closed by order of Marvin Zindler."

But the Chicken Ranch did not die. It was made into a popular musical (Miss Edna had a non-speaking part in the original Broadway production), a less-successful movie, and a ZZ Top song. When Zindler returned to La Grange some time later to film a segment on the benefit he had foisted upon the local population, Sheriff Flournoy roughed him up a bit, even stomping on the reporter's notorious (and quite obvious) toupee. Zindler sued the sheriff for $3 million, but settled out of court for a reported $10,000. Flournoy's supporters (most of the town) raised the funds through a charity barbecue and bumper sticker sale.

The Chicken Ranch building was moved to Dallas in 1977 and made into a disco/restaurant that specialized in—you guessed it—chicken dishes. It has since closed.

Route 71, La Grange, TX 78945

No phone

Hours: No longer there

Cost: Free

www.lagrangetx.org

Directions: Head east out of town on Travis St. (Rte. 71); the Chicken Ranch was located at the river.

Whose big idea?

Lake Jackson
Which Way?

Try to imagine the trouble folks living in one neighborhood of Lake Jackson must have when giving directions to visitors. "Head down That Way before taking a left at This Way . . . " "Which way?" "No, *That* Way!"

Ha, ha, ha. Very funny. Some smart-aleck developer named a few of the streets in Lake Jackson This Way, That Way, and Any Way. Residents on these thoroughfares are now condemned to a lifetime of Abbott and Costello routines. Thanks a lot.

This Way and That Way, Lake Jackson, TX 77566

No phone

Hours: Always visible

Cost: Free

Directions: One block east of Rte. 332 on Oyster Creek Dr., then two blocks south on That Way to This Way, or five blocks north to Any Way.

Moscow
Dinosaur Gardens

Donald Bean, like you, has taken his fair share of road trips. Back in the early 1960s, his family came across a dinosaur park on the way to Oregon, and Bean became obsessed: Why not build his own dinosaur park? Throwing caution and cash to the wind, Bean commissioned fiberglass sculptor Burt Holster to create 11 prehistoric critters that he could place around his property near Moscow.

Today you can follow the 1,000-foot trail back through the forest and imagine what it would be like to stumble across a dinosaur . . . and then do just that! Looking back, Bean should probably have had them constructed of concrete instead of fiberglass; some of these big beasts are in pretty sorry shape. Still, you should stop by for a visit, and perhaps catch the dinosaur-building bug yourself. Somebody needs to carry the kitschy torch forward to a new generation of wackos.

Dinosaur Gardens, Rte. 59 South, Moscow, TX 75960

(936) 398-4565

Hours: June–August, daily 10 A.M.–6 P.M.; September–December, Saturday–Sunday 10 A.M.–6 P.M.; March, daily 10 A.M.–6 P.M.; April–May, daily 10 A.M.–6 P.M.

Cost: Adults $2.50, Kids $1.50

Directions: On the south end of town along Rte. 59, near the intersection with Rte. 62.

MARSHALL
Composer **Scott Joplin** was born in Marshall on November 24, 1868.

Port Arthur
Janis Joplin Collection

Janis Joplin's childhood in Port Arthur was remarkably average. She was born here on January 19, 1943. She read her Bible, did paint-by-number portraits of Jesus, and learned how to use a slide rule. She attended Woodrow Wilson Junior High (1500 Lakeshore Drive) and Thomas Jefferson High School (2200 Jefferson Drive), graduating in 1960. Then she saw the rest of the world.

Joplin first attended Lamar State College of Technology in Beaumont, but in 1962 transferred to the University of Texas in Austin. There she began singing with the Waller Creek Boys. While at UT, a group of oh-so-handsome frat boys nominated her for the Ugliest Man on Campus Award, and she won. Joplin also went on a blind date with future virtues nag/compulsive gambler William Bennett, who was also a student. Is it any wonder she dropped out and split for California?

Her road to fame, coming out of the San Francisco music scene, was filled with nonstop booze and narcotics. When her 10-year high school reunion rolled around she returned "just to jam it up their asses," she admitted. "I'm going down there with my fur hat and feathers and see those kids who are still working in gas stations and driving dry cleaning trucks while I'm making $50,000 a night." Two months later, on October 5, 1970, she died of a drug overdose.

Today, Port Arthur's Museum of the Gulf Coast chooses to focus a fair amount on her pre-rock-'n'-roll days; they've got childhood letters to her mother, her slide rule, her 1960 Yellow Jacket yearbook, and other knickknacks. But they also have a replica of her psychedelic Porsche and one of her "nudie" stage costumes, and each January they host a Janis Joplin Birthday Bash. Better late than never.

The Museum of the Gulf Coast also celebrates the town's other celebrities, including J. P. "The Big Bopper" Richardson; they've got the hair brush, Zippo lighter, Bufferin bottle, and dice found on his body after he was killed in an Iowa plane crash. Tex Ritter fans can see the singer's blue pinstriped suit. And sports lovers can view displays on dozens of professional athletes, including footballer Charles "Bubba" Smith, Redskins' trainer Bubba Tyler, and boxer Bubba Busceme— it's a Bubbapalooza!

Museum of the Gulf Coast, Gates Memorial Library, 700 Procter St., Port Arthur, TX 77640

(409) 982-7000

Hours: Monday–Saturday 9 A.M.–5 P.M., Sunday 1–5 P.M.

Cost: Adults $3.50, Seniors $3, Kids (6–18) $1.50

www.museumofthgulfcoast.org

Directions: Six blocks northeast of Houston Ave. on Procter St., just north of the Sabine Neches Canal.

Saratoga
Bragg Road Light

Poor Jake Murphy. A brakeman on the Santa Fe railroad, Murphy slipped in the mud one rainy night, fell on the tracks, and was decapitated by a locomotive. The cleanup crew never found his head, but Murphy didn't give up so easily; if reports are true, Murphy is forever doomed to walk the old railroad bed with a lantern trying to find it. Don't believe me? Head on over to Bragg Road on some dark night and see for yourself.

The Santa Fe tracks were pulled up years ago, replaced by a dirt road connecting Saratoga and the now nonexistent town of Bragg. The road is eight miles long and doesn't curve, rise, or fall an inch on its entire length. As you drive north, look behind you and you will no doubt see Jake holding his lantern in the distance, directly over the road. Or it could just be headlights on Route 787.

Come to think of it, looking at a map, that's *exactly* what the Bragg Road Light is—Route 787 aligns perfectly with Bragg Road. All right, who came up with this cockamamie ghost story?

Bragg Rd., Saratoga, TX 77585

No phone

Hours: At night

Cost: Free

www.bigthicketdirectory.com/ghostroad.html

Directions: Head north out of Saratoga on Rte. 787, and when the road bends to the left take the dirt road that continues directly; that's Bragg Road (FM 1293).

SARATOGA

Musician **George Jones** was born in Saratoga on September 12, 1931.

About all that's left.

Texas City
A Big Bang

There's a riddle told in the chemical industry that asks, "What's the difference between a munitions depot and a fertilizer factory?" Answer: "The sign on the door." You don't have to tell that to the folks of Texas City.

On April 16, 1947, a fire started in the hull of the French freighter SS *Grandcamp* as it sat dockside in Texas City. The ship had been loaded with 2,300 tons of ammonium nitrate fertilizer, as well as shelled peanuts, agricultural equipment, and a few cases of handgun ammunition. In retrospect, the bullets were a bad idea. When the fire reached the ammo around 9 A.M., it triggered a massive explosion. The blast ignited a nearby oil refinery, the Monsanto chemical plant, the *Grandcamp*'s sister ship, the SS *High Flyer*, and a good portion of Texas City, which was then hit with a 15-foot-high wave. The *High Flyer* was also loaded with fertilizer, and it exploded a couple hours later.

Numbers vary, but at least 560 people perished, including 27 firefighters who were at the *Grandcamp* when it detonated. More than 2,500 residents were injured and/or left homeless. The *High Flyer*'s propeller marks the site of the original explosion (Loop 197 and Dock Road), while a formal memorial can be found on the other end of town, adjoining a cemetery where 59 unidentified victims, or parts of victims, were laid to rest. Here you'll see the *Grandcamp*'s impressive 3,200-pound anchor, which landed at 2000 S and 2160 E, about 1.62 *miles* from the demolished dock.

Texas City Memorial Park, N. 29th St. and Loop 197N, Texas City, TX 77590

No phone

Hours: Always visible

Cost: Free

ww.chron.com/content/chronicle/metropolitan/txcity/index.htm

Directions: At the corner of 25th Ave. (Loop 197N) and N. 29th St.

Warrenton
World's Smallest Catholic Church

St. Martin's Catholic Church, just north of Warrenton, claims to be the World's Smallest Catholic Church. The floor plan is 12 by 16 feet, and it seats a dozen parishioners. And, although this is a noteworthy claim, it's hardly a practical one since, when it was first built in 1888, many Catholic families had more than 12 members. Where could they all fit?

The original St. Martin's Church was torn down in 1915 . . . and replaced with a new sanctuary of the same size. Whose big idea—excuse me, *small* idea—was that?

St. Martin's Catholic Church, FM 237, Warrenton, TX 78961

No phone

Hours: Always visible

Cost: Free

Directions: On Rte. 237 just north of town.

Wharton
Dan Rather's Birthplace

When it comes to Horatio Alger stories, it's hard to beat that of CBS newsman Dan Rather. Born in a Wharton shotgun shack to Byrl and Irvin "Rags" Rather on October 31, 1931, young Dan had a tough early

life; he spent 5 of his first 10 years in bed with rheumatic fever. The family had moved to Houston by the time he got his first job as a paperboy for the *Houston Chronicle*. Rather sold papers at the corner of 18th Street and N. Shepherd Drive, where he routinely got in fistfights with other newsies. This training no doubt came in handy when he was assaulted years later in New York by a crazed man asking, "Kenneth, what is the frequency?" His father kept telling him "Courage!"—a phrase he later used when he signed off the *CBS Evening News*.

Rather landed his first journalism gig with KSAM radio while attending Sam Houston State College in Huntsville. From there he worked for UPI, the *Houston Chronicle*, and KTRH radio in Houston. He got his big break when Hurricane Carla slammed into Galveston in September 1961; reporting for KHOU-TV, Rather became the first person to broadcast a radar scan of a hurricane from the scene while the storm was in progress. That got him a job as the head of CBS's southwestern bureau, where he was the network's main reporter during the JFK assassination. A short time later he was off to New York.

Rather's Wharton birthplace was moved from its original location on College Street to the grounds of the local historical society, where you can visit it today.

Wharton County Historical Museum, 3615 N. Richmond Rd., Wharton, TX 77488

(979) 532-2600

Hours: Monday–Friday 9:30 A.M.–4:30 P.M., Saturday–Sunday 1–5 P.M.

Cost: Free

www.whartoncountymuseum.com

Directions: North of town on Rte. 183 (Richmond Rd.).

SHINER
Shiner claims to be the Cleanest Little City in Texas.

SPRING
Spring throws a Crawfish Festival each May.

The ways things used to be: cool.

Tee Pee Courts Motel

If you think all progress is for the better, perhaps you should give yourself a reality check in Wharton. On the north end of town you'll find the crumbling remains of the Tee Pee Courts, 10 tipi-shaped stucco units that once welcomed weary travelers. Each one-bedroom, one-bath tipi—excuse me, *tee pee*—was furnished with rustic furniture crafted from Colorado spruce, and the door handles were made from elk antlers. The structures were built in 1942 by Toppie and George Belcher and were originally known as Belchers Court.

But no more. Abandoned and in disrepair, they've changed hands several times in recent years, yet none of the owners have been able to begin restoration. If you want to spend the night in Wharton, you've got a few completely adequate, but completely boring, chain motels out along the bypass.

Some progress.

Tee Pee Courts, 4100 N. Richmond Rd., Wharton, TX 77488

No phone

Hours: Always visible

Cost: Free

Directions: North of town on Rte. 183 (Richmond Rd.), just past the museum.

Big and bony.

Wharton Brontosaurus

The Wharton Brontosaurus, with its bony shoulders and hips, looks more like an old mule than a dinosaur. The 20-foot-tall, 77-foot-long fiberglass statue was built in 1992 by Dana Steinheimer and guards the northern approach to the town's Colorado River bridge. Paleontologists will tell you there's no such thing as a brontosaurus, preferring to call the gigantic plant-eater an apatosaurus. Those know-it-alls have obviously never been to Wharton.

Riverfront Park, 400 W. Colorado St., Wharton, TX 77488

No phone

Hours: Always visible

Cost: Free

Directions: Just west of Richmond Rd. (Rte. 183), just north of the Colorado River.

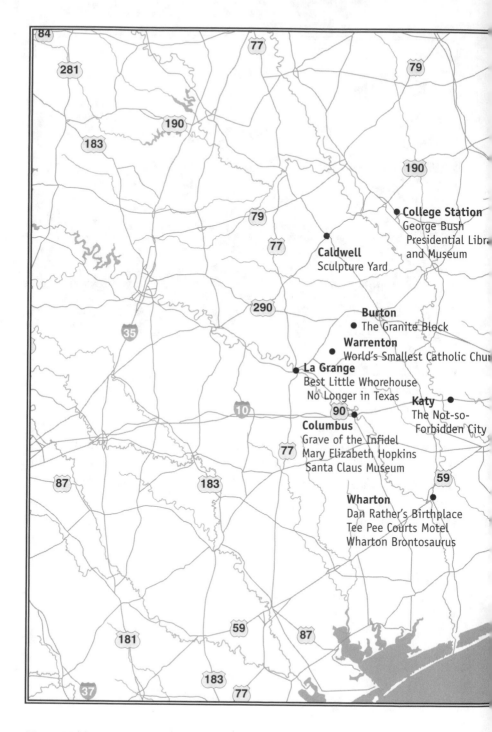

College Station
George Bush
Presidential Libr
and Museum

Caldwell
Sculpture Yard

Burton
The Granite Block

Warrenton
World's Smallest Catholic Chu

La Grange
Best Little Whorehouse
No Longer in Texas

Katy
The Not-so-
Forbidden City

Columbus
Grave of the Infidel
Mary Elizabeth Hopkins
Santa Claus Museum

Wharton
Dan Rather's Birthplace
Tee Pee Courts Motel
Wharton Brontosaurus

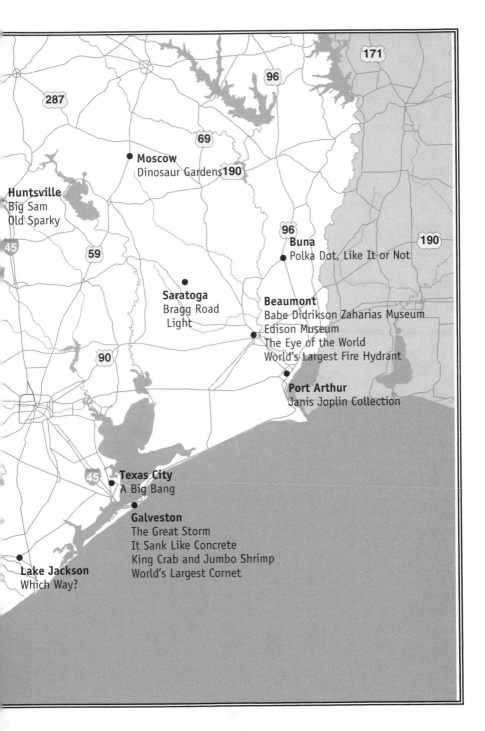

8

HOUSTON AREA

Most folks in Houston will tell you, whether you ask or not, the word "Houston" was the first word spoken on another celestial body. It was uttered by astronaut Neil Armstrong on July 20, 1969, when he announced, "Houston, the *Eagle* has landed." Exactly what this says about the city is unclear, other than that Lyndon Johnson was skilled at wrangling pork barrel for Mission Control out of the U.S. Congress.

Don't get me wrong—if I was the first person on the moon and I had to give a shout out to my favorite Texas city, I'd pick Houston. There's a Lone Star observation that goes something like "Dallas is the pretty sister with the bad personality, but Houston is the ugly sister who knows how to cut a rug." Where did George W. Bush live when he was "young and irresponsible"? Where did John Milkovisch drink enough beers that he could use the empties to side his entire house? Where did Janet Jackson's wardrobe malfunction? Houston, Houston, and Houston.

Houston
Art Cars

Take my advice: stop what you're doing, pull out your calendar, and go to the Orange Show's Web site to find out when their next Art Car Parade will be held. It typically coincides with Houston's International Festival, which is held sometime around Easter. If you do nothing else before you die, you *must* attend Houston's Art Car Parade.

The first parade was held in 1986, but only a few cars participated. It has since grown to a 300-car extravaganza of the most outlandish, weird, goofy, and original vehicles ever devised, cars with names such as Button Hearse, Cow-de-lac, Pepto Gizmo, Litter-Bug, Rocky Roadster, Spoon Truck, Oozemobile, Doom Buggy, Homage to Timothy Leary, Mirabilis Statuarius Vehiculum, and the Cosmic Ray Deflection Car. The lead car in the parade is always the Fruitmobile, a 1967 Ford station wagon encrusted with fake oranges, bananas, pineapples, and other plastic produce, driven by its creator Jackie Harris.

To truly appreciate the cars, arrive several hours early when they're lining up along the Allen Parkway. You'll need plenty of time to take in the cars and chat with the artists and drivers. Better still, come a day early for the Art Car Symposium, where you can learn how to make your own. Be sure to buy tickets for the Art Car Ball, which is held in a downtown parking garage the night of the parade, complete with bands and booze. During the ball judges present trophies to the participants for such categories as Contraption, Political Statement, Youth Group, Performance, and Daily Driver.

Sponsor: The Orange Show, 2401 Munger St., Houston, TX 77023

(713) 926-6368

E-mail: orange@insync.net

Hours: April; check Web site

Cost: Free

www.orangeshow.org

Directions: Along the Allen Pwy. between Shepherd Dr. and downtown.

It was only a matter of time before Houston's art car movement had a museum of its own. Known by many as the Garage Mahal for its chrome cupolas, the Art Car Museum opened in 1998. It has room for only a few

cars at a time, but they're constantly rotating in new vehicles. The museum is also a showcase for other contemporary art and has an impressive exhibit schedule.

Art Car Museum, 140 Heights Blvd., Houston, TX 77007

(713) 861-5526

E-mail: artcarm@swbell.net

Hours: Wednesday–Sunday 10 A.M.–5 P.M.

Cost: Free

www.artcarmuseum.com

Directions: Two blocks south of I-10 on Heights Blvd.

HOUSTON

"In Houston the air [is] warm and rich and suggestive of fossil fuel."
—Joan Didion

Robert Johnson recorded for one of his two known sessions in a room at the Gunter Hotel (205 E. Houston Street, (210) 227-3241) in Houston, between November 23 and 27, 1936.

George and **Barbara Bush** rent a suite at the Houstonian Hotel (111 N. Post Oak Lane) in Houston in order to maintain their Texas residency. It is here that they retreated following Bush's 1992 defeat, where Babs reportedly snapped at George, "Get over it!"

Houstonians eat out more than citizens of any other city, nearly five times a week.

Boxer **Muhammad Ali** was arrested for draft evasion in Houston in 1967.

Recycling at its most artistic.
Photo by author, courtesy of the Orange Show.

Beer Can House

The next time your significant other complains about all the beer you've been drinking, tell him/her the story of John Milkovisch. A retired upholsterer for the Southern Pacific Railroad, Milkovisch enjoyed his daily six-pack, but rather than toss the empties beside his La-Z-Boy, he put them to good use decorating his house. It started in 1968 as an alternative to expensive siding. He would trim off the tops and bottoms, then nail the flattened cans to his home, label-side out. Over the next 18 years he guzzled or collected about 50,000 cans, all of which he incorporated into the building.

Like Native Americans with buffalo, Milkovisch used every part of the beer can. He wove long curtains out of the trimmed tops and wired the bottoms together to create fences. He even fashioned earrings out of pull tabs for his incredibly supportive wife, Mary. On the off chance he purchased beer in bottles, he stacked the empties to make windows in a covered porch behind the house. And since he didn't want to be bothered with a lawn to mow, he covered his front and back yards in cement . . . embedded with about 14,000 marbles and discarded whatnots. The work didn't stop until shortly before he died in 1988.

When Mary Milkovisch passed away a few years ago, the Orange Show (see page 253) purchased the home and converted it into a combination gallery and artist's residence. The Beer Can House still has a ladder Milkovisch erected in his front yard—the Ladder of Success. He originally painted it black to show most people never make it. As a folk artist who has left a stunning legacy, Milkovisch could not be counted in this victoryless category.

222 Malone St., Houston, TX 77007

Contact: Orange Show Foundation, 2402 Munger St., Houston, TX 77023

(713) 926-6368

Hours: Daylight hours; view from street

Cost: Free

www.orangeshow.org

Directions: Two blocks north of Memorial Dr., three blocks east of Westcott St.

HOUSTON

It is against the law to buy Limburger cheese, rye bread, or goose livers on Sunday in Houston.

Hundreds of students ditched classes at several Houston junior highs in February 1983 when rumors circulated that evil blue Smurfs would attack and kill students.

Jack Nicholson's astronaut character in *Terms of Endearment* lived at 3068 Locke Lane in Houston; **Shirley MacLaine** lived in the home just to its right.

Two Houston women were kidnapped in December 1993 and forced to purchase Twinkies, and drive around town looking at Christmas lights. Their abductor said he was lonely.

Enron Country

The world needs more citizens like Sherron Watkins. As Enron's Vice-President for Corporate Development, Watkins thought something looked fishy and sent an e-mail to her boss, CEO Kenneth Lay, warning him, "I am incredibly nervous that we will implode in a wave of accounting scandals." She didn't know how right she was until a few months later; on December 2, 2001, Enron filed for bankruptcy, the largest business failure in U.S. history. The Watkins memo, unearthed by congressional investigators, proved that Lay had been made aware of looming problems as he continued to urge employees to invest in the company. At the same time, Lay made $123 million by cashing in his stock options.

When the house of cards came tumbling down, it took most of its employees' retirements with it, not to mention significant portions of several states' and unions' pension funds. A company that handled about a quarter of all domestic energy trades, valued at $74 billion in early 2001, and whose stock sold as high a $85 a share, was now worthless. Four thousand employees were let go at their 50-story Houston headquarters alone.

Former Vice-Chairman Cliff Baxter committed suicide in his new Mercedes in the median of a Sugar Land highway on January 25, 2002, shortly after being subpoenaed to appear before Congress. By all accounts, Baxter was one of the *good* guys at Enron and had left the previous May in an undisclosed disagreement with others in the company. Ken Lay and Jeff Skilling both testified before Congress by *not* testifying; both pled the fifth amendment.

The big, crooked E sign that Americans saw every night on the news was purchased at auction for $8,500 by Lou Congelio of Houston's Stan and Lou Advertising Agency. He also got Ken Lay's telescope. The company's former headquarters are still there.

1400 Smith St., Houston, TX 77002

No phone

Hours: Always visible

Cost: $1 billion and counting

www.enron.com

Directions: At the corner of Clay and Smith Sts., just east of I-45 on the west end of downtown.

Evel, Billie Jean, and Astroturf

When Houston's Harris County Domed Stadium—the Astrodome—opened in 1965, it was the first air-conditioned domed stadium in the world. Unfortunately, sunlight coming through the stadium's clear roof caused glare that distracted players on the field. The roof was then painted over, which caused the grass on the field to die. Workers tried painting the brown stubble green, but that strategy couldn't work forever. A year later Monsanto solved the problem with a new synthetic grass: Astroturf!

Over the years, the Astrodome has seen several historic pop culture events. On January 8, 1971, Evel Knievel cleared 13 cars on his motorcycle, setting a new jump record. And on September 20, 1973, 40 million television viewers in 36 countries tuned in to watch a best-of-five tennis competition between Billie Jean King and Bobby Riggs—billed as the "Battle of the Sexes." King handed Riggs his ass in the first three sets. Riggs reneged on his pledge to jump off a California bridge if he lost, so not only was Riggs a chauvinist pig, he was a chicken, too.

Reliant Astrodome (former Harris County Domed Stadium), 8400 Kirby Dr.,
Houston, TX 77001
(713) 799-9718
Hours: Always visible
Cost: Free
www.reliantpark.com/facilities/astrodome.asp
Directions: Two blocks north of Loop 610S on Kirby Dr.

HOUSTON

Musician **Carlos Santana** was arrested for marijuana possession at the Houston International Airport in June 1991.

A Houston man drew a 35-year prison sentence in 1984 for stealing a $2 can of Spam. In 1987 another man was fined $10,000 for stealing 80,000 rolls of toilet paper. But a year later a third criminal got only 30 days in jail for stealing a Trailways bus.

Funky Houston Homes

Thank heaven for Houston's lax zoning laws—they've allowed more than a few local visionaries to turn their humble abodes into genuine works of art. Two of these homes/shrines, the Beer Can House (see page 240) and the Orange Show (see page 253), are covered in detail elsewhere in this chapter. Here are three more houses worth a visit.

Fun with flowers.

Flower Man House

Around Houston, Cleveland Turner is known as the Flower Man. He starts most of his days by hopping on his Flowercycle, which is covered in plastic blooms, to search alleys and dumpsters for the cast-off items that will eventually decorate his house. Turner is a recovered alcoholic who made a pact with God: he promised to build "a thing of beauty" if the Big Guy could help him stay sober. Both Turner and God have kept their parts of the bargain.

Turner's first Flower Man House was located on Sauer Street, though it was destroyed by an ar(t)sonist. Turner moved to a new location on Sampson Street and started all over. His house is caked with junk: porch

railings, plastic rocking horses, birdhouses, scratching posts, broken clocks, kid's toys, heating grates, mirrors (to look to Heaven), horse bridles, and even a winch his father used to rescue him from a well he'd fallen down as a child. Oh, and flowers, lots and lots of plastic flowers.

3317 Sampson St., Houston, TX 77004

Private phone

Hours: Always visible

Cost: Free

Directions: One block south of Elgin St., three blocks west of Scott St.

O.K. Corral

The O.K. Corral was built by Howard Porter. It looks like an outdoor beer garden—tables and chairs fill the lot—but isn't. The corral is located on a former vacant lot that is wedged between two buildings on Houston's near-west side. Porter has painted the walls on either side in bright colors, and decorated them with dozens of old cowboy boots, hubcaps, and stringless guitars. The boots remind him of the old days, he says.

1912 Gillette St., Houston, TX 77019

Private phone

Hours: Always visible

Cost: Free

Directions: Just south of Gray St., three blocks east of Taft St.

Pigdom

While a few of Houston's other art environments can look a little junky (in a good way), Pigdom is no sty. Owner Victoria Herberta painted her home a stunning shade of purple and mounted hundreds of road signs from across the United States on its exterior walls, all very neat and orderly.

But why "Pigdom"? Herberta named her home in honor of Jerome, a prize pig who was a direct descendant of Priscilla the Pig, a plucky porker who rescued a retarded child from Lake Summerville on July 29, 1984.

Sadly, Jerome was cast out of Pigdom by a tight-assed Houston bureaucrat who denied Herberta the right to keep "livestock" on city property. But Jerome wasn't any old barn pig—he was *afraid* of other pigs, having been raised in the company of humans. Herberta also claimed Jerome knew how to pray, though sometimes his prayers went

unanswered; when Herberta could fight City Hall no longer, Jerome had to be retired to Aquarena Springs, where he spent his later years in the company of Ralph the Diving Pig.

4208 Crawford St., Houston, TX 77004

Private phone

Hours: Always visible

Cost: Free

Directions: Two blocks northeast of Wheeler St., four blocks southeast of San Jacinto St.

George W. Bush and the TANG

Boy, some guys get all the luck! Take George W. Bush: 12 days before his undergraduate student deferment from the Selective Service expired in 1968 (the day he was to graduate from Yale), four pilot slots opened with the Texas Air National Guard (TANG). Although the Guard had an 18-month backlog of 500 applicants, Bush managed to land a slot with the 147th Fighter Wing 111th Tactical Recon, stationed at Houston's Ellington Air Force Base.

Earlier that year Bush took an aptitude test for prospective pilots. He scored 25% on pilot aptitude, 50% on navigation, and 95% on "officer quality." His application asked him to list "background qualifications of value to the Air Force." Bush wrote "None." He also checked a box saying that he "[did] not volunteer" for overseas duty.

With such a lackluster resume and test performance, how did he snag one of those four coveted slots? Well, it wasn't *all* luck. In fact, his father had called Texas oilman Sidney Adger, a family friend, who then called the Texas Speaker of the House, Democrat Ben Barnes, who then got General James Rose on the phone. Rose was commander of the Texas National Guard. Meanwhile, the elder Bush also contacted Colonel Walter "Buck" Staudt, commander of the 111th Tactical Recon, just to say howdy. It was Staudt who approved Junior's application.

Unofficially, the 111th was known as "Air Canada," a bipartisan safe haven for the offspring of Texas politicians—such as the sons of Senators Lloyd Bentsen and John Tower, and Governor John Connally—and Dallas Cowboys football players. (There were *seven* in Bush's group.)

Staudt helped Bush after basic training in September 1968 by approving a rare "direct appointment" for Bush to become a second lieutenant,

allowing him to bypass Officer Candidate School. At the time Bush signed a Statement of Intent that said "I plan to return to my unit and fulfill my obligation to the utmost of my ability. I have applied for pilot training with the goal of making flying a lifetime pursuit."

Bush trained on the F-102 Delta Dagger at Moody Air Force Base in Valdosta, Georgia. After his first solo flight, his name appeared in a press release from the base that stated, "George Walker Bush is one member of the younger generation who doesn't get his kicks from pot, or hashish, or speed. . . . As far as kicks are concerned, Lt. Bush gets his from the roaring afterburner of the F-102." The last F-102 was phased out on June 30, 1970, six months after Bush got his wings, and was never used in Vietnam . . . but that too was probably just a coincidence.

When Bush got back to Texas, Commander Lt. Col. Jerry Killian recommended him for first lieutenant in November 1970. In May 1972, Bush tried to transfer to a position with the 9921st Air Reserve at Maxwell Air Base in Alabama, where he could also work on the Senate campaign of Winton "Red" Blount. There was only one problem: at the time the 9921st did not fly F-102s. Actually, it had *no* airplanes; it was a postal unit. Bush's transfer was not approved.

But by September Bush wrangled a transfer to the 187th TAC Recon Group at Dannelly Air Force Base in Montgomery. He didn't make much of an impression on the squadron at Dannelly; Commander Lt. Col. William Turnipseed later claimed, "Had he reported in, I would have had some recall, and I do not." But folks on Blount's senate campaign did remember Bush; they called him the Texas Soufflé, all puffed up with hot air.

But wait a second—*he didn't show up for duty*? The only person who recalls Bush reporting to Dannelly was John "Bill" Calhoun, the 187th's safety officer, who said Bush came to the base and read flight manuals and safety magazines to fulfill his Guard obligation. Calhoun's statement was later called into question—the dates he claimed to have seen Bush were three months *before* Bush arrived in Alabama. (None of this made much of a difference since only F-4s flew out of Dannelly, not F-102s, and Bush had been grounded in July for not taking his annual physical.) The only piece of paper to link Bush to the base in Montgomery was a dental visit in on January 6, 1973. In October of that year he received an honorable discharge from the Guard . . . seven months early.

Ellington Field, 510 Ellington Field, Houston, TX 77034
(713) 929-2221
Hours: Always visible
Cost: Free
http://efd.houstonairportsystem.org and www.awolbush.com
Directions: Southeast of Loop 8 off Old Galveston Rd. (Rte. 3).

CONFLICTING THOUGHTS ON NATIONAL SERVICE

"I was not prepared to shoot my eardrum out with a shotgun in order to get a deferment. Nor was I willing to go to Canada. So I chose to better myself by learning how to fly airplanes." —George Bush, *Houston Chronicle*, 1994

"I am angry that so many of the sons of the powerful and the well-placed . . . managed to wrangle slots in Army Reserve and National Guard units." —Colin Powell, *My American Journey* (Random House, 1995)

George W. Bush: Party Animal

Shortly after moving the family to Houston from Midland (see page 119) in 1959, George and Barbara Bush shipped off their oldest son, George, to an East Coast prep school: Phillips Academy in Andover, Massachusetts. After Phillips, Junior was admitted to his father's Ivy League alma mater, Yale, where he was asked to join the elite Skull and Bones society.

Bush didn't grow up much in his undergraduate years . . . or his early adulthood, for that matter. Bush has confirmed the characterization, without specific details: "When I was young and irresponsible, I behaved young and irresponsible [sic]." By his own account, Bush's youth ended on his 40th birthday . . . but that's getting ahead of the story.

After graduating from Yale, and pilot training with the Air National Guard (see above), Bush got an apartment at Houston's swanky Chateaux Dijon, "The Place to Live." Coincidentally his future wife, Laura Welch, lived here at the same time, but the two never met; there were 300+ units. Welch taught for two years at John F. Kennedy Elementary

(306 Crosstimbers Street), followed by a year as a librarian at the Kashmere Gardens Branch (5411 Pardee Street, (713) 393-2450) of the Houston Public Library.

Beside his Guard obligations, the only job Bush is known to have held during his two years in Houston—what he calls his "nomadic days"—was in 1972 as a youth counselor with the Professional United Leadership League, or P.U.L.L., an inner-city mentoring program for disadvantaged youth. Most reports claim he took the position on orders from his father, whom he had recently challenged to go "mano a mano" after a night of drinking in Washington. Other reports assert that it was part of a plea bargain from a drug arrest. Whatever the case, Bush, as a volunteer, had to sign in and out to keep track of his hours and was the only volunteer who had to do so.

Bush lived at Chateaux Dijon until the fall of 1973, when he left for Harvard Business School.

Chateaux Dijon, 5331 Beverly Hill St., Houston, TX 77056

(713) 626-3660

Hours: Always visible

Cost: Free

www.chateauxdijon.com

Directions: One block south of Richmond Ave., one block south of Rice St., just northwest of the Loop 610/Rte. 59 interchange.

HOUSTON

Aviator **Howard Hughes** was born on December 24, 1905, in a home that stood at 1404 Crawford Street in Houston. His family later moved to 3921 Yoakum Boulevard; that building still stands, and is used by St. Thomas University. Hughes died en route to Houston from Acapulco on April 5, 1976, and was buried at Houston's Glenwood Cemetery (2525 Washington Avenue, (713) 864-7886).

A man died on October 3, 1991, in a Houston motel after he was swarmed by a colony of Brazilian fire ants. His wife, who was sleeping in the bed beside him, survived.

Earthquake!!!

Indeterminate Facade

Tucked away in the corner of a Houston shopping mall is a dilapidated structure . . . bricks from the building's facade have collapsed into a pile on the awning above the entryway, and nobody is doing a damn thing about it!

Well, there's a reason it hasn't been repaired: it was *built* broken. Back in the 1970s, the Best Products retail chain commissioned several stores from S.I.T.E., a cutting-edge architecture firm. This Houston outlet was designed to look as if an earthquake had struck the Gulf Coast. The only tip-off that the damage wasn't real is the size of the pile; clearly there were more bricks in the rubble than could fit in the gaping hole in the facade.

Best Products sold the space years ago, and it has seen a variety of tenants. There's no telling who will be there when you show up, or whether it will be collapsing for real.

Alameda-Genoa Shopping Center, Kingsport Rd. and Kleckley Dr., Houston, TX 77075

No phone

Hours: Always visible

Cost: Free

Directions: Exit westbound on Alameda-Genoa Rd. from I-45; the mall is located just south of the intersection.

National Museum of Funeral History

This museum is to die for . . . literally. But have no fear, it's more than just coffins, hearses, and embalming tables. They've also got tributes to some of the greatest funerals in history, those of John F. Kennedy, Elvis Presley, and Abraham Lincoln, including a replica of Abe's 6-foot, 6-inch casket. They've also got the 1973 Mercedes hearse that carried the body of Princess Grace of Monaco to her final rest in 1982, as well as the funeral announcements from the burials of Judy Garland, John Wayne, Martin Luther King Jr., and John Candy.

And there's more! The museum owns Packard's one and only funeral bus, built in 1916. And a life-sized replica of King Tut's sarcophagus. And a collection of fantasy coffins from Ghana in the shapes of airliners, fish, and giant onions. But the strangest piece in its collection is a three-person casket for a couple distraught over the death of their young daughter; they planned to commit suicide and be buried with her body. As the empty casket attests, they didn't go through with it. Perhaps they heard this museum's motto, or something like it: "Any day above ground is a good one."

415 Barren Springs Dr., Houston, TX 77090

(281) 876-3063

E-mail: info@nmfh.org

Hours: Monday–Friday 10 A.M.–4 P.M., Saturday–Sunday Noon–4 P.M.

Cost: Adults $6, Seniors (54+) $5, Kids (3–12) $3

www.nmfh.org

Directions: Take the Airtex Exit west from I-45 to Ella Blvd., then right to Barren
   Springs Rd.

MORE FUNERAL FUN

When you walk out of the National Museum of Funeral History, you'll probably start dreaming of a special service of your own. So why not consider one of these Texas-based solutions:

Space Services Inc. of Houston (www.memorialspaceflights.com) offers several out-of-this-world options for your cremains. For a mere $12,500 they will land a lipstick-sized capsule of your ashes safely on the surface of the moon or put them into lunar orbit—your choice. Too pricey? How about $5,300 for the company's Flight Module Service? That'll get seven grams of ashes into Earth's orbit in a capsule inscribed with your name (24 characters maximum), a commemorative plaque, a DVD of the blast-off, and a personalized Web page. Bargain hunters can have a single gram's worth of their ashes launched into orbit for the low, low price of $995. Of course they have to book a full flight of ashes first, but at that point what's *your* hurry?

F & F Metal Products of Dallas holds the southwest's franchise for **Art Caskets** (www.artcaskets.com). They will decorate your coffin in a variety of designs, costing between $2,500 and $2,900. They offer angels, golf courses, 16-wheelers, fire trucks, the Virgin Mary, and much more.

If you plan to be cremated, Houston artist **Wayne Gilbert** might want to talk to you. He creates paintings using human cremains as a medium. He used to mix the ashes with oil paints, but then he discovered that each person's ashes turn a unique color when mixed with a special clear gel he has devised. Too bad you have to die before you find your true color.

HOUSTON

Houston has been called the Fashion Capital of the Nation, the Seamy Little Swamp Town, and the Sassy New Pittsburgh of the Southern Rim.

Reporter Anna Werner of KHOU-TV, Houston's CBS affiliate, first broke the story of the danger posed by Firestone tires on Ford Explorers on February 7, 2000.

Please don't compare it to the Apple Show.
Photo by author, courtesy of the Orange Show Center for Visionary Art.

The Orange Show

Jeff McKissack had a singular obsession: the orange, or as he called it, "the perfect food." McKissack believed the orange contained all the answers to a good life, including health and prosperity. He eventually compiled his observations regarding citrus in a book titled *How You Can Live 100 Years . . . and Still Be Spry.*

McKissack was deeply worried that nobody else shared his enthusiasm for the fruit. What could he do to get the word out? Then, while standing on his front porch in 1956, a little voice in his head whispered, "The Orange Show." That's it! He would build a monument to the orange on a lot across the street from his home.

McKissack began collecting scrap around Houston to build his dream world—wagon wheels, old porch railings, discarded tile, Astroturf, gears, umbrellas, mannequins, tractor seats . . . you name it. His fantasies about how the Orange Show would impact the world grew faster than the monument. "Take 100,000 architects and 100,000 engineers and not one of them or all of them could come up with a show like the Orange Show," he boasted. McKissack painted his concrete and steel monument with bright colors—mostly shades of orange (surprised?)—and mosaic signs spelling out his thoughts: "Love Oranges and Live," "Go Orange," and "Clown Found Happiness by Drinking Cold Fresh Orange Juice Every Day." Why should you listen to a clown? Another sign points out "Clowns Never Lie." The Orange Show's centerpiece was an amphitheatre that surrounded a pool where a paddlewheeler chugged around in a circle, representing the history, and shape, of his favorite fruit.

When the Orange Show opened to the public in 1978, attendance was not quite what McKissack had anticipated. He believed 8 of 10 Americans would eventually visit the site, but he was lucky if he had 8 or 10 visitors a day. Those who did show up were asked to sign a petition stating that they thought the Orange Show was better than the Astrodome—it is—and that it should be proclaimed the Seventh Wonder of the World.

McKissack died eight months after his life's dream opened to the public, and his ashes were scattered over the monument he spent 20 years building. The Orange Show might have been bulldozed were it not for a group of Houston art lovers who purchased and restored this unique structure in 1981. Today it is a Mecca for fun-loving, visionary artists and those who admire them, and it sponsors Houston's annual Art Car Parade (see page 238). They also have regular arts programs at the site—check out their schedule on the Web.

The Orange Show Center for Visionary Art, 2401 Munger St., Houston, TX 77023
(713) 926-6368
E-mail: oranges@orangeshow.org
Hours: Wednesday–Friday 9 A.M.–1 P.M., Saturday–Sunday Noon–5 P.M.;
   September–Mid-December and Mid-March–May, Saturday–Sunday Noon–5 P.M.
Cost: Adults $1, Kids (under 13) Free
www.orangeshow.org
Directions: Three blocks west of Telephone Rd. on the I-45 Frontage Rd., then 1 block
   south on Munger St.

Wardrobe Malfunction

Sandwiched between nonstop advertisements for gas-guzzling SUVs, boner pills, and beer, the Super Bowl XXXVIII halftime extravaganza at Houston's Reliant Stadium included a shocking—yes, shocking!—"wardrobe malfunction." In the final seconds of Janet Jackson and Justin Timberlake's performance, Timberlake reached over and pulled open Jackson's leather bustier, revealing the singer's pierced nipple.

Oh.

My.

God.

The shrill outrage at the February 1, 2004, stunt seemed a bit over the top, and more than a little disingenuous. The subsequent congressional hearings, FCC fines, and cable "news" yammering all focused on Jackson's bare breast, not the fact that Timberlake was simulating a sexual assault.

Interestingly, neither CBS nor MTV, who produced the show, were taken to task for Kid Rock's use of a ripped American flag as a rock 'n' roll poncho in another musical number, nor Aerosmith's pregame exploitation of the Space Shuttle *Columbia* disaster. "What about the children!?!" people cried. If kids were to learn that people have nipples, the thinking went, it should be up to the parents to inform them, and only when the kids are good and ready.

In levying its paltry $550,000 fine against CBS, the FCC cited the affront to the game's 90 million viewers, 89,999,995 of whom were either in the bathroom, at the buffet table, or outside having a smoke when the malfunction occurred. Thank goodness for videotape, for to be utterly incensed at such brazen immorality folks needed to inspect the footage, over and over and over again in slow motion, during the nation's weekslong, postgame I'm-Outraged-apalooza.

Reliant Stadium, 8400 Kirby, Houston, TX 77054

(800) 776-4995 or (832) 667-1400

E-mail: guestservices@reliantpark.com

Hours: Always visible

Cost: Free

www.reliantpark.com/facilities/stadium.asp

Directions: Two blocks north of I-610 on Kirby Dr.

Waiting for the World's Largest Saxophonist.
Photo by author, courtesy of Bob Wade.

World's Largest Saxophone

At first glance the World's Largest Saxophone appears to be just an over-sized rendition of a musical instrument, but on closer inspection you'll see it is also a salute to creative recycling. Built in 1993 by Bob Wade, the

70-foot-tall horn's stops are made from VW hoods and food service trays, the finger pads are hubcaps, and its reed is a surfboard. The bottom curve of the bell is an inverted Beetle.

The sculpture once marked the entrance of a jazz club, which has since closed its doors. Today the sculpture sits idle, waiting for the World's Largest Saxophonist to give it a blow.

6025 Richmond Ave., Houston, TX 77057

No phone

Hours: Always visible

Cost: Free

Directions: Just west of Fountain View Dr. on Richmond Ave.

Suburbs
Channelview
Pom-Pom-Mom Takes Out a Contract

Many sullen teenagers feel misunderstood and unsupported by their parents, and most are probably justified in thinking so. But that could not be said for Shanna Harper. Her mom, Wanda Halloway, was willing to *kill* for her daughter.

Halloway felt she had a good reason to hire a hit man: by bumping off her neighbor, Verna Heath, Shanna had a much better shot at making the freshman cheerleading squad at Channelview High School (828 Sheldon Road). Heath's daughter Amber had been a star cheerleader since junior high, and if she was distraught over her mother's untimely demise, well, perhaps she'd drop off the squad.

Now I know what you're wondering: why didn't Halloway just go after *Amber*? As it turned out, Halloway had an even bigger ax to grind with Verna Heath, who she felt had orchestrated Shanna's disqualification a year earlier for "campaigning" for a spot on the junior high squad. (Shanna had passed out pencils and rulers with her name on them.)

So Halloway asked her ex-brother-in-law, Terry Harper, to find her a goon. He went to the police instead. Harper met with Halloway in the parking lot of Grandy's Restaurant on January 28, 1991, to discuss the details. It would cost $7,500 for both mother and daughter, but only $2,500 for the mom. Halloway agreed to the latter, and pulled off her diamond earrings to pay for the job. She soon found out that Harper was wired.

Halloway was convicted of solicitation of capital murder and sentenced to 15 years in prison, though it was overturned on a mistrial. She then pleaded no contest to the same charge and drew a 10-year sentence. She served only six months in the slammer before being released and ordered to perform 1,000 hours of community service. Oh, and she was ordered to *stay away from the Heaths forever.*

Grandy's Restaurant, 8 Uvalde Ave., Channelview, TX 77015

(713) 451-3074

Hours: Always visible

Cost: Free

Directions: At the intersection of Wallisville Rd. and Uvalde Rd., west of the Sam Houston Pwy. (Loop 8).

Nausau Bay
Crazy Woman Driver!

On July 24, 2002, dentist Clara Harris ran over her husband David in the parking lot of the Nausau Bay Hilton. Three times. And then she parked her silver Mercedes-Benz on top of his body. Her initial statement to police? "It was an accident."

This would be hard to swallow even without knowing what had transpired only moments before. Harris had marched into the hotel lobby with 16-year-old Lindsey Harris (David's daughter by a previous marriage) to confront David and his mistress Gail Bridges. Lindsey beat her dad with a purse. Harris ripped off Bridges's blouse. The police were called. Then, after David walked Bridges to her car, Harris ran him down. And then ran him down again. And again.

You've no doubt seen the shocking footage on cable "news" programs. How did they capture the murder on film? In what turned out (in retrospect) to be a bad decision, earlier that day Clara Harris had hired a private eye from Blue Moon Investigations to tail her cheating hubby. The P.I. was at the Hilton doing his job, and ended up catching his own client.

Harris was defended by the same lawyer who defended Andrea Yates, with approximately the same results; she was convicted of murder and sentenced to 20 years in prison.

Nausau Bay Hilton Inn, 3000 NASA Pwy., Nausau Bay, TX 77058

(281) 333-9300

Hours: Always visible
Cost: Free
www.houstonnasaclearlake.hilton.com
Directions: Just west of Space Center Blvd. on Rte. 528 (NASA Pwy.).

Seabrook
Thayer's Folly

For six decades a strange little bait shop/icehouse named Curley's Corner sat on the tiny triangle formed by the intersection of Bayport Boulevard, Second Street, and NASA Road One in Seabrook. Then, in the 1980s, Alan Thayer bought the place and transformed it into a salute to Central American folk art. Thayer added mission bells and statues of saints and decorated terra cotta tiles. Before he was finished, he'd spent about $500 a square foot on the project. The place is only 200 square feet, but still, $100K is a lot of dough for a building that sits on an oversized traffic median. Locals stopped calling it Curley's Corner and started calling it Thayer's Folly.

And folly it was. The building was eventually sold off and today houses a law office. They've modified it a bit, adding details like a railing of diving dolphins, but Thayer's eccentric vision still shines through loud and weird.

Valentine Law, 1210 Bayport Blvd., Seabrook, TX 77586

(281) 291-9765

Hours: Always visible

Cost: Free

Directions: At the intersection of Rte. 146 (Bayport Blvd.) and NASA Rd. One.

9

San Antonio Area

Jou have to hand it to whoever came up with the idea for San
Antonio's Paseo Del Rio Mud Festival. Each January, when the
city drains the River Walk for cleaning, they turn the chore into
a celebration. College teams battle it out on mud-filled barges or
jump into mud pits along the canal. There's a Mud Parade, a Mud
Pie Ball, and a King and Queen Mud are crowned.

Granted, a mud-chucking festival isn't everyone's cup of tea.
That's why I've made a few additional suggestions. Do you love art?
Check out Barney Smith's Toilet Seat Art Museum. Science? Visit
the retirement home of America's first astrochimp. And history?
There's always that broken down old building that Ozzy Osbourne
thoughtlessly . . . um . . . *watered*.

Shall we dance? Do we have any choice?
Photo by author, courtesy of the Buckhorn Saloon and Museum.

San Antonio
Buckhorn Saloon & Museum

When Albert Friedrich first opened his Buckhorn Saloon in 1881, he made an offer to his patrons: "Bring in your deer antlers and you can trade them for a shot of whiskey or a beer." What a deal! In very short

order Friedrich had amassed a substantial horn collection. The best samples, including a record-setting 78-point pair from a whitetail buck, were mounted on the walls, and the rest were made into furniture by Friedrich's father. As the Buckhorn moved from one location to another around town, the collection expanded to museum size. But what museum allows you to carry an open bottle of brew on your visit? Only the Buckhorn, so buy a round on the ground floor before heading upstairs to the exhibits.

The Buckhorn is divided into several themed halls. The Hall of Horns is the largest, and it's here that you'll find a stuffed Old Tex, whose horns measure 105 inches from tip to tip—a world record! Also on display, a 4,000-deer-horn chandelier and a 62-buffalo-horn chair built for Teddy Roosevelt. Many other critters, without horns, can be found in the adjoining Hall of Feathers, where you'll find a stuffed passenger pigeon, and Hall of Fins, for fish lovers. The most fascinating specimens, however, are the genuine mutants found in random display cases, including a two-faced calf, a rabbit with four horn-like growths coming out of its skull, and a one-headed, three-eared, eight-legged lamb. Also, look for sideshow cast-offs of fleas dressed in tiny human clothing, a merman, and three, count 'em *three*, shrunken heads.

And finally, before you leave, be sure to see the Buckhorn's Hall of Texas History, a 14-scene wax museum left over from the 1968 World's Fair. One diorama shows a Comanche warrior scalping a settler. Brutal, yes, but the paleface probably had it coming.

Buckhorn Saloon and Museum, 318 E. Houston St., San Antonio, TX 78205

(210) 247-4000

E-mail: sales@buckhornmusem.com

Hours: June–August, daily 10 A.M.–6 P.M.; September–May, daily 10 A.M.–5 P.M.

Cost: Adults $9.99, Seniors (55+) $9, Kids (3–11) $7.50

www.buckhornmuseum.com

Directions: Two blocks north of Commerce St., one block east of Navarro St.

SAN ANTONIO
William Sydney Porter, better known as **O. Henry**, once lived at 904 S. Presa Street.

Dionicio Rodriguez's Concrete Sculptures

Dionicio Rodriguez was a mysterious man. He was born in Mexico City in 1891, and eventually became an accomplished sculptor after learning a little-known technique from a Spanish mason. The process involved dyeing mortar with secret chemicals and sculpting "bark" with modified knives, forks, and spoons, allowing him to turn ordinary cement into what looked like petrified wood. He always worked under a tent to protect his methods.

Rodriguez moved to San Antonio in the 1920s where he was hired by the San Antonio Portland Cement Company (later renamed Alamo Cement). In 1931 he finished a covered trolley stop on Broadway Street; its thatched grass roof is supported by three knotted tree trunks, which shade circular seats that appear to be stumps. Only on close inspection can you tell that it's made entirely of concrete. The trolley stop is used today as a bus shelter.

Bus Stop, 4901 Broadway St., San Antonio, TX 78209

No phone

Hours: Always visible

Cost: Free

Directions: Six blocks south of Austin Hwy. on Broadway St., at Patterson Rd.

Don't let the name fool you—this garden is Japanese.

One of Rodriguez's biggest commissions was the pagoda entrance to the Japanese Sunken Gardens. The gardens were built in 1919 to cover up a scar left over from San Antonio Portland Cement—it's the company's old quarry. The original landscaper, Kimi Eizo Jingu, lived with his family at the gardens, where they also ran a tearoom. But shamefully, just after Pearl Harbor, Jingu was driven off the property and the park's name was changed to the Chinese Tea Gardens. Rodriguez's gate reflects the new name.

Rodriguez died in San Antonio in 1955. The gardens he helped embellish were restored in 1983, and the name was changed back to the Japanese Sunken Gardens.

Japanese Sunken Gardens, Brackenridge Park, 3800 N. St. Mary's St., San Antonio, TX 78212

(210) 735-0663

Hours: Gate, always visible; Gardens, June–August 8:30 A.M.–10 P.M.; September–May 9:30 A.M.–5 P.M.

Cost: Free

http://hotx.com/sunkengarden/

Directions: Three blocks north from Rte. 281on St. Mary's St.

Drivers' Little Helpers

San Antonio teenagers all know the story: years ago a school bus driven by a nun was hit by a train at a southeast side railroad crossing. The driver survived, but the children did not. Distraught, the good sister returned later to kill herself on the tracks. While parked and waiting for the train that would seal her fate, the nun's car mysteriously lurched off the tracks. The dead children apparently didn't hold a grudge and saved her life.

The tragedy actually works to the advantage of present-day drivers. People claim that if your car stops on the tracks, a strange force will push it to safety before a train arrives. Some say if you sprinkle baby powder on your bumper, little handprints will appear. While I would never recommend you try this for yourself, if do you feel so compelled, use a rental car. But only if you accepted the collision insurance.

Strangely, nobody seems too concerned that there is no record whatsoever of a busload of kids being crushed by a train in San Antonio. You'd think this would be the kind of thing nobody would forget. Still, the rumors persist, including that Cindy Sue Way, Nancy Carole Way, and Laura Lee Way—three streets located just east of the crossing—were named after three of the unfortunate tots.

Villamain St., San Antonio, TX 78223

No phone

Hours: Always visible

Cost: Free

Directions: Just south of the I-410 overpass on Villamain St., as it turns into Shane St.

SAN ANTONIO

Wings, the first movie to receive an Oscar for Best Picture (1927), was filmed almost entirely in the San Antonio area. (The story was set in World War I France.)

It is illegal to wash or repair your car in San Antonio on a Sunday.

Fire away, kiddies!

Kiddie Park

Open since 1925, San Antonio's Kiddie Park is the oldest private amusement park in the United States, though it doesn't look a day over 70 years old. The park is smaller than a city block, but it contains a lot. There's a miniature Eiffel Tower, a dinky roller coaster, a mechanical school bus, tiny boats, and a plane ride where each airplane has a front-mounted, child-sized machine gun.

Kiddie Park's crown jewel, however, is the 1918 carousel built by the Herschell-Spellman Company of Tonowanda, New York. The merry-go-round toured the states with traveling carnivals until 1935 when it found a permanent home in San Antonio. The carousel has 36 hand-carved horses and two chariots and was featured on a 25¢ U.S. postage stamp in October 1989.

3015 Broadway, San Antonio, TX 78209

(210) 824-4351

Hours: Daily 10 A.M.–Dusk

Cost: Always visible; Rides extra

Directions: At the corner of Mulberry Ave. and Broadway St.

Ozzy Osbourne Peed Here

One blurry night on February 19, 1982, during his *Howl at the Moon* tour, a drunken Ozzy Osbourne found what he thought was a secluded corner off the street to "drain the radiator." A security detail quickly informed him that he was urinating on the Alamo Cenotaph . . . as they hauled him off to jail. To make matters worse, Ozzy was wearing his wife's green evening gown; she had taken away his clothes to head off just this type of problem.

Though it was an honest (if somewhat unsanitary) misunderstanding, Osbourne was blackballed from performing in San Antonio for a decade. Not until 1992, after he donated $10,000 to the Daughters of the Republic of Texas, was he allowed to return.

As bad as that was in the eyes of many Texans, something even *worse* happened two years earlier at the Alamo. On March 20, 1980, three members of the Revolutionary May Day Brigade of the Maoist Revolutionary Communist Party—a local organization, not the Chinese variety—invaded the shrine, lowered the Texas flag, and raised a red Communist banner. They claimed they did it to invite folks to their upcoming May Day protest. The revolutionaries held the fort, or at least the flag, for about 30 minutes. So here's the worst part: the Ku Klux Klan took it upon themselves to "help" defend the Alamo for several May Days to follow.

Gee, thanks.

The Alamo, 300 Alamo Plaza, PO Box 2599, San Antonio, TX 78299

(210) 225-1391

Hours: Monday–Saturday 9 A.M.–5:30 P.M., Sunday 10 A.M.–5:30 P.M.

Cost: Free

www.thealamo.org

Directions: If you can't find the Alamo in San Antonio, you're in trouble.

SAN ANTONIO

Newlyweds **Dwight and Mamie Eisenhower** lived at the corner of Dickman and New Braunfels Streets on Fort Sam Houston in 1941.

REMEMBER ALAMO TRIVIA!

Nobody's allowed to live in the Lone Star State without knowing a thing or two about the Alamo. Here are a few tidbits to impress your friends:

★ The structure's real name is the Mission San Antonio de Valero.

★ The mission was established in 1718, but didn't move to this location until 1724.

★ "Alamo" is Spanish for "cottonwood."

★ Only nine of the Alamo's 189 defenders were Texas residents.

★ One of the Alamo's nurses described Davy Crockett as "the strangest man I ever saw. He had the face of a woman, and his manner was that of a girl."

★ Legend has it that the remains of Davy Crockett, Jim Bowie, and Colonel William Travis were buried beneath the altar at San Fernando Cathedral (115 Main Plaza, (210) 227-1297). Workmen doing renovation of the altar in 1936 found charred human bones, which were placed on public display before being reinterred on May 11, 1938.

★ The battle cry associated with this defeat is "Remember Alamo!" not "Remember *the* Alamo!"

★ The familiar arched parapet was added 14 years *after* the battle took place.

★ The Texas flag captured at the battle is still in the possession of the Mexican government, and they plan to keep it.

★ The original Alamo mission bell, cast in 1722, can be found at the Haley Library and History Center in Midland (1805 W. Indiana Street, (432) 682-5785, www.haleylibrary.com).

★ The Alamo has no basement.

SAN ANTONIO

Labor leader **Samuel Gompers** died at the St. Anthony Hotel (300 E. Travis Street, (210) 227-4392) in San Antonio on December 13, 1924.

Heloise Bowles Reese of **Heloise Hints** is buried in San Antonio's San Jose Burial Park (6235 Mission Road, (210) 923-0272).

Tea time.
Photo by author, courtesy of Ripley's Believe It or Not!

Ripley's Believe It or Not! & Plaza Theatre of Wax

Here's a warning: the Alamo doesn't have central air. If you're in San Antonio in the summer, you might consider bypassing that broken-down old mission and head across the street to a place that's *really* cool: Ripley's Believe It or Not! & Plaza Theatre of Wax, located in the former Grand Opera House.

Ripley's contains more than 500 items from Robert Ripley's original collection of bizarre artifacts, including a vampire-killing kit, the world's largest gavel, a shrunken head, a six-legged calf, a two-faced pig, a cannibal's throne and ceremonial fork, a working pool table the size of a quarter, a replica of the White House made from 6,057 dimes, and a rodent tea party from the Children's Museum of England.

And there's more! Your ticket also allows you to visit the adjoining wax museum. It's divided into four main galleries, starting with Hollywood, The Dream Factory: Whoopi Goldberg, Yul Brynner, Demi Moore, Anthony Hopkins, Brad Pitt, Louie Armstrong, Ed Asner, Elizabeth Taylor, Shirley Temple, the Beverly Hillbillies, and more. Next, the Heroes of the Lone Star are divided between the Alamo Heroes—John Wayne et al.—and the Faces of Mexico. 'Fraidy cats can bypass the Theatre of Horrors, but they'll miss Frankenstein, Dracula, Mr. Hyde, the Planet of the Apes, and a mad scientist's laboratory where detached wax heads are being kept alive for who-knows-what diabolical purpose. Finally, there's a holy wax gallery called the Passion of Christ, which re-creates the greatest hits of the New Testament.

301 Alamo Plaza, San Antonio, TX 78205

(210) 224-WAXX

Hours: Monday–Thursday 9:30 A.M.–8 P.M.; Friday–Saturday 9 A.M.–10 P.M., Sunday 9 A.M.–8 P.M.

Cost: Combo/Single, Adults $17.95/$13.95, Kids (4–12) $9.95/$6.95

www.plazawaxmuseum.com

Directions: Across the plaza from the Alamo.

Space Monkey

History books will tell you Alan Shephard was the first American in space, but truth be known, he was only the first American *human* in space. On December 4, 1959, Sam the astrochimp blasted off from Wallops Island, Virginia, aboard a Mercury capsule, making him the first American mammal to rocket spaceward. Though called an astrochimp, he was actually a rhesus monkey, born in Austin two and a half years earlier. During his 12-minute flight, Sam flew 55 miles high before splashing back down in the Atlantic Ocean. Sam was weightless for three and a half minutes, during which time he pulled levers while lights flashed, allowing scientists to measure his disorientation (or lack of it) during free fall. He performed like a champ.

Sam was an immediate media darling, appearing on the cover of *Parade* magazine in 1960. But once Shephard took off on May 5, 1961, Sam faded from the limelight. You can see a replica of Sam's flight harness—Biopack Number 1—in Hangar 9 on his home air force base in San

Antonio. The building just happens to be the nation's last surviving wooden hangar from World War I. It has been converted into a museum named in honor of Edward H. White, one of the three astronauts to die on the launch pad aboard *Apollo I*. White was the first American astronaut to walk in space and was a San Antonio native. The museum houses astronaut Alan Bean's training suit, among other space and air force artifacts.

Hangar 9 / Edward H. White II Memorial Museum, Brooks Air Force Base, 8008 Inner Circle Dr., PO Box 35362, San Antonio, TX 78235

(210) 536-2203 or (210) 531-9767

Hours: Monday–Friday 8 A.M.–4 P.M., Saturday by appointment

Cost: Free

www.brooks.af.mil/history/historic_buildings.html

Directions: Enter Brooks from Military Dr. (Spur 13), two blocks west of I-37; follow the signs on base.

Sam lived at Brooks Air Force Base until 1971, when he was transferred to the San Antonio Zoo. Here he was given his own apartment at the Monkey House and was provided with a simian concubine. After Sam died on September 19, 1978, he was returned to Brooks for an autopsy and later cremated. A plaque honoring Sam can be found outside the Monkey House where he retired.

San Antonio Zoological Garden and Aquarium, 3903 N. St. Mary's St., San Antonio, TX 78212

(210) 734-7184

Hours: June–August, daily 9 A.M.–6 P.M.; September–May, daily 9 A.M.–5 P.M.

Cost: Adults $8, Seniors (62+) $6, Kids (3–11) $6

www.sazoo-aq.org

Directions: North on St. Mary's St. five blocks from Rte. 281.

SAN ANTONIO

Teddy Roosevelt recruited many of his Rough Riders at San Antonio's Menger Hotel Bar (204 Alamo Plaza, (800) 345-9285) in 1898. Today it is named the Roosevelt Bar. The Menger was also the onetime home of **Gutzon Borglum**, the sculptor of Mount Rushmore.

Make a pig of yourself.

Texas Pig Stand

Are you looking for somebody to blame (other than yourself) for those love handles? Try Jessie Kirby and Reuben Jackson, the Dallas entrepreneurs who opened the Texas Pig Stand along the Dallas–Forth Worth Highway in September 1921. Kirby, a tobacco executive who'd already made plenty of money off others' bad habits, made a keen observation regarding America's emerging automobile culture: "People with cars are so lazy that they don't want to get out of them to eat." He enlisted the financial support of Jackson, a wealthy physician, and the world's first restaurant with curbside service was born. (The original Texas Pig Stand in Dallas is long gone.)

And talk about fast food! As cars pulled into the Texas Pig Stand's lot, male servers would jump onto their running boards before the cars came to a halt, hence the origin of the word "carhop." The restaurant chain and its popular Pig Sandwich caught on, and new stores opened across the nation. One San Antonio restaurant was built in the shape of a 12-foot-tall pig. No longer in use, the concrete structure was relocated to the parking lot of a still-operating franchise and restored.

801 S. Presa St., San Antonio, TX 78210

(210) 227-1691

Hours: Always visible; Restaurant open 24 hours

Cost: Free

Directions: One block south of Alamo St. on Presa St.

THE BIRTH OF ONION RINGS

As with so many great inventions, onion rings were created by accident. One night a cook at a Dallas Texas Pig Stand dropped a ring from a sliced onion into a bowl full of batter. He tossed the gooey mess into the deep fryer, and a few minutes later, out popped the world's first onion ring! Cardiologists across the nation hailed the discovery, which today they refer to as "job security."

Wooden Nickel Museum and World's Largest Wooden Nickel

Whoever first warned people not to take any wooden nickels couldn't have been more wrong. The first wooden nickels were actually *not* nickels but 25¢, 50¢, and $1 denominations. They were issued in 1931 by the Chamber of Commerce in Tenino, Washington, after the Citizen's Bank in that town failed, creating a money shortage. The town's temporary scrip was printed on "slicewood" and was rectangular, like wooden dollar bills, not circular. In 1933 the folks of Blaine, Washington, issued round 5¢ wooden coins when their bank failed, and the wooden nickel was truly born. Those original nickels are worth a pretty penny today.

Later in the 1930s, starting in Chicago, traveling fairs began handing out wooden nickels for change, and fairgoers warned one another not to take the coins if they didn't plan on using them before the fairs moved to

the next town. You can trace the history of this curious currency at this one-of-a-kind museum, the private collection of Herb Hornung. He's got about 1.5 million wooden nickels, of which 10,000 are on display. Hornung runs the Old Time Wooden Nickel Company, founded in 1948, the oldest wooden nickel manufacturer in the United States. It produces more than 5 million nickels each year. Today they're primarily used as promotional giveaways.

Outside the museum you'll find the World's Largest Wooden Nickel; it's 13 feet, 4 inches in diameter, is 5.5 inches thick, and weighs 2,500 pounds. You couldn't take this wooden nickel if you tried.

345 Austin Rd., San Antonio, TX 78209

(800) 750-9915 or (210) 829-1291

Hours: Monday–Friday 10:30 A.M.–3:30 P.M.

Cost: Free

www.wooden-nickel.net

Directions: Three blocks east of New Braunfels Ave., two blocks south of Funston Pl.

BORN IN SAN ANTONIO

Carol Burnett—April 26, 1936

Joan Crawford (Lucille LeSueur)—March 23, 1908

Christopher Cross (Chris Geppert)—May 3, 1951

Paula Prentiss (Paula Ragusa)—March 4, 1939

Henry Thomas—September 9, 1972

Edward White—November 14, 1930

Big boots, big feet.
Photo by author, courtesy of Bob Wade.

World's Largest Cowboy Boots

You know what they say about big boots, don't you? Big boots, big feet. And if you were to guess who would have such big, ummmm, *feet*, wouldn't you suspect it would be a Texan? Well, not so fast—these boots are East Coast hand-me-downs.

That's right, the World's Largest Cowboy Boots, 40 feet tall and 30 feet from heel to toe, originally stood in Washington, D.C., funded in part by the National Endowment for the Arts. They were sculpted by Bob Wade in 1979 out of steel and urethane foam and are so sturdy Wade actually lived in one of the boots for a short time . . . but not with his old lady—she lived in a shoe. The big boots were eventually purchased by the North Star Mall and retired to this warmer climate.

North Star Mall, 7400 San Pedro Ave., San Antonio, TX 78216

(210) 340-6627

Hours: Always visible

Cost: Free

www.bobwade.com/pub.htm#

Directions: Exit I-410 south at Spur 537 (San Pedro Ave.), then turn east into the mall and follow the service road around to the north side of the mall.

SAN ANTONIO

San Antonio's Milam Square (Commerce and Santa Rosa Streets) is said to be haunted by skeletons in black robes, the spirits of Spanish settlers buried in a cemetery located beneath the sidewalk.

Marshall Herff Applewhite, aka "Do," the leader of the Heaven's Gate cult, is buried in San Antonio's Hillside Memorial Gardens (Mission Road and Military Drive SE).

Comedienne **Carol Burnett** grew up at 2803 W. Commerce Street and attended Crockett Elementary (2215 Morales Street).

San Antonio was determined to be the nation's sweatiest city by Procter and Gamble in 2002.

If you flirt in San Antonio, you may not use your eyes or hands, or you will be breaking the law.

They've never looked so good.
Photo by author, courtesy of Barney Smith.

Suburbs
Alamo Heights
Barney Smith's Toilet Seat Art Museum

Some artists work in oils. Others, pastels. But as far as art historians can document, Barney Smith is the only person to choose toilet seats (lids, technically) as his medium. Why toilet seats? Smith is a retired plumbing contractor who still has connections to an inexpensive industry supplier.

Smith made his first artwork in 1970 when he mounted a set of deer antlers on a toilet seat. He has since moved on to less dangerous subjects (the exception being the "They Shall Study War No More" seat with a defused hand grenade on it). They're all neatly mounted in his garage—more than 700 in all—some painted, others embellished with found objects. There are 50 state license plate seats, tributes to kitchen cabinet knobs and cosmetic dentistry, toilet seats reminding you to open a savings account, graphic representations of the devaluation of the dollar, and seats commissioned for his appearances on the *Today Show, Montel Williams,* and *The View.*

Barney's most famous seat contains a hunk of the insulation tile from the Space Shuttle *Challenger* that he found washed up on a Florida beach after the explosion, or so the story goes. And yes, there are a *lot* of stories. Want to hear the tale of his eye operation? It's commemorated on its own seat, along with his used eye patch, IV drip, surgeon's business card, and photograph of Smith being wheeled through recovery by his nurse. Smith will make toilet seat art out of *anything*, including handles from a coffin he said he dug up in the backyard that the city never came by to claim. Each seat is numbered and cataloged for posterity, so if you have a particular area of interest, just ask.

239 Abiso Ave., San Antonio, TX 78209

(210) 824-7791

Hours: By appointment, or whenever the orange traffic cone is placed in the driveway

Cost: Free

www.unusualmuseums.org/toilet

Directions: Two blocks west of Broadway, two blocks south of Normandy Ave.; the garage is entered from Arbutus St.

Elmendorf
Eaten Alive?

Joe Ball was not the type of person you wanted to mess with. The World War I vet ran an Elmendorf bar called the Sociable Inn where the Saturday night entertainment consisted of drunken patrons cheering on Ball as he tossed live animals—dogs, cats, possums—into an alligator pen behind the establishment. After a series of Ball's girlfriends, waitresses, and one wife disappeared, rumors circulated that he had fed them to the gators, too. When police received a report of a barrel reeking of rotten meat, they stopped by the Sociable Inn on September 24, 1938, to have a chat with Ball. After they invited him to take a ride with them to San Antonio for further questioning, Ball asked if he could have a beer while he closed up shop. He took a few swigs, went to the cash register and punched "No Sale," pulled out a .45, and shot himself in the heart.

Police found no body parts in the alligator pen, only a blood-spattered ax. But Ball's handyman friend, Cliff Wheeler, confessed: he had recently helped Ball bury Hazel "Schatzie" Brown on a bluff three miles from town. Wheeler had also dug the grave for "Big Minnie" Gotthardt, a girlfriend Ball shot a year earlier on a beach near Ingleside. But did Ball feed anyone to the gators? Wheeler didn't think so. He was eventually sentenced to two years in prison for his complicity, and Ball's five alligators were taken to the San Antonio Zoo (see page 272).

As the years rolled by, Ball's infamy . . . and list of alleged atrocities . . . began to grow. Just how many waitresses had he fed to the gators? Two? Ten? *More*? Police located most of the supposed victims, including Ball's wife, the former Dolores "Buddy" Goodwin, very much alive, but that didn't slow down the rumor mill. After making *The Texas Chainsaw Massacre*, director Tobe Hooper filmed *Eaten Alive*, based very loosely on the Ball case. Though many crime books suggest Ball was one of America's first serial killers—the Bluebeard of Texas, the Butcher of Elmendorf—he probably killed only two, which is two more than enough. Ball is buried in the St. Anthony of Padua Church Cemetery in Elmendorf.

Sociable Club, Old Route 181, Elmendorf, TX 78112

No phone

Hours: Torn down

Cost: Free

Directions: Along Borregas Rd./Corpus Christi Rd. (FM 327/Old Route 181), at the river.

Leon Valley
Gomer Pyle Drive

I'm no realtor, but I'd bet it would take a little convincing to get a home buyer to take a look at a place on Gomer Pyle Drive. Less so a house on Charlie Chan Drive. But who wouldn't want to live on Cary Grant Drive? To each his or her own. Luckily, in Leon Valley, you have options. Lots and lots of goofy options. There are streets named for George Burns, Danny Kaye, Errol Flynn, John Wayne, Ernie Kovaks, Edie Adams, Lon Chaney, and Billie Jean King. And there are shortened, but still familiar, names: McQueen, Cronkite, Bogart, Gleason, Presley, Prentiss, and Gabor—Zsa Zsa or Eva, it's not clear.

Who came up with this idea? Suspicion falls on an uncle of Monkee Michael Nesmith, one of the developers of this suburb. He was no doubt proud of his nephew, and named Mike Nesmith Way in his honor. Laugh all you want; it's still better than the equestrian-themed Leon Valley subdivision that includes Horse Whip Drive.

All Over Town, Leon Valley, TX 78238

No phone

Hours: Always visible

Cost: Free

www.ci.leon-valley.tx.us

Directions: Northeast of Rte. 14 (Bandera Rd.).

Schertz
Mighty Armadillo

The armadillo is the official Texas State Small Mammal, so the armadillo at Bussey's Flea Market in Schertz must be the official Texas State *Large Small Mammal*—it's 15 feet long! Don't worry, it isn't real, nor was it ever, just a fiberglass mascot to lure folks off the interstate.

And as long as we're on the topic of armadillos, did you know they always give birth in litters of four and that the offspring are identical quadruplets? Armadillos are also more likely than other animals to transmit leprosy, though you would have to be fairly intimate with one to contract the disease . . . such as eating one. *Raw.* Luckily during the Great Depression, when the animals were widely known as "Hoover Hogs," folks preferred their armadillos well-done, not sushi style.

Bussey's Flea Market, 18738 I-35N, Schertz, TX 78514

(210) 247-4000

Hours: Always visible

Cost: Free

Directions: Exit northbound from I-35 at Jack Hays Blvd., then follow the frontage road
   to the flea market.

SOUTH TEXAS

The Battle of Palmito Ranch in South Texas was the final skirmish of the Civil War. On May 12, 1865, Union troops under the command of Colonel Theodore Barrett advanced on Confederate forces near Brownsville, which were led by Colonel John "Rip" Ford. After two days of fighting the Rebs won, killing more than 30 Union soldiers in the process.

But then Ford learned an interesting piece of news from his Northern captives: General Robert E. Lee had surrendered in Virginia on April 9 . . . five weeks earlier. D'oh! After confirming the story, the Rebel victors surrendered to their Union captives.

What's the moral of this story? Things in South Texas are not always what they seem. Is that the Alamo in Brackettville or a clever forgery? Is the Pearsall Peanut as big a deal as the town claims it is? And is the killer bee invasion something to celebrate? Read on and find out. . . .

10

Brackettville
The Fake Alamo

As much as the folks of Texas wanted to see the Alamo story immortalized on film—by John Wayne, no less—they just couldn't be persuaded to let a bunch of Hollywood types trample the state's most sacred shrine. Wayne couldn't have shot his film in San Antonio even if he'd wanted to.

The Alamo was to be the Duke's directorial debut, mostly out of necessity; the pitch had been turned down by every major studio, so he put it together himself over several years. The production started in Mexico in the late 1950s, but it was moved to the States to *save* money. (How often does that happen?) It took two years, but J. T. "Happy" Shahan built a replica from the Alamo's original plans, and Wayne used it for the final battle scenes.

Critic Frank Thompson summarized the Duke's effort: "*The Alamo* is a stirring, heartfelt epic, but it maintains no contact with the facts. In fact, there is not a single incident in *The Alamo* that corresponds with the actual historical moment." Picky, picky, picky.

When the movie wrapped, Shahan had to figure out what to do with his new Alamo. The mission he'd built was a solid, sturdy reproduction, and he saw no sense in tearing it down, so he reopened it as a theme park and studio. It has been used as a backdrop for more than 30 films.

Alamo Village has a John Wayne Museum and has daily shoot-outs in the summer. Also, every year they stage a reenactment of the famous siege, just so nobody forgets. Call ahead.

Alamo Village Vacationland, FM 674, PO Box 528, Brackettville, TX 78832

(830) 563-2580

E-mail: happy@hilconet.com

Hours: June–August, daily 9 A.M.–6 P.M.; September–May, daily 9 A.M.–5 P.M.

Cost: Adults $8.60, Kids (6–12) $4.30

www.alamovillage.com

Directions: Seven miles north of town on FM 674.

ALICE
The water supply in Alice (Front and Reynolds Streets) is believed to be the World's Tallest Concrete Water Tower.

Not for the lactose intolerant.

Corpus Christi
Bottle Building

If you're heading over to see the USS *Lexington*, take a quick, two-block detour north on Surfside Boulevard once you exit Route 181. There you'll find the architectural remnant of an old dairy—a bottle-shaped building that has seen better days. The structure has had a variety of uses over the years, including its most recent incarnation as a storage shed for an RV park. This type of "programmatic" or "duck" architecture used to be more common on the American landscape, but yesterday's goofy sensibility has long since been pushed aside for more practical (and less interesting) designs.

4105 Surfside Blvd., Corpus Christi, TX 78402

No phone

Hours: Always visible

Cost: Free

Directions: Two blocks east of Rte. 181 at Surfboard Ave.

Selena Sites

Tejano superstar Selena (Selena Quintanilla Perez) was on the fast track to crossover megastardom after she picked up a Grammy for best Mexican-American album in 1993. But then she confronted the ex-president of her fan club, Yolanda Saldívar, about possible embezzlement on March 31, 1995.

Saldívar, who was staying at a Corpus Christi Days Inn, did not take it well. The two argued and Saldívar pulled a gun. Selena took off across the parking lot and Saldívar shot her once in the back. Selena managed to make it to the lobby and was rushed to a hospital, but the 23-year-old singer later died. Meanwhile, Saldívar held the police at bay for nine hours, threatening to kill herself. She finally surrendered.

Saldívar was convicted of murder and sentenced to life in prison. After the trial, the murder weapon was cut into 50+ pieces and dumped into Corpus Christi Bay. The Days Inn renumbered its rooms to discourage rubberneckers. People like *you*.

Days Inn, Room 158, 901 Navigation Blvd., Corpus Christi, TX 78408

(361) 888-8599

Hours: Always visible (though the room is now renumbered)

Cost: Free

Directions: Just south of I-37 on Navigation Blvd.

Although efforts have been made to erase the memories of Selena's untimely death, her career and image are very much alive in Corpus Christi. A museum has opened at the Q Productions Studio, where she recorded. The collection includes hundreds of awards she received over

the years, starting with her fifth grade spelling bee. You'll also get to see many of her outfits, her red Porsche, her collection of decorated eggs, and the movie script for *Selena*.

After leaving the museum, there are two more popular Selena sites in town. Down on the waterfront (N. Shoreline Boulevard and Peoples Street T Head) stands a memorial—*Miradores del Flor*—of a bosomy, life-sized Selena with a microphone in her hand. Farther south, in Seaside Memorial Park (4357 Ocean Drive, (361) 992-9411), fans can visit her gravesite.

Selena Museum, 5410 Leopard St., Corpus Christi, TX 78408

(361) 289-9013

Hours: Monday–Friday 9 A.M.–Noon and 1–5 P.M.

Cost: $1 donation

www.q-productions.com/museum.htm

Directions: Three blocks south of I-37, two blocks east of Rte. 358 (Padre Island Dr.).

ALICE
The ghost of Leonora Rodriquez, sometime called the Woman in Black, has been spotted on Route 281 south of Alice at the FM 141 underpass. She was reportedly murdered by her husband's vaqueros after he found out she was pregnant by another man.

ARANSAS PASS
Aransas Pass calls itself the Shrimporee City. (800) 633-3028, www.aransaspass.org

BRACKETTVILLE
Musician **Tom T. Hall** first met **Johnny Rodriguez** at Alamo Village in Brackettville, plucking the singer out of theme-park obscurity.

Reports of its demise were premature.

USS Lexington

The USS *Lexington* saw a lot of action in World War II, even though it was commissioned in 1943, a year and a half after the United States entered the conflict. It was it was hit by a kamikaze, and the Japanese Navy thought they'd sunk it twice. Tokyo Rose claimed it had been sunk on *four* separate occasions, but when it steamed into Tokyo Bay in September 1945, the reports of Lady Lex's demise were immediately debunked.

You can imagine, then, how its former crew reacted when movie crews filming *Pearl Harbor* decorated the ship to look like a *Japanese* aircraft carrier and even hoisted the flag of the Rising Sun over its conning tower. Let's just say the vets were not pleased.

The so-called "Blue Ghost" has been docked in Corpus Christi since 1992. Visitors are allowed to explore its 16 levels, but a word of warning: tourists have reported seeing the ghost of a mysterious seaman on the lower decks.

2914 N. Shoreline Blvd., PO Box 23076, Corpus Christi, TX 78403

(800) LADY-LEX or (361) 888-4873

Hours: Monday–Saturday 9 A.M.–5 P.M., Sunday 11 A.M.–5 P.M.

Cost: Adults $11.95, Military $9.95, Seniors (60+) $9.95, Kids (4–12) $6.95

www.usslexington.com

Directions: Exit Rte. 181 just north of the bridge over the Ship Basin.

THE FIRST AIRCRAFT CARRIER

The USS *Lexington* was not the first ship to ever launch an aircraft from its deck. That honor is held by the USS *Texas*, the last surviving World War I dreadnought. On March 10, 1919, Lt. Commander Edward McDonnell was launched in a Sopwith Camel—Snoopy's favorite plane—from a deck laid across the *Texas*'s gun turrets. The ship was anchored in Guantanamo Bay for the takeoff. Today you can visit the ship in La Porte (3527 Battleground Road, (281) 479-2431, www. tpwd.state.tx.us/park/battlesh/index.htm).

BROWNSVILLE

Actor/musician **Kris Kristofferson** was born in Brownsville on June 22, 1937.

Brownsville is the Chess Capital of Texas.

Hustler **"Fast Eddie" Parker** died during a pool tournament in Brownsville on February 2, 2001.

CORPUS CHRISTI

It's illegal for Corpus Christi residents to raise alligators in their homes.

Actress **Farrah Fawcett** was born in Corpus Christi on February 2, 1947.

I yam what I yam: a statue.

Crystal City
Popeye, the Statue Man

Spinach has long been the main cash crop around Crystal City, so when Popeye began telling children of the Blutto-beating and Brutus-bashing benefits of spinach, the citizens of this town were grateful. So grateful, in

fact, that they built a monument to the big-armed sailor in front of City Hall. It was dedicated on March 26, 1937, "To All the Children of the World," many of whom, ironically, *hate* spinach. Sure, a statue to a cartoon might have seemed extravagant during the Great Depression, but the folk here didn't see it that way. If anyone would pull them out of an economic slump, it would be Popeye.

The eight-foot statue still stands, and Crystal City—the Spinach Capital of the World—is still going strong, no doubt due to the muscle-buildin' properties of you-know-what. On the second weekend in November each year, Crystal City throws a Spinach Festival, where a Spinach Queen is crowned. And no, she does not have to look like Olive Oyl to win.

City Hall, 101 E. Dimmit St., Crystal City, TX 78839

No phone

Hours: Always visible

Cost: Free

Directions: One block north of Lake St. (Rte. 155), one block east of Zavala St. (Rte. 65).

CORPUS CHRISTI
Whataburger was founded in Corpus Christi by Harmon Dobson in 1950.

FULTON
Each March Fulton celebrates Oysterfest.

HARLINGEN
Harlingen was once nicknamed Six Shooter Junction.

The Iwo Jima Memorial in Arlington, Virginia, was based on a full-scale model that was erected in 1954 at the Marine Military Academy (320 Iwo Jima Boulevard, (956) 423-6006, www.mma-tx.org) in Harlingen. **Corporal Harlon Block**, one of the men depicted in the sculpture, is buried at its base.

Don Pedro Jaramillo, a sort-of saint.

Falfurrias
Don Pedro Jaramillo, Faith Healer

Sometimes you don't know your calling in life until it smacks you in the face. For Don Pedro Jaramillo, it happened when he was smacked in the face . . . by a tree branch . . . while riding a horse near Jalisco, Mexico. To ease the pain, he ran down to a pond and smeared his nose with mud. It seemed to help, and that night an angel came to him in a dream and told him that he would be allowed to cure the sick. There was a catch: he had to do it for God, not money.

Jaramillo moved to Texas in 1881 and settled on the Los Olmos Ranch. Word got around that the man with the scar on his nose was a *curandero* (faith healer) and folks were flocking to his small home. Jaramillo's *recetas* (prescriptions) usually involved water—baths or glasses of water—often taken in multiples of three, or mud packs applied somewhere on the ill person's body. Though he did not charge for his services, he did accept donations.

Jaramillo died here on July 3, 1907, but the healings continued. He is buried east of Falfurrias where his grave has become a shrine, even

though Jaramillo has not been recognized as a saint by the Catholic Church . . . and likely never will. The faithful leave coins on his grave, where some have claimed to see a hovering green light at night.

FM 1418, Falfurrias, TX 78355

(361) 325-2224

Hours: Always visible; Gift shop, daily 10 A.M.–5 P.M.

Cost: Free

www.emmultimedia.com/donpedrito

Directions: Head east two miles on Rte. 285, then north on FM 1418.

Freer
What's That About?

There's not a lot to look at along Route 59 northeast of Freer, so when you spot a fence covered with hundreds of hand-painted signs, you're bound to slow down and read them. But will you understand them? Not likely.

"Two thirds then 5-24-02 and two thirds 6-02-02 would leave U.S.A. defense looking like a puffed rice commercial." Uhhhh, OK.

"June 1, 2003 Bush calls medicine dispensing shelves and Red Adair's well heads, mobile chemical and biological weapons labs. He then claims them 'just cause' of war." Hmmmm, so *that's* why we went to Iraq.

"They don't care how much they insult intelligence. We obviously don't have any or our defense weaponry wouldn't be gone." Yeah. *Obviously.*

The signs go on and on, each one more cryptic than the next.

Star Route Box 6A, Route 59, Freer, TX 78357

Private phone

Hours: Always visible

Cost: Free

Directions: On Rte. 59 near the intersection with County Rd. 407.

KINGSVILLE

Pigs who have sex at the Kingsville Airport are breaking the law.

This is the safe one.

World's Largest Rattlesnake

Everything's bigger in Texas, even the stuff that'll kill ya. Take the seven-foot-tall western diamondback rattlesnake on the outskirts of Freer. Locals claim it's the world's largest, and are you going to argue with them? If uncoiled it would measure about 22 feet long. But it's not. It's reared up and ready to strike!

The concrete statue was designed by Peggy Stacy and built by Peter Hunter in 1976 to honor the town's annual Rattlesnake Round-Up. Each April thousands of tourists—more accurately called "morons"—descend on this west Texas town for the chance to capture live, wild rattlesnakes. Apparently some folks find this more entertaining than playing hacky sack on a busy freeway or five-bullet Russian roulette.

154 Route 59/44, Freer, TX 78357

No phone

Hours: Always visible

Cost: Free

Directions: Just west of the fairgrounds on Riley St. (Rte. 59/44), at the east end of town.

RATTLE ON!

There are 11 distinct varieties of rattlesnake in the Lone Star State and more than a few towns that have chosen to honor these deadly serpents. On average, two or three folks die of rattlesnake bites each year in Texas, so if you can't make it to Freer to tempt fate, here are a few more suggestions:

Sweetwater Rattlesnake Round-Up and Cook-Off (Newman Park, 1699 Cypress Street, (800) 658-6757 or (325) 235-5488, www.sweet watertexas.org): Since 1958, on the second weekend in March, the Panhandle town of Sweetwater has hosted an annual Rattlesnake Round-Up, organized by the Jaycees. Participants typically collect 6–7 tons of snakes, yielding 5,000+ pounds of meat (and are paid $3–$5/pound) for the Cook-Off. That's enough to feed 30,000 visitors. The celebration includes a Miss Snake Charmer Queen pageant where contestants are only required to charm the judges.

World Championship Rattlesnake Race (San Patricio, (361) 547-6112, www.sanpatricioedc.com): To honor the man who drove all the snakes out of Ireland—some of which, no doubt, ended up in Texas—the south Texas town of San Patricio hosts the World Championship Rattlesnake Race each St. Patrick's Day. Jockeys herd snakes along a track by pounding the ground on either side of the serpents.

National Rattlesnake Sacking Championship and Round-Up (Taylor, (512) 352-6364, www.taylorchamber.org): Each March the town of Taylor, near Austin, hosts the National Rattlesnake Sacking Championship and Round-Up. Two-person teams compete to be the first to sack 10 rattlesnakes. Contestants are assessed a five-second penalty each time they are bitten.

Bayou Bob's Brazos River Rattlesnake Ranch (I-20 and Route 281, Santo, (940) 769-2626, www.wf.net/~snake): Though the sign outside this roadside attraction claims there's a petting zoo, have no fear, the rattlesnakes are not part of it. Bayou Bob Popplewell does, however, give each of his paying visitors a free mouse to feed to the snakes. Bayou Bob has at least one specimen of every poisonous snake in North America, all housed in flimsy wooden crates and white plastic buckets. Got an extra snake in the trunk? Why not sell it? Bayou Bob promises, "We buy all snakes!"

Snake Farm (5640 I-35S, New Braunfels, (830) 608-9270): The Snake Farm has more than 500 reptiles in its collection, though its rattlesnakes are not part of the petting zoo. Stop by any Sunday at 3 P.M. and you can watch handlers feed the alligators. This New Braunfels institution also has a modest non-reptile menagerie that includes zebras, monkeys, llamas, and baboons.

Dallas Zoo (621 E. Clarendon Street, (214) 670-5656, www.dallas-zoo.org): The Dallas Zoo's reptile house is home to the world's largest collection of rattlesnakes.

KINGSVILLE
The King Ranch (formerly the Santa Gertrudis Ranch) near Kingsville encompassed about 1,250,000 acres at its peak, a world record. Today it covers a piddly 825,000 acres in six counties, which is still larger than Rhode Island. Its fence could stretch from Corpus Christi to Boston. The entrance is just west of town. (King Ranch Museum, 405 N. Sixth Street, (361) 595-1881)

Kingsville flea market operator Leonoso Canales tried to change the town's official greeting from "Hello" to "Heaven-o."

LAREDO
Congressman Tom Delay was born in Laredo on April 8, 1947.

Laredo is completely surrounded by one ranch.

Nothin' to worry about. Really . . .

Hidalgo
World's Largest Killer Bee

We were warned. Throughout the 1970s and '80s we were told that the killer bees were headed northward, that it was just a matter of time before the aggressive "Africanized" bees swarmed across our southern border and invaded the United States. And then, on October 15, 1990, the first colony was discovered in Hidalgo.

Most towns would try to downplay that they had been infested with deadly insects. Not Hidalgo! In 1992 the city contracted with F.A.S.T. of Sparta, Wisconsin, to build the World's Largest Killer Bee. Sculptor Jerome Vettrus crafted a 10-foot-tall, 21-foot-long badass buzzer that was mounted on a flatbed. After years of being pulled around town in parades, the bee has found a permanent home atop a small hill adjacent to the Hidalgo Municipal Building. If you want to fight city hall, you might think twice in this town.

Hidalgo Municipal Building, 704 E. Texano Dr., Hidalgo, TX 78557

(956) 843-2734

Hours: Always visible

Cost: Free

www.hidalgotexas.com/killer%20bee.htm

Directions: At the corner of Texano Dr. and Eighth St., two blocks south of Rte. 241.

Los Ebaños
Crossing the Old-Fashioned Way

Looking for an interesting way to cross the U.S.–Mexican border, but are tired of bridges? Then try the Los Ebaños ferry, the last hand-pulled ferry across the Rio Grande. The trip aboard the *Victoria* takes about four minutes, depending on how quickly the operators pull the rope. The ferry can only take three cars at a time, but a few more pedestrians. Once on the Mexican side you'll realize that you're not really anywhere—no town, nothing, though Ciudad Diaz Ordaz is a couple miles away—so you'll have to turn around and head back. With turnaround time it'll probably eat up about 15 minutes of your vacation, but imagine the stories you'll be able to tell when you get home!

Los Ebaños Ferry, FM 886, Los Ebaños, TX 78565

No phone

Hours: Daily 8 A.M.–4 P.M.

Cost: Car + driver $1.50, Passengers 50¢

www.valleychamber.com/visitor-guide/attractions~unusual.shtml

Directions: Two miles south of Rte. 83 on FM 886.

Los Fresnos
Little Graceland

Simon Vega served in Germany with the U.S. Army in the late 1950s, and so did Elvis Presley. Vega and the King became friends, so when Presley received a medal for good conduct, he gave it to Vega. Today, that medal forms the centerpiece of a shrine to the dead rock 'n' roller in a one-room museum over Vega's garage in Los Fresnos.

The shrine is called Little Graceland, though it bears little resemblance to the Memphis mansion, except for the front gate. Vega has built a downsized replica of Presley's Tupelo birthplace and placed it in his front yard. His museum is mostly filled with Elvis merchandise, though not Elvisabilia, from commemorative plates to King dolls. Even if the museum is closed on your visit, the view from the curb is worth a stop. Vega also hosts an Elvis Fest each August.

W. Ocean Blvd., Los Fresnos, TX 78566

Contact: Rte. 1, PO Box 94, Los Fresnos, TX 78566

(956) 233-5482

Hours: Always visible; Interior, Saturday–Sunday 9 A.M.–5 P.M., or by appointment

Cost: Free

Directions: On Rte. 100 (Ocean Blvd.); look for the gate.

LAREDO

Since 1898, Laredo has celebrated George Washington's Birthday with a 10-day, citywide party each February. A statue of the first president by Roberto Garcia Jr. stands downtown at 1110 Houston Street. (800) 361-3360, www.visitlaredo.com

---

Laredo has the largest inland port in the United States.

MCALLEN

McAllen is the Square Dance Capital of the World.

PLEASONTON

Pleasanton claims to be the Birthplace of the Cowboy. A cowboy statue stands in front of City Hall (108 Second Street).

PEARSALL

Musician **George Strait** was born in Pearsall on May 18, 1952.

POTEET

Poteet is named for Poteet Canyon, a character in Milt Caniff's *Steve Canyon* comic strip.

ROCKPORT

Thousands of ruby-throated hummingbirds descend on Rockport each September as they migrate to Mexico.

ROMA

Viva Zapata! was filmed in Roma.

As close to Bikini Bottom as you're likely to get.

Seven Seas

Fans of *SpongeBob SquarePants* who long to live in Bikini Bottom now have a place to go where they don't need a scuba gear: Seven Seas. You enter this marine tchotchke megastore between two three-story, pink-and-tan conch shells. Across the parking lot, along Ocean Boulevard, stands an oversized coral wonderland populated with eels and sunfish and one very large shark—perfect for photo ops!

But Seven Seas would be special enough *without* the sculptures out front. The store is crammed with aisle after aisle of coconut fishermen and monkeys, ships in bottles, island scenes made entirely of shells, alligator claw backscratchers, dried starfish, and millions of thingamabobs you'll wonder why you purchased the second you get home. And save your back, and hours of time, walking the beach looking for shells—just buy them in bulk from the bottomless bins at Seven Seas. Who back home will know the difference?

U.S. Shell Wholesale Division, 36451 Ocean Blvd., Los Fresnos, TX 78566

(956) 554-4500

E-mail: usshellsales@aol.com

Hours: Always visible; Store, daily 9 A.M.–7 P.M.

Cost: Free

www.usshell.com

Directions: At the east end of town on Rte. 100 (Ocean Blvd.).

SHARK ATTACKS!

Besides Seven Seas, South Texas has at least two other opportunities to pose inside the mouth of a giant fake shark. You enter South Padre Island's Jaws Souvenir Shop (815 Padre Boulevard, (956) 772-9719) through the open mouth of a Great White or you can pose inside the gaping maw of another shark near the entrance to the USS *Lexington* (Shoreline Boulevard) in Corpus Christi.

Mission
Tom Landry Mural

Former Dallas Cowboys head coach Tom Landry was born in Mission, which makes this town a gridiron Bethlehem in the minds of many Texans. The holy event took place on September 11, 1924, when three Wise Men, guided by a big Texas star, bore gifts for their savior: a football, a playbook, and a hat.

OK, so that's not entirely how it went. Landry did play quarterback for the Mission High School Eagles (1201 Bryce Drive) and received a scholarship to the University of Texas in 1942, but his career was interrupted by World War II. Landry flew 30 bombing missions over Europe in a B-17, then returned to college and a stint with the New York Giants. After four seasons as that club's defensive coach, he was hired in 1960 to lead an expansion team known as the Dallas Cowboys, where he met with some success.

In 1995 Landry dedicated a 95-by-18-foot mural in his old hometown. The artwork traces his life from his humble beginnings to his induction into the Pro Football Hall of Fame. His handprints, signature, and shoeprints are embedded in cement, though sadly nobody thought to make an impression of his hat. Several players, including Tony Dorsett, Ed "Too Tall" Jones, and Robert Newhouse, have left their footprints on the mural's sidewalk as well.

101 E. Tom Landry Ave., Mission, TX 78572

(800) 580-2700

Hours: Always visible

Cost: Free

www.missionchamber.com/tomlandrymural.html

Directions: Just east of Conway Ave. (Rte. 107) on Rte. 83 (Tom Landry Ave./Tenth St.).

World's Largest Red Grapefruit

While the common grapefruit is not native to Texas, the red grapefruit is. In 1929 a mutant Thompson pink grapefruit tree in McAllen started producing red fruit, and through selective breeding this new variety was born. In 1993 the state legislature named the red grapefruit the Texas State Fruit. There are several red varieties, including the Red Blush, Rio Red, Rio Star, and the Ruby Red.

No town in Texas loves the grapefruit more than Mission, the Home of the Ruby Red Grapefruit. In 1982 it commissioned an eight-foot diameter grapefruit sculpture from artist Suter Warren. The piece is somewhat stylized, looking more like a skinned propane tank than a giant fruit, but it has been painted red and yellow to assist the less imaginative.

As if the sculpture were not enough, Mission hosts the Texas Citrus Fiesta each January. The highlight of the event is the Miss Citriana Pageant where contestants wear gowns made of local agricultural products for the Products Style Revue. People come from miles around to check out the entrants' melons.

La Placita Park, 801 Conway Ave., Mission, TX 78572

No phone

Hours: Always visible

Cost: Free

www.missionchamber.com/citrusgroves.html

Directions: Two blocks south of Rte. 8 (Tom Landry St./Tenth St.) on Rte. 107 (Conway Ave.).

Runner-up in gargantuan goobers.

Pearsall
World's Second Largest Peanut

Don't believe the bold claim on the base of this six-foot cement goober. Pearsall's peanut is actually only the World's *Second* Largest Peanut; the World's *Largest* Peanut is on a mighty pedestal in Ashburn, Georgia. Sure, it's tough for Texans to admit when citizens from a smaller state have bested them, especially when it comes to matters of size, but this type of peanuts envy is inexcusable, not to mention false advertising!

What's worse, even though farms around Pearsall produce 55 million pounds of peanuts each year (if you can trust the rest of the sign), the town doesn't throw a party in their honor. Yet it does have another annual agriculture shindig. A *Potato* Festival.

Randall Preston Produce, 1005 S. Oak St., Pearsall, TX 78061

(830) 334-4195

Hours: Always visible

Cost: Free

Directions: South of downtown on Oak St., at Pecos St.

ANOTHER BIG PEANUT

The five-foot peanut outside the Wilson County Courthouse (Fourth and D Streets) in Floresville might not be as big as Pearsall's, but the locals treat it a whole lot better. Potato Festival? Oh please—try a *Peanut Festival*, held each fall on the second weekend in October. As with any grand celebration, a King and Queen Peanut are crowned, but they're named King Reboog and Queen Tunaep. (Hint: read the titles backward.)

SAN PATRICIO

A headless cowboy ghost rides a steaming horse near the Old City Cemetery in San Patricio. This cattle rustler was beheaded when the posse that caught him couldn't find a hanging tree.

SOUTH PADRE ISLAND

It is against the law to wear a tie or socks on South Padre Island. This ordinance has nothing to do with the unofficial island motto that boasts "On South Padre, Girls Flash More Than a Smile."

Rocker **Bill Haley**'s ashes were scattered over the Gulf of Mexico off South Padre Island.

Each October, South Padre Island celebrates Sand Castle Days.

UVALDE

Actor **Matthew McConaughey** was born in Uvalde on November 4, 1969.

Rock on!
Photo by author, courtesy of Smitty's Jukebox Museum.

Pharr
Smitty's Jukebox Museum

The sound quality from a CD player might be exceptional, but where is the *style* in a digital device? A jukebox, on the other hand, is a classy piece of hardware. Dennis and Leo Schmidt—both called Smitty by those who know them—have been repairing classic jukeboxes in south Texas for years, and have amassed an impressive collection in the process.

You can see 70+ restored machines in this combination museum/ business in downtown Pharr. They've got a 1929 Electra Muse (the first to automatically change disks), Rock-olas, Select-O-Matics, Singing Towers, and models from RCA and Edison. The jewel of their collection, however, is a fully functioning 1942 Wurlitzer "950 Satyr" Bubbler, one of only 150 known to still exist. Now there's a work of art—who cares what kind of music it plays? (And might I add, it sounds just fine.)

116 W. State St., Pharr, TX 78577

(956) 787-0131

Hours: Monday–Friday 9 A.M.–4 P.M.

Cost: Free, Jukeboxes 25¢

Directions: A half block west of Rte. 281 (Cage Blvd.), one block north of Rte. 83 on the north side of the tracks.

Port Aransas
Scaley Walls

Here's something you're not likely to see on *Trading Spaces*: decorating a wall with fish scales. Most fish are covered in scales too small to use, but not the tarpon. This fish has two- to three-inch scales. If you catch one while staying at the Tarpon Inn in Port Aransas, tradition dictates that you take the largest scale, write your name on it, and stick it to the wall in the lobby. Over 7,000 have been attached to the walls over the years. Even FDR has done it, though his is framed under glass. (When the president was vacationing here, he also sent his condolences to Adolf Hitler for the *Hindenburg* crash.) The inn also has scales signed by Hedy Lamarr, Edward Teller, and Aimee Semple McPherson.

The Tarpon Inn has been around since 1886, though it burned to the ground in 1900 and its replacement was blown away in a hurricane in 1919. As long as it survives it'll accept tarpon scales from guests, though they're not as easy to come by as they once were. By law, you must throw back any tarpon under 80 inches long.

Tarpon Inn, 200 E. Cotter Ave., Port Aransas, TX 78353

(800) 365-6784 or (361) 749-5555

E-mail: info@thetarponinn.com

Hours: Always visible

Cost: Free

www.thetarponinn.com

Directions: One block east of the north end of Alister St. (Rte. 361).

Yep, it's a real reel.

Port Isabel
World's Largest Fly Rod and Reel

As you can imagine, the *Guinness Book of World Records* has strict standards as to what it will even consider listing in the book. A roadside attraction like the World's Largest Killer Bee (see page 297) is never listed because, to be nit-picky, it's not a *real* killer bee. It's fiberglass.

Well la-di-da!

Tiney Mitchell knew the rules when he set out to build the World's Largest Fly Rod and Reel in the 1990s. The 71-foot, 4.5-inch-long rod was built from fiberglass, the 4-foot-diameter reel was manufactured from aviation grade aluminum, and if you could find a dozen or so strong men, or one large Texan (so says the sign), they could use it to pull whales out of the adjacent Laguna Madre. That's right, this is a fully functioning fly rod and reel!

On June 12, 1999, the folks at *Guinness* made it official and announced that Tiney Mitchell had indeed built the World's Largest Fly Rod and Reel. It is mounted on the shore facing South Padre Island, awaiting a large Texan who can reel in that big one. And no, the 20-foot fiberglass tarpon suspended in midair just offshore does *not* count. Just ask the fussbudgets at *Guinness*.

Pirate's Landing Fishing Pier, 1100 N. Garcia, Port Isabel, TX 78578

Contact: Laguna Madre Fly Fishing Association, PO Box 2729, South Padre Island, TX
  78597

(956) 943-3663

Hours: Always visible

Cost: Free

www.portisabel.org

Directions: One block north of the Rte. 100 bridge to South Padre Island.

UVALDE

Actress **Dale Evans** was born Frances Octavia Smith in Uvalde on October 31, 1912.

Uvalde's **John Nance Gardner**, aka Cactus Jack, was FDR's vice president for two terms. He once reflected that being second in command "[wasn't] worth a bucket of warm spit." He died here at 333 N. Park Street in 1967.

Berry big.

Poteet
Big Strawberries

With 40 percent of the state's strawberries being grown on farms around Poteet, is it any wonder that the town calls itself the Strawberry Capital of Texas? In order to show folks they are serious about their fruity designation, the citizens of Poteet have erected no less than *four* monuments to the berry around town. The first sculpture, a 5-foot, 1,600-pound concrete strawberry outside the volunteer fire department, was designed and erected by Alfred Hesse in 1965. A smaller concrete berry sits in front of the local genealogical society (Avenue H and Seventh Street). Five more jumbo strawberries decorate the billboard at the city fairgrounds (Route 16), and the town's 130-foot water tower north of town has been painted red and green to resemble a . . . well, you probably already know.

None of Poteet's big strawberries is edible, so if you plan on showing up with an appetite, come in April for the annual Strawberry Festival where you're invited to participate in the Strawberry Eating Contest. A berry-shaped mascot named Freckles is the event's official goodwill ambassador.

First Strawberry Statue, Poteet Fire Department, Ave. H and Fifth St., Poteet, TX 78605
(830) 742-8144 or (830) 276-3323
Hours: Always visible
Cost: Free
www.strawberryfestival.com
Directions: On FM 476 (Ave. H), one block east of FM 282 (Fourth St.).

San Juan
A Miracle!

Since 1623 people have been flocking to the Church of San Juan de los Lagos near Guadalajara, Mexico, to venerate a small wooden icon of the Immaculate Conception. Earlier that year a young girl from a family of acrobats had broken her neck while practicing their act, but when a priest held the statue over her body, she sprang back to life . . . or so the story goes. Locals dubbed the statue Our Lady of San Juan, and pilgrims were soon traveling hundreds of miles to request miracles of their own.

Father Jose Azpiazu, pastor of a parish in San Juan, Texas, knew a good thing when he saw it. More than 300 years after the acrobat was resurrected, he commissioned a copy of Our Lady of San Juan for a chapel he wanted to build in his hometown. That shrine was dedicated on May 2, 1954. Then, on October 23, 1970, an insane pilot named Francis Alexander, hell-bent on killing either Catholics or Methodists (whichever church he saw first), flew his plane into the shrine while 130 people, including 50 priests, were celebrating mass inside. Amazingly, only the pilot was killed, and though the entire building was consumed by fire, the icon survived the blaze. The faithful saw this as a case of the shrine being 1 percent unburned, not 99 percent burned—it was a miracle!

The structure was rebuilt, bigger and better, and was rededicated on April 19, 1980. The icon was placed in an elaborate chancel behind the altar, where you can still see it today.

Basilica of Our Lady of San Juan del Valle–National Shrine, 400 N. Nebraska Ave., PO Box 747, San Juan, TX 78589

(956) 787-0033

E-mail: jnicoulauSJB@aol.com

Hours: Daily 6 A.M.–7 P.M.

Cost: Free

www.sanjuanshrine.com

Directions: Just south of Rte. 83 on FM 1426 (Nebraska Ave.).

MORE TEXAS MIRACLES

Our Lady of San Juan's rescue from a kamikaze attack was just one incident in long history of Texas miracles. Here's a sampling of other hard-to-explain holy events:

Mary on a Camero (PO Box 1335, Elsa, (956) 262-3616): In December 1993 Santiago Quintero and his brother-in-law, Dario Mendoza, noticed the image of the Virgin of Guadeloupe on the rusty bumper of his 1982 Camero. Rather than scrub it off, Quintero built a shrine in his garage. You can see the Holy Camero of Elsa if you make an appointment or visit during the celebration hosted each September. Quintero also honors her on December 12, the Feast Day of its patron saint.

Mary in an Auto Parts Store (Progresso): On December 3, 1990, Ray Trevino spotted the Virgin Mary on the floor of his auto parts store in Progresso, in back, by a shower stall. Trevino tried to scrub her off, to no avail. Praise the Lord! Word got around and soon 14,000+ people were filing through his business *each week*. Unfortunately, not enough of these people bought auto parts, and the business later closed its doors.

Mary Cries Bloody Tears (Sacred Heart Church, 5909 Reicher Drive, Austin, (512) 926-2552): A foot-tall ceramic statue of the Virgin of Guadalupe, owned by Candy Gonzalez of Austin, began crying blood on August 13, 2000. When neighbors complained about the steady stream of pilgrims coming to her home, the statue was moved to Sacred Heart Church. A week later, after 10,000 people had flocked to see it, the church returned the icon and declined to verify its authenticity.

The Chapel of Miracles (Solado Street, San Antonio): Built in the 1870s by a group of immigrants from the Canary Islands, El Capilla de Miragolas—the Chapel of Miracles—contains a 400-year-old crucifix known as El Señor de los Milagros. The statue was moved here from the San Fernando Cathedral after an 1813 fire. Many blind, deaf, crippled, and otherwise injured folks claim to have been cured after visiting this chapel.

Oozing Myrrh (Christ of the Hills Monastery, 1 Monastery Road, Blanco, (830) 833-5813): On May 7, 1985, a 13-by-15-foot icon of the Virgin Mary in the chapel of this Byzantine monastery began weeping myrrh. Mary seemed to ooze fastest when a troubled soul came into her presence. As the shrine's brochure notes, "The Monks do not believe that the Mother of God is weeping because she is happy." Good point.

Drippy Jesus and Friends (St. Mark's Coptic Orthodox Church, 424 Mulberry Lane, Bellaire, (713) 669-0311): Twelve-year-old Isaac Ayob of Bellaire was given three months to live after being diagnosed with leukemia in 1991. He started praying, and soon a portrait of Jesus on the wall of his family's home began weeping. Pilgrims flocked to the house to see the miracle—over 20,000 people in two months. Then, on November 12, 1991, Isaac was declared free of the disease. The portrait was then moved to St. Mark's Coptic Orthodox Church where it continued to ooze oil. Soon other paintings placed near the portrait began weeping, at least temporarily. The well has since gone dry, but oily cotton balls are still available for sale at the church.

Miracle Cottage (School Road, Hunt): Otis Ward's physician told him he would never walk again, but Ward proved the doctor wrong by building a Miracle Cottage on his property. The day he finished the building, he returned to the doctor and showed him what he'd done. The crutches Ward no longer needed were embedded on the outside wall of the structure. The chapel is now a bed-and-breakfast.

The Rio Grande Valley Snowball (Laguna Vista): In January 2005 a snowball went up for sale on eBay, and within a short time the bids were up to the $20,000 range. What was so special about this four-inch-diameter glob of snow? According to the individual who posted the item, his Indonesian wife had prayed and prayed for a Christmas Day snowstorm, and on December 25, 2004, Mother Nature (or somebody) delivered. According to weather reports, snow had not fallen in this area for the previous 109 years—so this isn't any old snowball!

Mary in the Sky with Jesus (St. John Neumann Catholic Church, 5802 22nd Street, Lubbock, (806) 799-2649): Pilgrims claimed Jesus, the Virgin Mary, and astral doves appeared in the sky above Lubbock's St. John Neumann Catholic Church on August 15, 1988. Others believed their rosaries turned from silver to gold, while the Virgin's crown on a statue in the chapel started to spin.

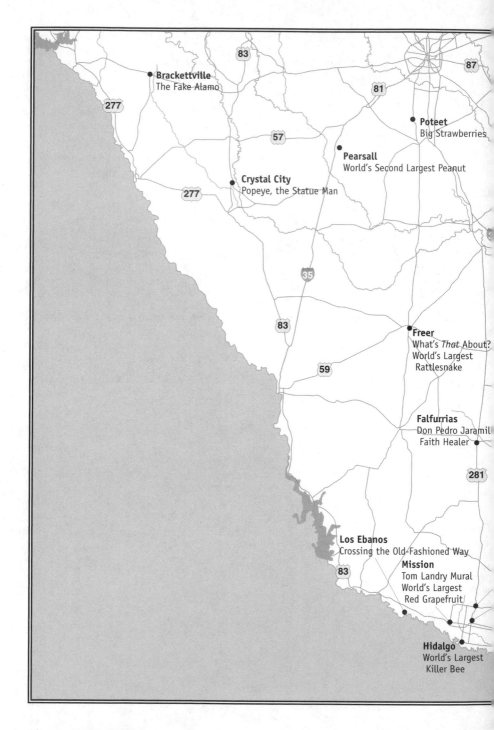

Brackettville
The Fake Alamo

83

277

87

81

Poteet
Big Strawberries

57

Pearsall
World's Second Largest Peanut

Crystal City
Popeye, the Statue Man

277

35

83

Freer
What's *That* About?
World's Largest
Rattlesnake

59

Falfurrias
Don Pedro Jaramil
Faith Healer

281

Los Ebanos
Crossing the Old-Fashioned Way

Mission
Tom Landry Mural
World's Largest
Red Grapefruit

83

Hidalgo
World's Largest
Killer Bee

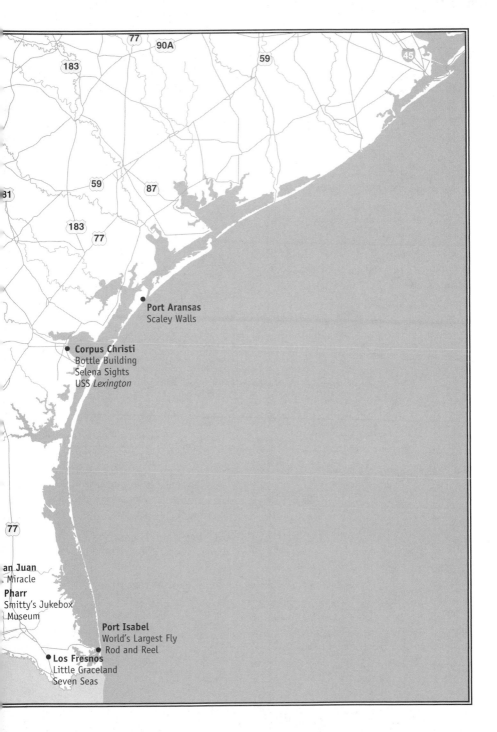

77
90A
183
59
45

59
87
183
77

81

Port Aransas
Scaley Walls

Corpus Christi
Bottle Building
Selena Sights
USS *Lexington*

77

an Juan
Miracle
Pharr
Smitty's Jukebox
Museum

Port Isabel
World's Largest Fly
Rod and Reel

Los Fresnos
Little Graceland
Seven Seas

11

THE JFK TOUR

$\mathcal{A}$ lot of Texans would just as soon everyone forget about the Kennedy assassination, which is somewhat unrealistic when you consider that anyone over age 50 knows *exactly* where he or she was when they heard the news from Dallas. Most Americans suspect that Lee Harvey Oswald was not the only person responsible, and there have been more than 3,500 books written to feed their suspicions. Correction: more than 3,501—you didn't think I'd leave it out, did you?

The best part about this special tour is that so many of the locations from 40 years ago are still around, as if trapped in the amber of the nation's collective memory. The Texas School Book Depository. The triple underpass. Parkland Memorial Hospital. The Texas Theatre. The Trade Mart. The grassy knoll. Compare a photo from November 22, 1963, to the ones you'll take on your trip—I challenge you to tell the difference. It's almost as if these places are *begging* to be explored.

So give in to your ghoulish urges. Drive the motorcade route. Wave to the crowds. You can't say Dallas doesn't love you. . . .

A Dark Day in Dallas

Before discussing any conspiracy theories, it's worthwhile to backtrack to that infamous day in Dallas to relay a few facts or, depending on your point of view, "facts."

President Kennedy had come to Texas to mend political fences within the state Democratic Party before his reelection campaign got into full swing. He brought Jackie with him, the first time she'd ventured out of Washington since their son Patrick died shortly after birth.

The couple spent the night of November 21–22 in Fort Worth at the Texas Hotel (now the Radisson Hotel, Seventh Floor, 815 Main Street, (817) 870-2100). Before they left the hotel that morning for the short flight to Dallas, Jack saw a full-page ad in the local paper accusing him of treason, and remarked to Jackie, "We're really in nut country now." Before long, most of the rest of the world would concur, though few have ever agreed whether it was *lone* nut country.

Air Force One left Fort Worth's Carswell Air Force Base and landed at Dallas's Love Field at 11:40 A.M., pulling up in front of Gate 28. The first couple spent a few minutes greeting local politicians before the presidential motorcade departed for downtown. Kennedy was scheduled to give a lunchtime speech at the Dallas Trade Mart (2100 Stemmons Freeway), but before that he would greet the citizens of Dallas. The weather was beautiful, so the Secret Service, on instructions from Bill Moyers, didn't mount the protective bubbletop on the limousine. Jack and Jackie sat in the back seat; Governor John Connally and his wife Nellie sat on the jump seat just in front of them.

Love Field, 8008 Cedar Springs Rd., Dallas, TX 75235

(214) 670-6073

Hours: Always visible

Cost: Free

www.dallas-lovefield.com

Directions: Northwest of Mockingbird Lane, west of Lemmon Ave.

The motorcade headed southeast on Cedar Springs Road, took a left (northeast) onto Mockingbird Lane, a right (southeast) onto Lemmon Avenue, a right (south) onto Turtle Creek Boulevard, a glancing left (south) back onto Cedar Springs Road, and a left (southeast) onto Harwood Street

Dealey Plaza today.

into downtown. At City Hall it took a right (west) onto Main Street.

After cruising through downtown, the motorcade entered Dealey Plaza heading west on Main, then took an immediate right (north) onto Houston Street. (You're not allowed to make the same turn today.) There, just moments before the first shot rang out, Nellie Connally observed, "Mr. President, you can't say Dallas doesn't love you," to which he replied, "No, you sure can't."

As the limousine made a long, slow left onto Elm Street in front of the Texas School Book Depository (TSBD), a shot rang out. For a variety of not very good reasons, nobody, including the Secret Service, paid the blast much mind—most thought it was just a car backfiring, or perhaps fireworks. As the limousine began to accelerate down Elm, a second bullet hit the president in the back of the neck, exited the front while clipping his necktie, passed completely through Governor John Connally at chest level, *and* through his wrist, before embedding in his knee. This shot, based on both its curious trajectory and the amount of damage inflicted, was later dubbed the "magic bullet" by Warren Commission detractors.

The Zapruder film captured Kennedy reaching for his throat while Jackie leaned in to see what was the matter. Hearing the second shot, the limo driver, Secret Service Agent Bill Greer, slowed the vehicle briefly and looked over his shoulder at the president, unknowingly giving the assassin an easy third shot. As Kennedy leaned forward and to the left, a bullet struck him on the right side of the head, blowing away a good portion of his skull and brains. Jackie rose up from her seat just at the moment Greer accelerated and she slid back onto the trunk. Luckily for her, Secret Service Agent-Come-Lately Clinton Hill was jumping onto the limo from behind and was able to push Jackie back into her seat and cover both of their bodies with his own. The limo raced off toward the Stemmons Freeway.

Texas School Book Depository, 411 Elm St., Dallas, TX 75202

No phone

Hours: Always visible

Cost: Free

Directions: On the northwest corner of Elm and Houston Sts., on the north side of Dealey Plaza.

The grassy knoll.

Policeman Robert "Bobby" Hargis, the motorcade's rear-left motorcycle escort, dropped his bike and rushed up the grassy knoll to the right of the parade route and looked over the stockade fence. He claimed he found no one. Dallas policeman Clyde Haygood was also driving a motorcycle in the motorcade, but farther back. He too rushed up the grassy knoll, but saw nothing suspicious.

Witnesses later revealed there were two people behind the concrete retaining wall directly in front of the stockade fence: a young African American couple who were having lunch and rose to watch the motorcade as it passed. Immediately following the gunshots, one of the pair dropped a glass Coke bottle that exploded on impact, perhaps resulting in another "pop" that others might have interpreted as a gunshot. Marilyn Sitzman, Abraham Zapruder's secretary, who was steadying her boss as he filmed from atop the left pedestal in the concrete pergola, witnessed the Coke-dropping incident. These two individuals could have provided valuable evidence regarding events on the grassy knoll that day, but they have never come forward.

Of the 266 witnesses to the actual killing in Dealey Plaza who identified themselves, 121 claimed to know where the shots came from: 32 believed the shots came from the TSBD, while 51 claimed the sounds emanated from the grassy knoll; the remaining 38 were unsure.

The Grassy Knoll, 400–500 Elm St., Dallas, TX 75202

No phone

Hours: Always visible

Cost: Free

Directions: On the north side of Elm St., just west of the TSBD.

The third shot.

Officer Haygood was approached by a man who was wounded on his right cheek (not the left, as is often reported). His name was James Tague, and he had been watching the motorcade from the triple underpass along Commerce Street when he was struck in the face by a small projectile. Many believe it was a fragment of the first bullet that ricocheted off the Main Street curb or perhaps a piece of concrete. (The chipped section of the curb was later removed, but you can still see where the curb was replaced, about 23 feet east of the triple underpass on the south side of the street.)

The Triple Underpass, Commerce, Main, and Elm Sts., Dallas, TX 75202

No phone

Hours: Always visible

Cost: Free

Directions: On the west side of Dealey Plaza.

Parkland Memorial Hospital's emergency entrance, looking the same today as it did then.

President Kennedy was rushed to Parkland Memorial Hospital, arriving at 12:35 P.M., and was taken into Trauma Room #1. In an effort to help the president breathe, doctors performed a tracheotomy and, in the process, destroyed the exit wound—or was it an entry wound?—on the front side of his throat.

John Connally was taken into Trauma Room #2, and a tube was inserted into his chest to prevent his lung from collapsing. Shortly after the move, the so-called Magic Bullet, Exhibit 399, virtually undamaged though slightly flattened from the side, was discovered on the governor's gurney.

The president was declared dead at 1:00 P.M. After being cleaned and placed in a casket, his body was taken to Love Field around 2:15 P.M., over the objections of Dr. Earl Rose, the county medical examiner. By Texas law, Rose was supposed to do an autopsy before the body was taken away, but nobody was stopping the Secret Service.

Parkland Memorial Hospital, 5201 Harry Hines Blvd., Dallas, TX 75235

(214) 590-8000

Hours: Always visible

Cost: Free

www.parklandhospital.com

Directions: Two blocks southeast of Inwood Road on Harry Hines Blvd., two blocks north of I-77.

Oswald's rooming house—and it's still for rent!

Meanwhile, back in Dealey Plaza . . .

Jack Ruby, Oswald's eventual killer, was around the corner from Dealey Plaza at the *Dallas Morning News* when the shots were fired. He was there to purchase an ad for his Carousel Club (1312½ Commerce Street, torn down) and liked to hang out in the lunchroom, talking up the staff. Though most folks went over to watch the motorcade, Ruby did not. When the newspaper staff returned following the gunshots, they found Ruby talking on the phone, sobbing, and looking out the window toward the TSBD. Before leaving he placed his ad, announcing that his strip club would be closed through Sunday, out of respect for the fallen leader.

Ten minutes after the shots were fired, Oswald boarded the Marsalis bus at the Murphy Crosswalk. The bus was being driven by Cecil McWatters, headed west on Elm Street toward the Oak Cliff section of town. Oswald still had a bus transfer on him when he was arrested. Early reports said that Oswald laughed uproariously when a rider mentioned the president had been shot, but that story later turned out to be false—it was 16-year-old Milton Jones who laughed at the news.

When the bus got tied up in traffic a few blocks later, Oswald exited the bus at Poydras Street, walked to the corner of Commerce and Lamar Streets, and hailed a taxi driven by William Whaley. The cabbie took him to the corner of Beckley Avenue and Neely Street. Oswald then walked the last four blocks back to his rooming house, arriving about 1:03 P.M.

In the few minutes Oswald was in his room, housekeeper Erlene Roberts claimed a police squad car pulled up in front of the house, beeped its horn twice, and left.

Oswald's Rooming House, 1026 N. Beckley Ave., Dallas, TX 75203

Private phone

Hours: Always visible

Cost: Free

Directions: Just south of Zang Blvd. on Beckley Ave.

After retrieving his handgun and changing clothes, Oswald headed off on foot through Oak Cliff, where he was stopped at about 1:15 P.M. by Officer Jefferson Davis "J. D." Tippit. The policeman called to Oswald, then got out of his squad car. Oswald shot Tippit three times across the hood of the cruiser, then once in the head as Tippit lay in the street. Witnesses claimed Oswald then reloaded his gun as he walked across a vacant lot, heading west.

Tenth and Patton Sts., Dallas, TX 75203

No phone

Hours: Always visible

Cost: Free

Directions: One block north of Jefferson Blvd., two blocks west of Marsalis Ave.

The next time Oswald was spotted, he was ducking into the entryway of Hardy's Shoe Store (now Liz Bridal & Quinceañera, 213 W. Jefferson Street) to avoid being spotted by another police cruiser. Inside, manager Johnny Brewer observed Oswald's suspicious behavior, so he followed him down the sidewalk until Oswald ducked inside the Texas Theatre without paying. A double feature was playing: *Cry of Battle* and *War Is Hell*.

Brewer asked the box-office cashier, Julia Postal, to call police. They arrived in force a few moments later. At 1:50 P.M., the police marched in while the lights came up. From the stage Brewer fingered Oswald, who

Off work early, Oswald decided to take in a movie.

rose to his feet, raised his hands, and mumbled, "Well, it's all over now." Oswald then punched Officer Maurice "Nick" McDonald in the face while reaching for his own gun. It misfired. Oswald was apprehended, though roughed up a bit by the police as he struggled to break free.

Texas Theatre (Aisle 2, Row 3, Seat 5), 231 W. Jefferson St., Dallas, TX 75208

No phone

Hours: Always visible; closed to business

Cost: Free

Directions: Two blocks north of 12th St., just west of Zang Blvd.

Oswald was taken to the Dallas city jail in the Municipal Building where he was first charged with the murder of Officer Tippit. On him, police found a phony Selective Service card with the name Alek James Hidell typed on it. As they would later learn, it was the same name Oswald used to purchase a Mannlicher-Carcano rifle via mail from a store in Chicago, the same rifle found on the sixth floor of the TSBD.

That evening, Oswald appeared at a press conference in a basement of the jail. Jack Ruby attended the press conference, disguised in black horn-rimmed glasses, claiming he was a translator for the Israeli press. After Oswald answered a few questions and was taken away, Dallas County District Attorney Henry Wade first spoke to the press about Oswald's possible involvement in the Kennedy murder.

Old Dallas City Jail, 2014 Main St., Dallas, TX 75201

No phone

Hours: Always visible

Cost: Free

Directions: Downtown, at the corner of Main and Harwood Sts.

Lee Harvey Oswald, Lone Nut?

To understand the Kennedy assassination, it is important to understand Lee Harvey Oswald . . . his history, if not his motivation.

Lee Harvey Oswald was born in New Orleans on October 18, 1939, two months after his biological father, Robert Oswald, died of a heart attack while mowing the lawn. His mother, Marguerite, moved the family five times over the next four years and shipped out several of her children to the Evangelical Lutheran Bethlehem Orphan Asylum when they became too much to handle. Or, more accurately, more than she *wanted* to handle.

But in January 1944 Marguerite pulled the kids out of the home and headed off to Fort Worth with her new husband, Edwin Eckdahl. During the next seven years, Marguerite bounced Lee through seven homes and six schools around Fort Worth, Benbrook, and Covington, Louisiana, as she and Eckdahl separated, reconciled, and separated again.

In August 1952 the family moved to New York City, where Lee became a chronic truant. Eventually he was remanded to Youth House, where a psychologist evaluated the 13-year-old: "Lee has to be diagnosed as 'personality pattern disturbance with schizoid features and passive-aggressive tendencies.' Lee has to be seen as an emotionally, quite disturbed youngster who suffers under the impact of really existing emotional isolation and deprivation, lack of affection, absence of family life, and rejection by a self-involved and conflicted mother." And how.

The family returned to New Orleans in January 1954, but eventually landed back in Fort Worth at 4936 Collinwood Avenue in July 1956, where Lee enrolled at Arlington Heights High School (now Forest Oak Middle School, 3221 Pecos Street). He dropped out before the end of September. In October he reported for Marine Corps basic training in San Diego, California.

★

What exactly happened during Oswald's adult life—who he met and what he was up to—is open for speculation. For the most part, researchers can trace *where* he was. After basic training he was shipped off to Japan aboard the USS *Bexar*. In September 1957, while stationed in Atsugi, he shot himself with a derringer, for which he was court-martialed. He would be court-martialed once more—this time for fighting with a sergeant—before being released from duty on September 11, 1959.

A little more than a month later he was in Moscow, trying to defect. The Soviets were wary of a potential spy, so they declined to make him a citizen; Oswald went back to the Hotel Berlin and tried to kill himself by slashing his wrists. But by January he was in Minsk, working at a radio factory. The KGB was convinced he was a CIA plant and monitored his movements around the clock.

Just add assassin.

In Minsk Oswald met Marina Prusakova, his soon-to-be wife. The couple gave birth to a daughter, June, on February 15, 1961, and were married on April 30. Eventually Oswald grew disillusioned with his new, dreary Soviet life, and in the summer of 1962 decided to return with his family to the United States. The Oswalds lived briefly with his brother Robert in Fort Worth, and then his mother, before moving to a home at 2703 Mercedes Street in August. Three months later they moved 604 Elsbeth Street in Dallas.

In March 1963 Oswald mail-ordered a rifle and a pistol from Klein's Sporting Goods in Chicago using the name A. Hidell. The package arrived shortly after the couple moved to a new home on Neely Street. Here, in the backyard beside the stairway to the second floor, Oswald posed for two infamous photos with his deadly new toys. The backyard today looks almost unchanged.

214 W. Neely St., Dallas, TX 75208
Private phone
Hours: Always visible
Cost: Free
Directions: One block north of Davis St. (Rte. 180), one block west of Zang Blvd.

From the spring of 1963 to the assassination in November, Oswald's life unraveled at a rapid pace. On April 10 he tried to murder Major General Edwin A. Walker using his soon-to-be-famous Mannlicher-Carcano rifle. Walker was sitting in a chair in his Dallas home when a bullet came through the window behind him, was deflected by the frame, and just missed his head. Oswald was not captured at that time, but the bullet he fired would match those fired at Kennedy seven months later. Marina Oswald later produced a cryptic "If I die tonight . . ." letter her husband wrote and left with her the night of the Walker shooting. (Marina later told the Warren Commission that Oswald had hoped to bump off Richard Nixon, to no avail.)

Walker Residence, 4011 Turtle Creek Blvd., Dallas, TX 75219
Private phone
Hours: Always visible
Cost: Free
Directions: The second home north of Avondale Ave. on Turtle Creek Blvd.

Mrs. Paine's garage.

Two weeks after the Walker assassination attempt, Oswald left for New Orleans and Marina moved in with Ruth Paine, a friend of hers who lived in Irving. Ruth Paine was recently separated from her husband Michael and appreciated Marina's company.

Marina eventually followed Lee to Louisiana, but after he was arrested on August 9 for passing out leaflets for the Fair Play for Cuba Committee (a committee of one: him), Marina started making plans to return to Irving. She left for Texas on September 23. Lee traveled to Mexico City on September 25 and tried to defect to the Soviet Union . . . again. The Soviet embassy turned him away. The Cubans didn't want him either, so he returned to the United States, and Dallas, on October 3.

Marina initially would not have Lee back. Lee rented a room at a Dallas boarding house for $8 per week (see page 324). When Marina and Ruth Paine learned through a neighbor of a job possibility at the Texas School Book Depository, Paine arranged an interview for Lee with Roy Truly, the building's superintendent, on October 15. Oswald was hired as a temporary worker and started the next day.

The Oswalds' second child, Rachel, was born in Irving on October 20, 1963. Her parents were still living separately, but Lee was stopping by more often. Oswald spent the night before the assassination in Irving, and in the morning loaded a brown paper bag filled with "curtain rods" into the trunk of coworker Buell Wesley Frazier's car for the ride to the TSBD . . . and infamy. Oswald left what little money he had, and his wedding ring, in Marina's room that morning.

Later that day, with Oswald behind bars, police went to search the Paine residence. Here they found the backyard photographs of Oswald posing with the murder weapon they'd just found at the TSBD. Police showed the incriminating photos to Oswald, but he dismissed them as fakes. His wife Marina said otherwise; she claimed she had taken the snapshots at their home on Neely Street (see page 329), on or around March 31, 1963.

Paine Residence, 2515 W. Fifth St., Irving, TX 75060

Private phone

Hours: Always visible

Cost: Free

Directions: Five block south of Rock Island Rd., one block west of Story Rd.

Jack Ruby "Snaps"

On the morning of November 24, Oswald was to be transferred to the Dallas County jail on Dealey Plaza, which the FBI hoped would be more secure. As Oswald was being handcuffed to Officer Jim Leavelle, the policeman joked, "Lee, if anyone shoots at you, I hope they're as good a shot as you are." In fact, strip-club owner Jack Ruby was even *better.* Ruby used his close relationship with the Dallas Police Department to gain entry to the underground garage at the station. Here, while the cameras rolled, Ruby fired a single shot into Oswald's stomach at point-blank range. It was the first live murder ever seen on U.S. television.

Curiously, Ruby's actions just before he shot Oswald do not indicate an act of premeditation. Ruby stopped at a Western Union office (2030 Main Street) to wire money to Fort Worth stripper Little Lynn, and he left his beloved dachshund Sheba in his car.

Old Dallas City Jail, 2014 Main St., Dallas, TX 75201

No phone

Hours: Always visible

Cost: Free

Directions: On the corner of Main and Harwood Sts.; Ruby accessed the building
  through the Main St. entrance ramp.

Oswald was rushed off to Parkland Memorial (see page 323), where he died in Trauma Room #2. An ambulance driver stole Oswald's toe-tag on the way to the city morgue, along with a lock of his hair. Both were auctioned off in 1992.

After the autopsy, his body was sent to the Miller Funeral Home (5805 Camp Bowie Boulevard) in Fort Worth. On November 25 he was buried under the name William Bobo, the same name as a recently deceased cowboy/drifter. It took court action before the Oswald family could get Lee reinterred in the family plot.

Shannon Rose Hill Memorial Park, 7301 E. Lancaster Ave., Fort Worth, TX 76112

(817) 451-3333

Hours: Daylight hours

Cost: Free

Directions: On Rte. 180 (Lancaster Ave.), 11 blocks east of Rte. 820.

Jack Ruby went on trial for killing Oswald, starting on February 17, 1964, in the courtroom of Judge Joe Brown. He was defended by Melvin Belli. Ruby claimed he "snapped" on seeing the sneering Oswald at the midnight press conference at the Dallas city jail (see page 327).

Ruby was found guilty of first-degree murder on March 14. That conviction was overturned on October 5, 1966, and a new trial was ordered. Two months later, on December 9, Ruby fell ill in his cell; he died of cancer less than a month later on January 3, 1967.

Jack Ruby's Apartment, 223 S. Ewing St., Apartment 207, Dallas, TX 75203

No phone

Hours: Torn down

Cost: Free

Directions: One block south of Eighth St., two blocks east of Marsalis Ave.

JUST A COINCIDENCE, HMMMMM?

Exactly who first noticed the parallels between the Kennedy assassination and the Lincoln assassination is not known, but whoever it was, that person had a little too much time on his or her hands. A cottage industry has developed around the list, available wherever fine conspiracy materials are sold.

★ Abraham Lincoln's secretary was named John Kennedy; John Kennedy's secretary was named Evelyn Lincoln.

★ John Kennedy (the secretary) told Abraham Lincoln not to go to Ford's Theater; Evelyn Lincoln told John Kennedy (the president) not to go to Dallas.

★ Lincoln and Kennedy were both shot on a Friday.

★ Lincoln and Kennedy were both shot in the head from behind.

★ Lincoln and Kennedy were both shot while sitting next to their wives.

★ Lincoln was sitting on his wife's left, and was shot on the left side of his head; Kennedy was sitting on his wife's right, and was shot on the right side of his head.

★ Lincoln was shot in Ford's Theater; Kennedy was shot while riding in a Ford Lincoln.

★ Booth shot Lincoln in a theater and fled to a warehouse (actually, a tobacco barn); Oswald shot Kennedy from a warehouse and fled to a theater.

★ Booth shot Lincoln with a pistol and was killed with a rifle; Oswald shot Kennedy with a rifle and was killed with a pistol.

★ Booth and Oswald were both killed before being brought to trial.

★ Booth was born in 1839; Oswald was born in 1939.

★ John Wilkes Booth and Lee Harvey Oswald both contain 15 letters.

★ Lincoln and Kennedy were both succeeded by southern politicians named Johnson.

★ Andrew Johnson was born in 1808; Lyndon Johnson was born in 1908.

★ Andrew Johnson and Lyndon Johnson both contain 13 letters.

★ Lincoln was first elected to Congress in 1846; Kennedy in 1946.

★ Lincoln was elected president in 1860; Kennedy in 1960.

★ Lincoln and Kennedy both contain seven letters.

The sniper's nest at the Sixth Floor Museum.

The Sixth Floor Museum

Six weeks after the assassination, the TSBD's owner, Colonel David Harold "Dry Hole" Byrd, removed the window frame from the sniper's nest and mounted it on a wall inside his home. Byrd sold the TSBD in 1970, then bought it back in 1972. Many civic leaders in Dallas wanted the infamous building torn down, and two arsonists tried to do it the old-fashioned way, but Byrd would have none of that—like it or not, the building had a place in history.

The building was purchased by the county in 1977 and converted into the Dallas County Administration Building. One of the county's goals was to avoid it falling into the hands of somebody who might try to exploit the assassination. That was *their* job.

In 1989 the Sixth Floor Museum opened its doors. The exhibit traces the story from the president's decision to go to Texas to the explosion of conspiracy theories following the assassination. In addition to hundreds of photographs, diagrams, and maps, you'll see artifacts related to the murders: John Kennedy's St. Christopher medal, Lee Harvey Oswald's re-created sniper's nest (and window frame, on loan from the Byrd family), Officer Jim Leavelle's cowboy hat and the handcuffs that bound him to Oswald when he was shot, Abraham Zapruder's movie camera and 12 other cameras that snapped photos in Dealey Plaza that day, and the elaborate FBI scale model of the assassination site used by the Warren Commission. As you leave the museum, you'll pass the building's old freight elevator, which some believe Oswald used as he fled the building. Or not.

The Sixth Floor Museum, 411 Elm St., Dallas, TX 75202

(214) 747-6660

E-mail: jfk@jfk.org

Hours: Daily 9 A.M.–6 P.M.

Cost: Adults $10, Seniors (65+) $9, Kids (6–18) $9; Audio Tour, add $3

www.jfk.org

Dealey Plaza Cam (aka Sniper's Nest Cam): www.earthcam.com/jfk/

Directions: On the northwest corner of Elm and Houston Sts.

The Kennedy Memorial

In 1970 Dallas erected a cenotaph-like memorial along the motorcade route, two blocks from Dealey Plaza. It was designed by Philip Johnson to invoke the image of an empty tomb. Some city leaders objected to the memorial, fearing it might stymie business development in the western downtown. They withdrew their objections when an underground parking garage was added to the plan. Gosh, weren't they sentimental?

Kennedy Memorial, Commerce, Market, Main, and Record Sts., Dallas, TX 75202

No phone

Hours: Always visible

Cost: Free

Directions: Two blocks east of Houston St. on Commerce St.

The Conspiracy Museum

No trip to Dallas's assassination sites would be complete without a visit to the Conspiracy Museum, three short blocks from the we-don't-take-sides Sixth Floor Museum. It's the brainchild of "assassinologist" R. B. Cutler, who has detailed his many theories with photocopied affidavits, grainy photographs, and a 108-foot mural. As he sees it, the JFK assassination is part of a larger conspiracy run by the Shadow Government and is tied to the killings of Robert Kennedy, Martin Luther King Jr., and the UFO crash at Roswell. Cutler raises some interesting questions, but whether any of it makes any sense depends on your ability to look beyond certain well-established facts and to adjust your tinfoil hat to the proper frequency.

The Conspiracy Museum, 110 S. Market St., Dallas, TX 75201

(214) 741-3040

Hours: Daily 10 A.M.–6 P.M.

Cost: Adults $9, Seniors $8, Kids (9–12) $3

Directions: Two blocks east of Houston St., between Main and Commerce Sts.

CONSPIRACY CORNER

There's no way to do justice to the hundreds of conspiracy theories surrounding the Kennedy assassination. Was the CIA involved? The FBI? Lyndon Johnson? Fidel Castro? The Soviets? Richard Nixon? Or was there some combination of these dark, sinister forces? And then there are all the nagging questions of the evidence itself. Something just doesn't add up.

Well, you'll have to do your own research on the major theories; a list of books appears on page 358 of Recommended Reading. But for your entertainment, here are a few of the most . . . oh, what would you call them? . . . *screwball* theories.

Oswald Shot Kennedy, but Was Aiming at Governor Connally: John Connally, when he was in the U.S. Navy, was the officer who denied Oswald an honorable discharge from the Marines. The disgruntled Oswald chose the president's visit as the perfect moment to exact his revenge . . . and slightly missed his intended target.

Oswald Was High on Coke When He Shot Kennedy: No, not cocaine. *Coca-Cola*. Ninety seconds after the motorcade was fired upon, Oswald was spotted in the second-floor lunchroom of the TSBD, sipping a Coke. It was the smoking bottle, according to J. I. Rodale, editor of *Organic Gardening and Farming*. Oswald's ". . . brain was confused because he was a sugar drunkard."

The "Umbrella Man" Paralyzed Kennedy so That CIA Snipers Could Shoot Him: Louie Steven Witt, aka the Umbrella Man, was standing in front of Abraham Zapruder, pumping his umbrella up and down as an odd form of protest. (It was intended to recall Chamberlain's appeasement of Germany while standing beneath an umbrella on the eve of World War II.) Author Robert Cutler has suggested that Witt shot a paralyzing dart from beneath his umbrella—not unlike the Penguin might—from his vantage point in front of the Stemmons Freeway sign. This caused Kennedy to stiffen upright, making a clear headshot possible.

The Secret Service Shot Kennedy . . . by Accident: Sure, Oswald was blasting away at Kennedy from the TSBD, but he didn't fire the *fatal* shot. That job was done by none other than Secret Service agent George Hickey who was riding on the running board of the car just behind the president's. Startled by the sound of gunfire, Hickey accidentally discharged his AR-15, which unfortunately was aimed at the man he was supposed to protect. Embarrassed by its agent's mistake, the Secret Service suppressed evidence and failed to acknowledge the error on any of Hickey's performance reviews.

Oswald Shot Kennedy Because He Was Angry That Marina Wanted to Buy a Washing Machine: Oswald family friend George de Mohrenschildt claimed Lee and Marina had gotten in an argument the night before the assassination after Marina threatened to leave Lee if he didn't buy her a washing machine. This caused Oswald, a devout Communist, to snap.

The British Killed Kennedy Under Orders from Queen Elizabeth: Ever-wacky Lyndon LaRouche pins the Kennedy assassination on the British. Why? Well, aren't they responsible for all that is evil, including that mastermind of the international heroin trade, the Queen of England? Why certainly!

Kennedy Crossed the Church of Satan: Writer David Icke has posed the theory that the president screwed with the wrong people, so to speak. Among JFK's many bedroom conquests, three women stand out: Marilyn Monroe, Jayne Mansfield, and Zsa Zsa Gabor, all of whom also slept with Anton LaVey, founder of the Church of Satan. But while it is not hard to fathom somebody being driven to a jealous rage over Marilyn Monroe, would anyone do the same over Zsa Zsa Gabor?

Kennedy Was Offed in a "Killing of the King" Rite: Kennedy was shot as part of a secret ritual of the Scottish Rite Freemasons. The three tramps arrested in the railyard after the shooting performed the roles of Jubal, Jubelo, and Jubelum, the "unworthy craftsmen" who appear in the Scottish Rite's 33rd-degree Masonic ritual. Dealey Plaza, situated near the *triple* underpass and the *Trinity* River, 10 miles south of the *33rd* parallel, was the optimal location for the ritual. Notice all the threes? The goal of the murder was to destroy Americans' morale, thereby allowing Freemasons to retain their secret control of the world.

Aliens Killed the President: OK, technically speaking, aliens didn't pull the trigger; that was assigned to the motorcade's limo driver William Greer. According to John Lear, son of the founder of Lear Jet, the U.S. government made a pact with the alien "Gray" culture back in the 1940s, following the Roswell crash. The U.S. government was given advanced technology in exchange for a few cattle rectums and a human guinea pig every once in a while. During the 1950s the MJ-12 Group, the supersecret government agency in charge of human–alien relations, found that the aliens were overstepping the ground rules by impregnating female abductees and implanting control chips in the nasal cavities of other subjects. Angry at being double-crossed, Kennedy threatened to expose the whole program. MJ-12 got agent Greer to shoot the president while driving on a crowd-lined Dallas street, using a nickel-plated .45 pistol. What—no death ray?

And Finally, Kennedy Didn't Die in Dallas: None other than Truman Capote once suggested that Kennedy *survived* the assassination, but not by much. He was taken to a Swiss clinic where he lived on in a vegetative state and was occasionally visited by family members on their way to skiing vacations. Capote later denied he'd said any such thing.

EPiLOGUE

Nothing lasts forever in Texas, except the Alamo, and even that was in danger of being destroyed until Clara Driscoll purchased the old mission in 1903. (She turned it over to the Daughters of the Republic of Texas two years later.) But the Encountarium F/X Theatre just across the plaza, home of *The Texas Adventure*, a robot-filled multimedia retelling of the birth of Texas, didn't fare as well; it closed its doors a few years back. How can one fully appreciate the courage of the Alamo's defenders without witnessing their struggle in robot form? You tell me.

The list of lost Texas attractions is almost too heartbreaking to recount. Corpus Christi's International Kite Museum has blown away. San Antonio's Church of Anti-Oppression Folk Art has been suppressed. Eastland's Kendrick Religious Museum has met its maker. And Arlington's Sewing Machine Museum and World's Largest Sewing Machine have both disappeared, probably outsourced to China.

Gone is the gold De Lorean in the lobby of the Snyder National Bank, the *Charlie's Angels* van and the rest of the Alamo Classic Car Museum, and the trash-eating clowns (with the vacuum mouths) at San Antonio's Playland Park. Somebody even removed the stuffed armadillo from the moon crater at the Bob Bullock Texas State History Museum in Austin. If that's "history," count me out.

Let me tell you a sad little story. On my first visit to Texas, I stopped with my friends at San Marcos's Aquarena Springs, home of the World's Only Submerging Theater, and Ralph, the Diving Pig. We were informed by the ticket seller that Ralph's first show wasn't for another few hours, so we decided to press on to Houston. Ralph was an institution—certainly he still would be performing on our next Lone Star visit.

Wrong! Southwest Texas State University purchased Aquarena Springs in 1994 and Ralph was shipped off to a slaughterhouse. Or a retirement home for diving pigs. Where he ended up isn't really the point. The point is that I know that I will likely go to my grave having never seen a pig do a half gainer, and it bothers me. Big time. If you never saw Ralph perform either, it should bother you, too.

The Aquarena Springs of the world don't last forever. Get in your car and see them while you can.

ACKNOWLEDGMENTS

*M*y best friend from childhood, Gordon Wells, wasn't born in Texas, nor did he grow up there, but his parents were Texas natives. Each summer they'd visit the Lone Star State and Gordon would return with a drawl as thick as Lyndon Johnson's. I never understood the infectious nature of all things Texan until I visited as an adult, and I've got to confess: Texas is impossible not to love. Sure, it reeks of petroleum and its politics are borderline Cro-Magnon, but the folks are friendly and the food is fantastic. And any state that has given the world Barbara Jordan, Willie Nelson, Ann Richards, and Dr Pepper is OK in my book. Connecticut, on the other hand . . .

This book would not have been possible without the assistance, patience, and good humor of many individuals. My thanks go out to the following people for allowing me to interview them about their roadside attractions: Claudia Anderson (Lyndon Baines Johnson Library and Museum), Michael Bodham (Cockroach Hall of Fame), Pig Cockrell (Cockrell's Creations), Larry and Sherry Dennis (World's Largest Rocking Chair), Amo Paul Bishop Roden Drake (Branch Davidian Compound), Barbara Gladden (The Bush's Odessa Home), Harvey Gough (Goff's Charcoal Hamburgers), Dan Hamilton (Frontiers of Flight Museum), Vance Hannemann (Cathedral of Junk), Jackie Harris (Fruitmobile), Shannon Harris (Museum of the Gulf Coast), Bevin Henges (Buckhorn Saloon and Museum), Victoria Herberta (Pigdom), Doug Hill (Stonehenge II), George Hilton (Bicycle Tree), Beatrice Jimenez (Concrete Zoo), Shirley Klepfer (Frontier Times Museum), Lightnin' McDuff and Debby Carey (Carey-McDuff Contemporary Art), Charles and Sandra McKee

(Munster Mansion), Nancy McKinley (Midland County Historical Society), Mary Milkovisch (Beer Can House), Ira Poole (Concrete Map), Leo Schmidt (Smitty's Jukebox Museum), Barney Smith (Toilet Seat Art Museum), Joe Smith (Sculpture Yard), Steve Thomas (North America's Second Largest Cross), Cleveland Turner (Flower Man House), Jim Willett (Texas Prison Museum), and Fred Wilson (Washing Machine Museum).

For research assistance, I am indebted to the librarians in the Texas communities of Abilene, Alice, Amarillo, Angleton, Anson, Athens, Austin, Beaumont, Big Spring, Brownsville, Cisco, Columbus, Corpus Christi, Dallas, Del Rio, Denton, Dublin, Eastland, El Paso, Fort Worth, Galveston, Gonzales, Hereford, Houston, Leon Valley, Liberty, Lockhart, Lubbock, Marfa, Midland, Mineral Wells, New London, Odessa, O'Donnell, Ozona, Palestine, Pampa, Paris, Pecos, Port Arthur, Post, San Angelo, San Antonio, Seabrook, Seguin, Seminole, Shamrock, Snyder, Sugar Land, Sulphur Springs, Taylor, Texarkana, Texas City, Uvalde, Vernon, Waco, Waxahachie, Weatherford, and Wharton.

Thanks also to the Visitors Bureaus and/or Chambers of Commerce in Abilene, Amarillo, Arlington, Austin, Bandera, Beaumont, Boerne, Brownsville, Bryan, Buna, Carthage, Cisco, Clute, College Station, Comfort, Corpus Christi, Corsicana, Crawford, Crockett, Crystal City, Dallas, Del Rio, Denison, Eastland, El Paso, Elgin, Floresville, Fort Stockton, Fort Worth, Fredericksburg, Freer, Galveston, Goliad, Gonzales, Granbury, Grand Saline, Grapevine, Harlingen, Hico, Hidalgo, Houston, Huntsville, Hutto, Iraan, Irving, Kerrville, La Grange, Lajitas, Langtry, Laredo, Lockhart, Lubbock, Luling, Marble Falls, Marfa, Marshall, McLean, Mexia, Midland, Mineral Wells, Mission, Mt. Vernon, Muleshoe, New Braunfels, Odessa, Paris, Pharr, Pittsburg, Plano, Port Arthur, Port Isabel, Poteet, San Angelo, San Antonio, San Juan, San Marcos, Seguin, Shamrock, Snyder, South Padre Island, Stephenville, Stonewall, Texarkana, Texas City, Turkey, Vernon, Waco, Waxahachie, Weatherford, Wichita Falls, and Wink.

Thank you, Stanley Marsh 3 (through Melba), for permission to photograph the Cadillac Ranch. Bob Wade, creator of the World's Largest Six Shooter, the World's Largest Saxophone, and the World's Largest Cowboy Boots (which grace this book's cover), you're my oddball hero. Jean Fung, wherever you are, thanks for giving Jim and I a great excuse for our first

Texas road trip. Barney Smith, you were a great model. And Garrett Black of Discount Tire in Lubbock, I appreciate your help getting me back on the road after the prairie dogs puncture my tire.

My deepest gratitude to everyone at Chicago Review Press, particularly Cynthia Sherry, Brooke Kush, Allison Felus, and Gerilee Hundt who all worked on this book.

To my Texas friends—Bernestine Singley, Gordon Wells, Caroline Wells, and Dinah Zike—I hope I did right by your state. And to Jim Frost, who has traveled with me often to the Lone Star State, my deepest gratitude.

Recommended Sources

If you'd like to learn more about the places and individuals in this book, the following are excellent sources.

Introduction
Texas (General)
Texas Off the Beaten Path, Fourth Edition by June Naylor (Guilford, CT: Globe Pequot Press, 2002)

A Comprehensive Guide to Outdoor Sculpture in Texas by Carol Morris Little (Austin, TX: University of Texas Press, 1996)

52 Offbeat Texas Stops by Bob Phillips (Dallas, TX: Phillips Productions, 1993)

52 More Offbeat Texas Stops by Bob Phillips (Dallas, TX: Phillips Productions, 1997)

Texas Curiosities, Second Edition by John Kelso (Guilford, CT: Globe Pequot Press, 2004)

Good Times in Texas by Larry Hodge (Plano, TX: Republic of Texas Press, 1999)

Unique Texas by Sarah Lovett (Santa Fe, NM: John Muir Publications, 1994)

Kinky Friedman's Guide to Texas Etiquette by Kinky Friedman (New York: Cliff Street Books, 2001)

Backroads of Texas by Ed Syers and Larry Hodge (Houston, TX: Gulf Publishing, 1993)

Texas (History)
A Treasury of Texas Tales by Webb Garrison (Nashville, TN: Rutledge Hill Press, 1997)

Unsolved Texas Mysteries by Wallace O. Chariton, Charlie Eckhardt, and Kevin R. Young (Plano, TX: Republic of Texas Press, 1991)

Roadside History of Texas by Leon C. Metz (Missoula, MT: Mountain Press, 1994)

Why Stop? by Betty and Claude Dooley (Lanham, MD: Lone Star Books, 1999)

Legendary Texans, Volume II by Joe Tom Davis (Austin, TX: Eakin Press, 1985)

Texas Cemeteries by Bill Harvey (Austin, TX: University of Texas Press, 2003)

Texas Unexplained by Jay W. Sharp (Austin, TX: University of Texas Press, 1999)
Mysteries & Miracles of Texas by Jack Kutz (Corrales, NM: Rhombus Publishing Company, 1994)

Texas (Trivia)

At Least 1836 Things You Ought to Know About Texas but Probably Don't by Doris Miller (Plano, TX: Republic of Texas Press, 1995)

Uncle John's Bathroom Reader Plunges into Texas by the Bathroom Readers' Historical Society (San Diego, CA: Portable Press, 2004)

Eventfully Texas by Jim Bradford (Bedford, TX: Classic Publishing, 2000)

The Truth About Texas by Anne Dingus (Houston, TX: Gulf Publishing, 1995)

First in the Lone Star State by Sherrie S. McLeRoy (Plano, TX: Republic of Texas Press, 1998)

Muleshoe & More by Bill and Clare Bradfield (Houston, TX: Gulf Publishing, 1999)

Tremendous Texas by Barbara Bartels (Nashville, TN: Premium Press America, 2002)

Texas High School Hot Shots by Alan Burton (Plano, TX: Republic of Texas Press, 2003)

A Treasury of Texas Trivia by Bill Cannon (Plano, TX: Republic of Texas Press, 1997)

A Treasury of Texas Trivia II by Bill Cannon (Plano, TX: Republic of Texas Press, 2000)

1. The Panhandle
Texas Meat

Mad Cowboy: Plain Truth from the Cattle Rancher Who Won't Eat Meat by Howard Lyman (New York: Touchstone, 1998)

Cadillac Ranch, the Ant Farm, and Stanley Marsh 3

Ant Farm, 1968–1978 by Constance Lewallen, Steve Seid, Michael Sorkin, Caroline Maniaque, and Chip Lord (Berkeley, CA: University of California Press, 2004)

No Dancing!

No Dancin' in Anson by Ricardo C. Ainslie (Northvale, NJ: Jason Aronson, Inc., 1995)

Buddy Holly

Buddy Holly: A Biography by Ellis Amburn (New York: St. Martin's, 1995)

Rave On by Philip Norman (New York: Simon and Schuster, 1996)

Texas Music by Rick Koster (New York: St. Martin's 1998)

Devil's Rope Museum

The Wire That Fenced the West by Henry and Frances McCallum (Norman, OK: University of Oklahoma Press, 1965)

The Devil's Rope: A Cultural History of Barbed Wire by Alan Krell (London: Reaktion Books, 2003)

2. North Texas

Dead Alien

"Once Upon a Time in Aurora" in *Fortean Times* by Jeff Gorvetzian (October 1998, Issue 115, pp. 34–38)

Santa Steals

The Santa Claus Bank Robbery by A. C. Greene (New York: Tudor, 1972)

The Santa Claus Bank Robbery by the First National Bank (Cisco, TX: Longhorn Press, 1958)

Dr Pepper

Dr Pepper, King of Beverages by Harry Ellis (Dallas, TX: Dr Pepper Company, 1979)

The Legend of Dr Pepper/7-Up by Jeffrey Rodengen (Ft. Lauderdale, FL: Write Stuff Books, 1995)

Old Rip

The Story of Old Rip by H. V. O'Brien, Jr. (Cisco, TX: The Longhorn Press, 1965)

O Ye Legendary Texas Horned Frog by June Rayfield Welch (Irving, TX: Yellow Rose Press, 1993)

Downtown Eastland Walking History Tour by the Eastland Chamber of Commerce (Eastland, TX: Self-published, Date unknown)

Creation Evidence Museum

Why Do Men Believe in Evolution Against All Odds? by Carl E. Baugh (Oklahoma City, OK: Hearthstone, 1999)

Evolution: The Fossils Say NO! by Duane T. Gish, Ph.D. (San Diego, CA: Creation-Life Publishers, 1978)

John St. Helen or John Wilkes Booth?

Return of Assassin John Wilkes Booth by W. C. Jameson (Plano, TX: Republic of Texas Press, 1999)

The Escape and Suicide of John Wilkes Booth by Finis L. Bates (Memphis, TN: Bates Publishing, 1907)

Modern Mummies by Christine Quigley (Jefferson, NC: McFarland & Company, 1998)

Mary Martin as Peter Pan

My Heart Belongs by Mary Martin (New York: William Morrow, 1976)

3. Dallas/Fort Worth Area

Dallas (General)

Dallas Uncovered, Second Edition by Larenda Lyles Roberts and Kay Threadgill (Plano, TX: Wordware, 1998)

133 Things to Do in Dallas/Fort Worth by Karen Foulk (Sugar Land, TX: Into Fun, 2000)

Introduction (Chen Tao)

"Spirit in the Sky" in *Fortean Times* by Rodney Perkins and Forrest Jackson (April 1998, Issue 109, pp. 24–26)

Big Tex and the Texas Fair

The Great State Fair of Texas by Nancy Wiley (Dallas, TX: Taylor Publishing, 1985)

Bonnie and Clyde

The Strange Story of Bonnie and Clyde by John Treherne (New York: Cooper Square Press, 1884)

Running with Bonnie and Clyde by John Neal Phillips (Norman, OK: University of Oklahoma Press, 1996)

The Family Story of Bonnie and Clyde by Phillip W. Steele and Marie Barrow Scoma (New York: Pelican, 2000)

Ambush: The Real Story of Bonnie and Clyde by Ted Hinton and Larry Grove (Bryan, TX: Shoal Creek Press, 1979)

The True Story of Bonnie and Clyde by Emma Parker and Neil Barrow Cowan (New York: New American Library, 1968)

The Lives and Times of Bonnie and Clyde by E. R. Milner (Carbondale, IL: Southern Illinois University Press, 1996)

The Bonnie & Clyde Scrapbook by B. Gelman and R. Lackmann (New York: Personality Posters, 1990)

Mary Kay
Miracles Happen by Mary Kay Ash (New York: Perennial, 2003)
More Than a Pink Cadillac by Jim Underwood (New York: McGraw-Hill, 2002)

George Bush and the Texas Rangers
Shrub by Molly Ivins and Lou Dubose (New York: Vintage Books, 2000)
Fortunate Son by J. H. Hatfield (New York: Soft Skull Press, 2000)

Lake Worth Monster
The Field Guide to Bigfoot, Yeti, and Other Mystery Primates Worldwide by Loren Coleman and Patrick Huyghe (New York: Avon Books, 1999)

Dallas and Southfork Ranch
25 Years of Dallas by Barbara Curran (College Station, TX: Virtualbookworm, 2004)

Cockroach Hall of Fame
What's Buggin' You? by Michael Bohdan (Santa Monica, CA: Santa Monica Press, 1998)
The Cockroach Papers: A Compendium of History and Lore by Richard Schweid (New York: Four Walls Eight Windows, 1999)

Bug Man (Tom DeLay)
The Hammer by Lou Dubose and Jan Reid (New York: Public Affairs, 2004)

4. West Texas
Goat Testicles
The Bizarre Careers of John R. Brinkley by R. Alton Lee (Lexington, KY: University Press of Kentucky, 2002)

John Wesley Hardin
Gunfighter: The Autobiography of John Wesley Hardin by John Wesley Hardin (New York: Creation Books, 1896, 2001)
John Wesley Hardin: Dark Angel of Texas by Leon Metz (Norman, OK: University of Oklahoma Press, 1996)
"Texas's Original Serial Killer" in *Texas Bad Boys* by J. Lee Butts (Plano, TX: Republic of Texas Press, 2002)

U.S. Border Patrol

Patrolling Chaos: The U.S. Border Patrol in Deep South Texas by Robert Lee Maril (Lubbock, TX: Texas Tech University Press, 2004)

On the Line by Eric Krauss (New York: Citadel, 2004)

Judge Roy Bean

Judge Roy Bean Country by Jack Skiles (Lubbock, TX: Texas Tech University Press, 1996)

Judge Roy Bean Almanac by Emilie and Fritz Toepperwein (Boerne, TX: Highland Press, 1967)

Marfa Lights

Night Orbs by James Bunnell (Cedar Creek, TX: Lacey Publishing, 2003)

The Marfa Lights by Judith M. Brueske (Alpine, TX: Ocotillo Enterprises, 1989)

Aviation Art Gallery and the American Airpower Heritage Museum

Vintage Aircraft Nose Art by G. Valant (Osceola, WI: Motorbooks International, 1987)

Confederate Air Force: Celebrating 40 Years by Peter R. March (Midland, TX: Confederate Air Force, 1997)

George Bush in Midland and Odessa

"Driving Tour of Presidents Bush Homes in Odessa and Midland" by the Presidential Museum (Odessa, TX: Pamphlet, 2001)

George and Laura: Portrait of an American Marriage by Christopher Anderson (New York: Morrow, 2002)

Barbara Bush: A Memoir by Barbara Bush (New York: Scribner, 1994)

Barbara Bush: Matriarch of a Dynasty by Pamela Kilian (New York: Crown, 1999)

The Family by Kitty Kelley (New York: Doubleday, 2004)

Made in Texas by Michael Lind (New York: Basic Books, 2003)

Bush on the Couch by Justin A. Frank, M.D. (New York: ReganBooks, 2004)

Texas Prostitution

Texas Bad Girls: Hussies, Harlots and Horse Thieves by J. Lee Butts (Plano, TX: Republic of Texas Press, 2001)

Etta Place: Her Life and Times with Butch Cassidy and the Sundance Kid by Gail Drago (Plano, TX: Republic of Texas Press, 1996)

Roy Orbison

Dark Star: The Roy Orbison Story by Ellis Amburn (New York: Carol Publishing Corporation, 1990)

Mary of Ágreda

"The Flying Nun" in *Fortean Times* by Gerard DuBois (December 2003, Issue 177, pp. 34–39)

"The Mysterious Lady in Blue" in *Arizona Highways* by E. H. Evans (September 1959, pp. 1–26)

5. Central Texas

General

Day Trips from Austin, Third Edition by Paris Permenter and John Bigley (Guilford, CT: Globe Pequot Press, 2004)

Bonfire Bunnies

"Show Me the Bunny" in *Fortean Times* by Paul Slade (September 2001, Issue 149, p. 49)

Brushy Bill Roberts or Billy the Kid?

The Hico Legend of Billy the Kid by Bobby E. Hefner (Hico, TX: Self-published, 1996)

Billy the Kid: Beyond the Grave by W. C. Jameson (Dallas, TX: Taylor Trade Publishing, 2005)

Waiting for Guffman

Best in Show: The Films of Christopher Guest and Company by John Kenneth Muir (New York: Applause, 2004)

Anna Nicole Smith

Great Big Beautiful Doll: The Anna Nicole Smith Story by Eric and D'eva Redding (New York: Barricade Books, 1996)

David Koresh and Waco

Massacre at Waco, Texas by Clifford Linedecker (New York: St. Martin's Paperbacks, 1993)

The Davidian Massacre by Carol Moore (New York: Legacy Communications, 1995)

The Ashes of Waco: An Investigation by Dick J. Reavis (Syracuse, NY: Syracuse

University Press, 1998)

Inside the Cult by Marc Breault (New York: Signet, 1993)

A Place Called Waco: A Survivor's Story by David Thibodeau (New York: Public Affairs, 1999)

6. Austin Area
Charles Whitman, Sharpshooter
A Sniper in the Tower by Gary M. Lavergne (New York: Bantam, 1997)

Lyndon Johnson
Lyndon B. Johnson: Portrait of a President by Robert Dallek (New York: Oxford University Press, 2003)

Madalyn Murray O'Hair
Ungodly by Ted Dracos (New York: Free Press, 2003)

Madalyn Marie O'Hair by Jon Rappoport (San Diego, CA: Truth Seeker, 1998)

Wacky Texas Legislature
Molly Ivins Can't Say That, Can She? by Molly Ivins (New York: Random House, 1991)

Bats
America's Neighborhood Bats by Merlin D. Tuttle (Austin, TX: University of Texas Press, 1997)

The Bat in My Pocket by Amanda Lollar (Santa Barbara, CA: Capra Press, 1992)

7. East Texas
General
101 Things to Do on the Texas Coast by Karen Foulk (Sugar Land, TX: Into Fun, 1999)

Babe Didrikson Zaharias
This Life I've Led by Babe Didrikson Zaharias and Harry Paxton (New York: Barnes, 1955)

Babe Didrikson by Lena Y. DeGrummond and Lynne DeGrummund (Indianapolis, IN: Bobbs-Merrill, 1963)

The Great Storm
Isaac's Storm by Erik Larson (New York: Vintage, 1999)

Galveston's 1900 Storm by Keitha MacDonald (Galveston, TX: MacDonald Publishing, Date unknown)

Sam Houston
The Raven by Marquis James (New York: Bobbs-Merrill, 1929)

Texas Capital Punishment
Have a Seat, Please by Don Ried (Huntsville, TX: Texas Review Press, 2001)
Set Free by Karla Faye Tucker (Colorado Springs, CO: Shaw, 2000)
The Rope, the Chair, and the Needle by James W. Marquart, Sheldon Ekland-Olson, and Jonathan Sorensen (Austin, TX: University of Texas Press, 1998)
Within These Walls by Re. Carroll Pickett (New York: St. Martin's 2002)
Texas Death Row by the Sun River Cartel (Marietta, GA: Longstreet Press, 2000)

Best Little Whorehouse No Longer in Texas
The True Story of the Best Little Whorehouse in Texas by Jan Hutson (San Jose, CA: Authors Choice Press, 1980)

Janis Joplin
Scars of Sweet Paradise by Alice Echols (New York: Owl Books, 2000)
Piece of My Heart by David Dalton (New York: Da Capo, 1991)

A Big Bang
City on Fire by Bill Minutaglio (New York: HarperCollins, 2003)
The Texas City Disaster by Hugh W. Stephens (Austin, TX: University of Texas Press, 1997)

Dan Rather
The Camera Never Blinks by Dan Rather (New York: William Morrow, 1977)

8. Houston Area
Houston (General)
Day Trips from Houston, Seventh Edition by Carol Barrington (Old Saybrook, CT: Globe Pequot Press, 1998)
147 Things to Do in Houston by Karen Foulk (Sugar Land, TX: Into Fun, 2003)

Art Cars
Art Cars by Harrod Blank (Asheville, NC: Lark Books, 2004)
Art Cars: Revolutionary Movement by the Ineri Foundation (Houston, TX: The Ineri Foundation: 1997)

Enron

Power Failure by Mimi Schwartz and Sherron Watkins (New York: Doubleday, 2003)

The Smartest Guys in the Room by Bethany McLean and Peter Elkind (New York: Portfolio, 2003)

Pipe Dreams by Robert Bryce (New York: Public Affairs, 2002)

Anatomy of Greed by Brian Cruver (New York: Carroll & Graf, 2002)

George Bush and the TANG

A Charge to Keep by George W. Bush and Karen Hughes (New York: Harper-Collins, 1999)

Deserter: Bush's War on Military Families, Veterans, and His Past by Ian Williams (New York: Nation Books, 2004)

Unfit Commander by Glenn W. Smith (New York: ReganBooks, 2004)

Funeral History

Corpses, Coffins, and Crypts: A History of Burial by Penny Colman (New York: Henry Holt, 1997)

Pom-Pom Mom Takes Out a Contract

Mother Love, Deadly Love by Anne McDonald Maier (New York: Birch Lane Press, 1992)

Crazy Woman Driver!

Driven to Kill by Cliff Linedecker (Boca Raton, FL: AMI Books, 2003)

9. San Antonio Area

San Antonio (General)

San Antonio Uncovered by Mark Louis Rybcyk (Plano, TX: Republic of Texas Press, 2000)

West of the Creek: Murder, Mayhem and Vice in Old San Antonio by David Bowser (San Antonio, TX: Maverick Publishing, 2003)

122 Things to Do in San Antonio by Karen Foulk (Sugar Land, TX: Into Fun, 1999)

The Alamo

The Truth About the Burial of the Remains of the Alamo Heroes by the San Fernando Cathedral (San Antonio: Artes Graficas, 1938)

Alamo Traces by Thomas Ricks Lindley (Lanham, MD: Republic of Texas Press, 2003)

Death of a Legend: The Myth and Mystery Surrounding the Death of Davy Crockett
by Bill Groneman (Plano, TX: Republic of Texas Press, 1999)

Texas Pig Stand
Drive-In Deluxe by Michael Karl Witzel (Osceola, WI: Motorbooks International,
1997)

10. South Texas
General
101 Things to Do on the Texas Coast by Karen Foulk (Sugar Land, TX: Into Fun,
1999)

Selena
Selena: Como La Flor by Joe Nick Patoski (New York: Little, Brown & Company,
1996)
Selena's Secret: The Revealing Story Behind Her Tragic Death by María Celeste
Arrarás (New York: Fireside, 1997)

Don Pedro Jaramillo, Faith Healer
The Faith Healer of Los Olmos, Fourth Edition by the Brooks County Historical
Survey Committee (Falfurrias, TX: Self-published, 1990)
The Folk Healer by Eliseo Torres (Albuquerque, NM: Nieves Press, Date
unknown)

Rattlesnakes
Rattlesnakes: Their Habits, Life Histories, and Influence on Mankind by Laurence
Klauber (Berkeley, CA: University of California Press, 1997)

Killer Bees
Killer Bees: The Africanized Honey Bee in the Americas by Mark L. Winston (Cam-
bridge, MA: Harvard University Press, 1993)

Tom Landry
Landry: The Legend and the Legacy by Bob St. John (Nashville, TN: W Publishing
Group, 2000)

A Miracle!
Basilica of Our Lady of San Juan del Valle–National Shrine by Monsignor Juan
Nicolau (San Juan, TX: Self-published, 1999)

11. The JFK Tour

A Guide to the Sites of November 22, 1963 by John M. Nagel (The Colony, TX: Tinker Productions, 1999)

The JFK Assassination: The Facts and the Theories by Carl Oglesby (New York: Signet, 1992)

Who Shot JFK? by Bob Callahan (New York: Fireside, 1993)

The Assassination of John F. Kennedy: A Complete Book of Facts by James P. Duffy and Vincent L. Ricci (New York: Thunder's Mouth, 1992)

Murder in Dealey Plaza by James H. Fetzer (ed.) (Peru, IL: Catfeet Press, 2000)

Dealey Plaza National Historic Landmark by Conover Hunt (Dallas, TX: The Sixth Floor Museum, 1997)

Who Killed JFK? by Carl Oglesby (Berkeley, CA: Odonian, 1992)

Mrs. Payne's Garage by Thomas Mallon (New York: Pantheon Books, 2002)

INDEX BY CITY NAME

Mary Cries Bloody Tears (Sacred Heart Church), 312

Matthew McConaughey Arrest Site, 197

Naked in Austin, 196

Slacker Sites, 190

Stevie Ray Vaughan Statue, 134

Texas Military Forces Museum, 3

That Wacky Texas State Legislature (State Capitol), 197

To the Bat Bridge! (Congress Avenue Bridge), 199

UFO Sighting, 35

Waiting or Guffman Auditorium, 158

Bandera

Frontier Times Museum, 140

Beaumont

Babe Didrikson Zaharias Museum, 202

Edison Museum, 203

Eye of the World, The (Lone Star Steakhouse Seafood & Grill), 204

World's Largest Fire Hydrant (Fire Museum of Texas), 205

Bellaire

Drippy Jesus and Friends (St. Mark's Coptic Orthodox Church), 312

Big Spring

Heritage Museum in Big Spring, The, 264

Blanco

Oozing Myrrh (Christ of the Hills Monastery), 312

Boerne

Cascade Caverns, 168

Cave-Without-a-Name, 168

Brackettville

Fake Alamo, The (Alamo Village Vacationland), 284

Brady

Heart of Texas Country Music Museum, 134

Brownwood

Famous Rooms (Douglas MacArthur Academy of Freedom), 63

Buna

Polka Dot, Like It or Not, 206

Burnet

Longhorn Caverns State Park, 169

Crockett

   Clyde Barrow Prison (Eastham Prison Farm), 77

   Lightnin' Hawkins Statue (Camp Street Café), 133

Crystal City

   Popeye, the Statue Man, 290

Dallas

   America Won . . . Burgers! (Goff's Charcoal Hamburgers), 72

   American Museum of Miniature Arts, 81

   Art Caskets, 252

   Biblical Arts Center, 74

   Big Giraffe Statue (Dallas Zoo), 217

   Big Longhorn, 75

   Big Tex (Fair Park), 74

   Birthplace of Onion Rings (Texas Pig Stand), 274

   Birthplace of the Frozen Margarita (Mariano's), 113

   Blanche Barrow Grave (Grove Hill Memorial Park), 80

   Bonnie and Clyde, 76

   Children's Medical Center Train, 81

   Conspiracy Corner, 338

   Conspiracy Museum, The, 337

   Dallas Zoo, 217, 296

   Grassy Knoll, 321

   Hands of the Masters (Baylor University Medical Center), 82

   Hindenburg Junk (Frontiers of Flight Museum), 84

   J. D. Tippit Murder Site, 325

   Jack Ruby's Apartment, 333

   JFK Presidential Limo Tour, R.I.P., 337

   Kennedy Assassination Sites, 317

   Kennedy Memorial, The, 336

   Kennedy/Lincoln Coincidence, 334

   Lee Harvey Oswald Homes, 327

   Love Field, 318

   Medieval Times, 85

   Mount Vernon, 63

   Old Dallas City Jail, 327, 332

   Oswald Grave, 333

Muleshoe

National Mule Memorial, 25

Natural Bridge Caverns

Natural Bridge Caverns, 169

Nausau Bay

Crazy Woman Driver! (Nausau Bay Hilton Inn), 158

New Braunfels

Snake Farm, 296

Oatmeal

World's Largest Oatmeal Box, 164

Odessa

George, Babs, and Georgie (Presidential Museum), 124

Odessa Meteor Crater, 126

Presidential Museum, 125, 126

Shakespeare's Globe Theatre, 128

Stonehenge Replica, 155

World's Largest Jackrabbit, 129

O'Donnell

Blocker Head (O'Donnell Museum), 26

Pampa

Woody Guthrie's "This Land Is Your Land" Fence, 133

Paris

Eiffel Tower, Texas Style (Love Civic Center), 51

Jesus in Cowboy Boots (Evergreen Cemetery), 53

Parker

Southfork Ranch, 96

Pearsall

World's Second Largest Peanut (Randall Preston Produce), 303

Pharr

Smitty's Jukebox Museum, 305

Piedras Negras, Mexico

Birthplace of Nachos (Victory Club), 113

Pittsburg

Ezekiel Airship (Cotton Belt Depot Museum), 54

Plano

Cockroach Hall of Fame (The Pest Shop), 98

Wonder World, 167

San Patricio

World Championship Rattlesnake Race, 295

Santo

Bayou Bob's Brazos River Rattlesnake Ranch, 295

Saratoga

Bragg Road Light, 228

Schertz

Mighty Armadillo (Bussey's Flea Market), 281

Seabrook

Thayer's Folly, 259

Seguin

Big Pecans (Guadeloupe County Courthouse and Pape Pecan House), 170

Shamrock

Blarney Stone, The, 28

Irish Inn, 28

Sherman

Bonnie and Clyde Crime Site, 78

Snyder

Albino Buffalo (Scurry County Courthouse), 29

Sonora

Caverns of Sonora, 168

South Padre Island

Big Shark, 301

Stephenville

Cow Town (Erath County Courthouse), 56

Stonewall

LBJ National and State Historic Parks, 194

Sugar Land

Bug Man, 99

Sulphur Springs

Cow Town (Southwest Dairy Center and Museum), 57

Music Box Gallery (Sulphur Springs Public Library), 58

Sweetwater

Sweetwater Rattlesnake Round-Up and Cook-Off, 295

Taylor

National Rattlesnake Sacking Championship and Round-Up, 295

INDEX BY SITE NAME